The Agile Leader

The Agile Leader

Leveraging the Power of Influence

Zuzana Šochová

✦✦Addison-Wesley

Boston • Columbus • New York • San Francisco • Amsterdam • Cape Town
Dubai • London • Madrid • Milan • Munich • Paris • Montreal • Toronto • Delhi • Mexico City
São Paulo • Sydney • Hong Kong • Seoul • Singapore • Taipei • Tokyo

For information about buying this title in bulk quantities, or for special sales opportunities (which may include electronic versions; custom cover designs; and content particular to your business, training goals, marketing focus, or branding interests), please contact our corporate sales department at corpsales@pearsoned.com or (800) 382-3419.

For government sales inquiries, please contact governmentsales@pearsoned.com.

For questions about sales outside the U.S., please contact intlcs@pearson.com.

Visit us on the Web: informit.com/aw

Library of Congress Control Number: 2020944463

Copyright © 2021 Pearson Education, Inc.

Cover image: Zuzana Šochová

ISBN-13: 978-0-13-666042-2
ISBN-10: 0-13-666042-8

1 2020

CONTENTS

FOREWORDS

Foreword by Johanna Rothman

We hear a lot about agile leadership these days. The good news is that everyone realizes they need some agility in their organizations. The bad news is that too few people understand how to change their behaviors to become agile leaders.

What does agile leadership really mean?

In *Agile Leadership*, Zuzana Šochová explains—clearly and with examples—how each of us might think about agile leadership. She helps us navigate agile leadership by explaining the various organizational structures, how agile leadership might work, and the overall agile leadership journey.

As you read, she encourages you to take notes and experiment. Do so. You might learn about yourself—an excellent idea for any leader. You might select some experiments to try for yourself, your team, and your organization.

You will learn to look for feedback at every opportunity, to consider how transparent you can be, and how to try new things.

I particularly like that every chapter offers suggestions for books to read. And there's an extensive bibliography at the back. When I read books like this, I sometimes want to investigate a topic more fully. This book encourages us to do so.

Are you ready to be an agile leader? You can lead from anywhere in the organization. And if you want your organization to become an agile organization, you *must* lead. When leaders change themselves, the rest of the organization will follow.

I hope you enjoy this book. I did.

—*Johanna Rothman,*
author of Modern Management Made Easy *and other books*

Foreword by Evan Leybourn

Never before in the history of humanity has there been such a demand for business leaders to be truly agile. Leaders who create alignment in the people around them when all is changing. Leaders who face volatility and ambiguity with confidence in their own—and their team's—ability to adapt. And leaders who see, and embrace, the complexity in the systems around them. Throughout history, there have always been visionary and agile leaders—the great architects, generals, and explorers who have seen opportunity in adversity and found innovation to be the key to achieving their goals.

At the turn of the century, something changed. The drive for predictability, efficiency, and scale drove a new kind of leadership. Systems such as scientific management emerged to help leaders plan, repeat, and grow. And for a while it seemed like we were bringing order to our chaotic world, but we only hid the chaos under a layer of process and bureaucracy.

You can hide for only so long. In the hundred years between 1900 to 2000, the world population grew by 275 percent from 1.6 to more than 6 billion, while global total gross domestic product (GDP; also known as gross world product [GWP]) increased by more than 3,600 percent (from $1.1 trillion to $41 trillion in 1900 US dollars). Complexity grew. Today, we find ourselves needing leaders who are more visionary than scientific, who see the systems for what they are and not what we want them to be.

Given the scale of growth, leadership is no longer for the exclusive few who, by luck or circumstance, find themselves in a position to inspire and lead. Today, there are hundreds of thousands of companies in need of such leadership.

And so, the leader of today must be developed and grown, not found. Which brings us, very neatly, to agile leadership.

—Evan Leybourn,
founder of the Business Agility Institute

PREFACE

In the last two decades, a powerful movement has revolutionized the world of work.

Agility is the idea that we can put people before processes, focus on creating value, work in self-organizing teams, and cooperate directly with our customers to iteratively build increasingly useful and valuable products. Various organizations have grown to support this movement, including the Scrum Alliance, which offers training on the agile mindset and best practices. The movement has grown so popular so quickly that *agile* is now recognized as a key requirement for managing the modern workplace

I was fortunate to get into agile and Scrum in the early days. After completing my studies in computer science, I earned increasingly responsible roles. Becoming a manager of others opened my eyes to the reality of the modern work world and how agile could change everything, given proper leadership.

I became a sort of evangelist, introducing agile practices to companies, and a Scrum trainer, organizing and speaking at conferences, eventually being elected to the Scrum Alliance Board of Directors.

How did a young woman with colorful hair from a little-known country in the center of Europe achieve this? Certainly not by luck or wishful thinking. It's been hard and often uncomfortable work, constantly questioning conventional wisdom, stretching and challenging myself and others.

I've already written blogs, articles, and books about agile, including *The Great ScrumMaster: #ScrumMasterWay*, where I present my ideas and experiences with servant leadership and how to guide teams on their journey to agility.

In all this time, I've increasingly been called an "agile leader." And yet, I've repeatedly had to ask myself: What does being a leader in agile really mean? Is it an oxymoron, when we are supposed to be self-organizing, to even seek leadership? Who is an agile leader, and what does an agile leader do?

Answering these questions eventually led to the creation of the Certified Agile Leadership program at the Scrum Alliance.

Over the years, I've collected so much information about leadership, most of it common sense, some of it contradictory or counterintuitive, that it became obvious I had to write it all down and put it into some sort of order. The result is this book.

This book is *not* a collection of recipes that, if followed, can transform anyone, step by step, into an agile leader ready to change the world. Rather, you may consider this to be more like a tasting menu or buffet where you can sample the various concepts and principles of agile leadership, so you can build your own set of tools and skills that works for you. There is no one-size-fits-all approach. Your leadership style must suit your unique personality, circumstances, and constraints. This book aims to help you find the ideas that will guide you in your own personal journey.

So, feel free to skip around, browse this book, and take what works for you. Maybe when you're feeling stumped, or in a rut, needing a bit of inspiration, this book can help. I've included exercises, assessments, examples, and real-world stories of agile transformation. Take what works for you, and feel free to skip over what doesn't.

In the end, leadership is about providing a shared vision and changing organizations and cultures to achieve this vision. You will find a wealth of ideas, techniques, and hopefully inspiration so that you know you are not alone in your agile leadership journey.

WHO SHOULD READ THIS BOOK

This book is intended for anyone who has the **courage to challenge the status quo of traditional organizational design and become an agile leader.**

It's for managers, directors, executives, entrepreneurs, and anyone who is willing to take over the responsibility and ownership and become a leader. It's for anyone who has a passion to change things and anyone who cares about improving the agility at the organizational level. Leadership is a state of the mind; you don't need to have any positional power to become an agile leader.

This book guides you through your very first steps on the agile leadership journey, bringing the tasting menu of the relevant agile leadership concepts to help you decide where you would like to grow as a leader and how you can help your organization to achieve a higher level of the business agility.

Each chapter contains several assessments, exercises, and practical examples that will help you to connect the theory with your day-to-day life and reflect on your personal leadership style and organizational agility. If you don't like to write directly in the book, you can always use Post-it Notes for the exercises and assessments.

The book doesn't explain what agile, Scrum, and Kanban are or how to scale agile. It's not about frameworks, practices, or tools. It's also not for people who are confident that their way of working doesn't need any significant change.

The book summarizes my experience from leadership positions—entrepreneur, managing director, director of engineering, HR director, director of the board, and from one additional role that people often miss when speaking about leadership: a

ScrumMaster, which is a great example of servant leadership. It also builds on top of my coaching experience helping organizations on their agile journey and coaching executives on their agile leadership journey. Last but not least, it builds on top of my experience from running the Certified Agile Leadership program (Scrum Alliance), which is an almost year-long program where I work with a variety of leaders across the world and across different industries on their agile leadership transformation.

HOW TO READ THIS BOOK

This book is divided into two parts. The first part, The Agile Leader—Unleash Your Leadership Potential, guides you through the steps of becoming an agile leader, and the second part, The Different Parts of an Agile Organization, shows practical cases of how different parts of agile organization works.

Part I: The Agile Leader—Unleash Your Leadership Potential

Chapter 1, How It All Started: I share my story about the beginning of my agile leadership journey, changing one organization to a flat structure based on self-organized teams.

Chapter 2, Leadership Is a State of Mind: We cover the basic reasons for agile leadership, implementing agile at the organizational level, the difference between leader and manager, and why being an agile leader is important for the success of agile at the organizational level.

Chapter 3, Organizational Evolution: We look into the organizational development from a traditional Organization 1.0 to a knowledge Organization 2.0 to an agile Organization 3.0.

Chapter 4, The Agile Leader: We talk about different models and types of leaders so you can reflect on your style and preferences.

Chapter 5, The Agile Leadership Model: We describe the key model for agile leadership based on seeing an organization as a system.

Chapter 6, Competencies: We focus on agile leader competencies. This chapter, and especially the self-evaluation at the end, shows you nice opportunities to grow as an agile leader.

Chapter 7, Meta-skills: We look at high-level cognitive skills and abilities through the Me, We, and World domains.

Chapter 8, Agile Organization: We focus on agile organizational design, structure, and culture.

Part II: The Different Parts of an Agile Organization

Chapter 9, Business Agility: We describe how the executive team, the board of directors, and the CEO roles can change in an agile organization.

Chapter 10, Agile HR and Finance: We go deeper to the practical agile application in HR, covering the typical HR functions of recruiting, evaluations and performance review, career paths, and salaries and describe how agile changes the budgeting processes.

Chapter 11, Tools and Practices: We look into the practical tips, tools, and practices that are common in an agile organization, such as large-group facilitation, systems coaching, building trust, enhancing transparency, and forming great teams and communities.

Chapter 12, Summary: We put together an overview of different concepts mentioned in the book and show them all together in context.

Let me invite you to join this degustation of a variety of concepts, carefully designed by me, as chef, to inspire agile leaders. Taste different chapters as courses, feel the mixture of ideas as various flavors, let the assessments and exercises become the aroma sensed in your nose, enjoy the real-life stories as a secret spice. Having a great meal is a unique experience, and I hope this book brings you a unique experience of becoming an agile leader.

—*Zuzana (Zuzi) Šochová*

Register your copy of *The Agile Leader* on the InformIT site for convenient access to updates and/or corrections as they become available. To start the registration process, go to informit.com/register and log in or create an account. Enter the product ISBN (9780136660422) and click Submit. Look on the Registered Products tab for an Access Bonus Content link next to this product, and follow that link to access any available bonus materials. If you would like to be notified of exclusive offers on new editions and updates, please check the box to receive email from us.

ACKNOWLEDGMENTS

Special thanks to my family for their support; without them I would not have been able to finish this book.

ABOUT THE AUTHOR

Zuzana Šochová, Agile Coach, Certified Scrum Trainer (CST), and Certified Agile Leadership Educator (CALE), has more than 20 years of experience in the IT industry. She led one of the very first agile international projects in the Czech Republic, focusing on distributed Scrum teams, working in different time zones between Europe and the United States. Now she is a leading  expert on agile and Scrum practices in both startups and big corporations. She has experience with agile adoption in telco, finance, health care, automotive, mobile, and high-tech software companies. She's been helping companies with agile and Scrum across Europe, India, Southeast Asia, and the United States.

Zuzi has worked in various positions, starting as a software developer for life- and mission-critical systems, continuing as a ScrumMaster and director of engineering and director of HR. She has been working as an independent agile coach and trainer since 2010, specializing in leadership, organizational and team coaching, facilitations, and culture change using agile and Scrum.

Zuzi is a well-known international speaker. She is a founder of the Czech Agile Community, which organizes the annual Agile

Prague Conference. She is a CST and CTC with the Scrum Alliance. She received her MBA from Sheffield Hallam University (Great Britain) and her master's in computer science and computer graphics from the Czech Technical University. She is the author of the book *The Great ScrumMaster: #ScrumMasterWay* (Addison-Wesley, 2017) and coauthor of *Agile Methods Project Management* (Computer Press, 2014), written in the Czech language. She is a member of the Board of Directors of the Scrum Alliance (USA), was recognized as one the Top 130 Project Management Influencers in 2019, and is included in the Lean In Agile 100 (LIA 100), an initiative to identify women making significant contributions in lean and agile spaces across the globe.

twitter: @zuzuzka
web: sochova.com
blog: agile-scrum.com

1
. . .
AGILE LEADER—UNLEASH YOUR LEADERSHIP POTENTIAL

Being Agile leader is not about positional power, but your ability to leverage the power of influence.

1

. . .

HOW IT ALL STARTED

One summer afternoon in 2010, I was given three departments of software developers, software testers, and hardware designers and was asked to form one new department of engineering from them—a department with high collaboration and flexibility to build cross-functional teams across those three domains. The department would serve our customers better, with higher flexibility, creativity, and innovations, while keeping our technical excellence and living the company's vision: "Added-Value Solutions." I was asked to come up with my own idea of how I wanted to run my new department by the following week.

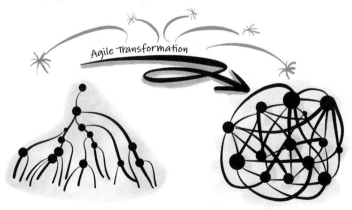

I went home, sat in the garden, and thought about it. My first feeling was "Wow! I can make a difference!" And then it faded. . . . The image of 120 people coming to me every day with their questions, requests, and approvals was overwhelming. I felt tired before I had even started. It felt like the beginning of a storm: thunder and lightning, dark with no hope. I started to think about names and hierarchy.

The next day brought new energy. Later that week, at the next executive meeting, I got the courage to present a very different structure based on a network of self-organizing teams with only Scrum Masters rather than managers and a new position structure of only team members instead of people's original roles. I was both excited and nervous about my presentation of a flat team.

Our chairman was a typical traditional manager with a hierarchy hardcoded in his DNA. He always wore a suit and kept his distance, and he had the aura of a person who could never be wrong. On the day of the executive meeting, he was clearly in a good mood, sitting in front, making jokes. Then he started a meeting: "Let's start with the engineering structure. We need to know who you expect to be in the management roles."

"Sure, let me connect to the projector," I said. My mind was exploding: *Management? I don't have any. . . . What if he . . . ? No, that's not going to happen. . . . He is not going to fire me in my first week. . . . What if I . . . ? No time to change that. . . . Here it is, I need to start.*

I took a deep breath and started: "You asked me to come up with my own vision of the new engineering department, but let me first summarize the goals we need to achieve with this new department." It was good, I had their interest, so I continued: "The department should have high flexibility and a fast-learning environment, and it should deliver added value solutions through innovations, creativity, and technical excellence. Is that correct?" I paused and looked around the room. They were nodding, seemingly in agreement. The chairman started to become impatient—his eyes were saying *yes, we all know that, move on.*

So I continued. "I did research about companies that are similar to us, read several case studies and articles about the way they work, and came up with an organization that is a flat structure based on self-organizing teams with no management in the department."

"With NO MANAGEMENT?" the chairman asked with raised eyebrows.

"Yes, no management," I continued. I had to be fast and deliver a simple message. "No management actually enables the empowerment, motivation, and creativity we need in the department. It's a natural continuation of the agile team structure with Scrum Masters we currently have in the development part of the organization."

"So you want to make us all agile?" he asked, as though he'd just heard a joke that made him smile, clearly recovering his good mood.

"Yes . . .," I said slowly, still puzzled by the turn of his mood.

"Let's do that," he continued. "After all, we've chosen you because we need a change, right?" There was nodding around the room. "We've been stagnating too long and have to turn this company around to be much more flexible than we are now. We have to attract new, talented people. Frankly speaking, we want to be a modern organization that attracts people in the region and is a model for other organizations to follow. Let's talk this afternoon about how you plan to do it."

The meeting continued, but I don't remember the rest. We were done with the team-level experimenting phase on our agile organization journey. I still don't know why the chairman said yes to this crazy idea, as he was generally very conservative, hated experiments, and had been fighting this flat structure with emergent leadership almost every day. I think part of it was that I was able to link my plan with our strategic goals, which resonated with him. Agile was not our goal, but it was the best way to achieve our strategic goals. It was a hard journey for everyone, as we all needed to change significantly, but if I had to go back, I would do it again. It worked and we made it. We achieved our dream goals, and only one person left the organization because of the change. It was a lot of work, and I'm glad I had this opportunity to learn and grow as an agile leader.

> *Agile is not your goal—it's only the best way to achieve your goals.*

THE NEED FOR CHANGE

In most organizations, you realize that to bring about change, you first need to fight the pharaoh syndrome, where the shared feeling is, "We don't need to change. We are a successful organization, and nothing can happen to us." Such overconfidence stands in the way of any change. And agile requires quite a hard change in the way we work and in our mindset. The very first step of the eight-step process for leading change described by Kotter [Kotter12] is to create a sense of urgency. Simply ask why. *Why do we have to change in the first place? What is the need behind it? What would happen if we don't change?* And unless we can find a good enough strategic reason, maybe we should not even start.

Agile is not your goal—it's the way you can achieve your strategic goals. I reiterate this statement at the beginning of this book because without a really important reason for change and without a sense of urgency, no organization will move, no leaders will change their habits,  and no change will happen. Let me quote Mike Cohn from his keynote speech at Agile2010 in Orlando, Florida: "The goal is not to become agile; the goal is to understand how to be more agile. Agility is a result of a mindset, not a process. An enterprise will never finish 'becoming agile' because it will always find ways to improve its operations" [Kessel-Fell19].

Before you start reading, do this exercise to make sure you have a sense of urgency yourself.

Why do we have to change? What is the need behind it? What would happen if we don't change?

Your notes ...

2
. . .
LEADERSHIP IS A STATE OF MIND

Many books focus on leadership, but not that many focus on *agile leadership*. Why does that matter? Because leadership has changed significantly over the past few decades. What used to be an effective leadership style in a traditional  organization might be counterproductive in agile environments. The most effective leaders, who had been great working with individuals in traditional structures, might be struggling or completely failing to work with teams and systems. But let's answer some questions before we deep-dive into the change.

WHAT IS AGILE?

What does *agile* mean in the first place? Let's first clear up some of the most common misconceptions and misunderstandings. Agile is a mindset, a philosophy, a different way of working. It changes the way you think and how you approach tasks, team mates, and work in general. It's not a process, method, or framework to be implemented, which makes it very flexible. It's all about culture and changing the way you think about business. It's based on transparency, team collaboration, a higher level of the autonomy, and creating impact through frequent value delivery.

When I first heard about agile and Scrum, I didn't like them. It felt like a process overkill. We were putting too much focus on the practices and not much on the mindset and culture, which is actually a very common mistake. I still remember when, as a new ScrumMaster, I introduced agile to the team and my only argument was that we have to use it because our customer required it. I could not have cared less about being agile. *Just get the work done and move on,* I thought. However, it turned out that even "technical agile"—before we understood the mindset and instead took it as only a set of practices, processes, and rules—helped us in areas where we thought we were already great. It was a big surprise for us.

A few years later, when I had some experience in building agile organizations, I was a managing director of a small web studio, and we used agile not only to deliver our products and services and build relationships with customers but also as an overall way to design strategy and inspect and adapt our business model. Interestingly, though the delivery process improvement was outstanding— we shortened the time to market from a couple of months to just a few days—the business impact was not relevant until we fully embraced agility at all levels and started experimenting with the business model and strategic decision-making process. Agility at a single-team level can create a huge impact on team members' motivation and efficiency, but the business impact is usually limited. Agility at the organizational level has much bigger potential.

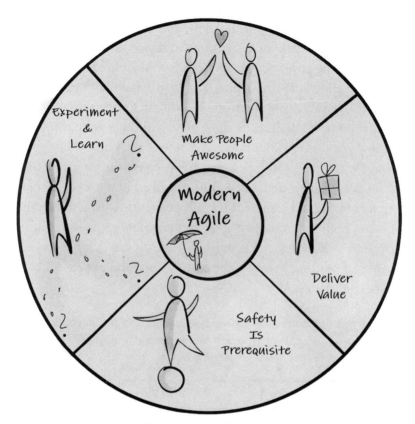

In one word, *agile* stands for "adaptiveness." Although agile started in the software development, it's widely applicable anywhere you can imagine. Over the years, agile has spread from IT toward other parts of the business: agile HR, agile finance, agile marketing, business agility, and agile leadership, where the Modern Agile [Kerievsky19] concept created by Joshua Kerievsky is more relevant than the original Agile Manifesto.[1]

Modern Agile has four principles: make people awesome, experiment and learn rapidly, deliver value continuously, and make safety a prerequisite. Making people awesome is a starting point for the mindset change. It's all about relationships.

---

1. Agile was popularized by the Manifesto for Agile Software Development: http://agilemanifesto.org.

Let's make people successful, happy, and content and make their lives better—this applies to everyone in the organizational ecosystem, including customers, employees, and shareholders. The next two principles are about helping people to collaborate and to learn about the business and their way of working through small experiments in how to deliver the right value. All three groups are supporting one other and building on top of each other. The fourth principle is a precondition. Safety is a prerequisite for any agility. If you don't have a high level of trust, agile will not work. People will feel far from awesome, they will be afraid to experiment and to come up with innovative and creative solutions, and the value delivered will suffer. Agile needs a "safe to fail" culture where people take failure as an opportunity to learn and improve, not to blame, judge, or punish.

Good agile needs all four segments. Imagine your organization. How agile are you according to the four Modern Agile principles? On a scale 1 to 10, where do you see your organization?

	1	10	
People are taken as resources who do the job.	←——————→		We care about making people awesome.
We follow processes and guidelines.	←——————→		We experiment and learn rapidly.
We focus on task efficiency.	←——————→		We focus on delivering value continuously.
Failure is only an opportunity to blame.	←——————→		We make safety a prerequisite, and we learn from failures.

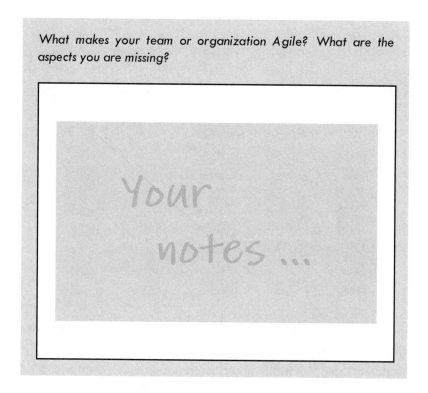

What makes your team or organization Agile? What are the aspects you are missing?

Why Agile?

Agile is a response to new business realities and challenges. It brings flexible business models and allows organizations to succeed in today's constantly changing world. Most of the modern management and organizational design traces its roots back to the early 1900s [Kotter12], when the problems organizations were solving were very different. If you look at how business has changed in just the past twenty years and how many originally successful organizations failed to keep up and consequently went out of business, you cannot doubt that organizational change is a requirement for success.

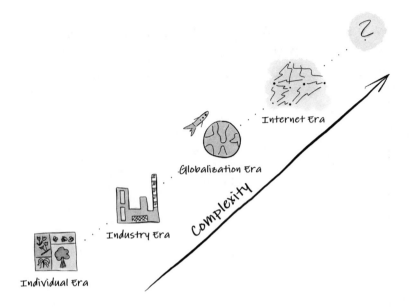

Let's take a step back and look at how the world has changed over the past centuries. Hundreds of years ago, in the individual era, the world was quite stable and simple. Every family had its own field. Most towns had only one restaurant, one shop, one hotel. People were less dependent on each other. The businesses were local, people worked as individuals. And then the world changed: the Industrial Revolution made impossible things possible, faster, and more complicated. People didn't like the change at first, but it didn't matter—the world was not asking their opinions, and the change happened anyway. Sabotaging machines in the factories didn't prevent it; trying to preserve the old world by using horses instead of cars didn't stop it either. The old way of doing business became too slow and was not competitive. The pressure was unstoppable, and companies either kept up to speed and survived or disappeared forever.

The Industrial Age gave birth to management as we know it now. Taylorism was born. All the management practices oriented toward task optimization, planning, and control have their roots in this period. But the world was not static and continued changing even faster. The new era ushered in by globalization and followed by the Internet completely changed not only the business world but our lives. It doesn't matter anymore where your company office is. You don't even need one. Instant communication and accessibility have redesigned everything. Companies such as Google and Facebook created the new virtual business, which companies such as Uber and Airbnb took to the next level. None of that would be possible without the Internet. Similar to the public resistance seen at the beginning of the industrial era, we may not like this change, we may try to fight with it and block Uber and Airbnb from running their services, but the trend is not stoppable. These exact companies may disappear, but the world is not going back. Day after day it becomes faster and increasingly complex. We not only can't stop the upcoming new eras, but we can't predict them either. We don't know what's next.

I still remember when my friend asked me during my computer science studies (in the mid-1990s) if I wanted an email address. Why would I need an email? I asked him. You have to have it, he said. And now, can you imagine a life without it? It has become an integral part of our lives. It's the same with globalization. When our teachers at the MBA program were talking about globalization as a critically important trend, I didn't believe them. It would affect a few companies, yes. But would it be a major game changer? Not really. And now, we might not like it, but it is our current reality. The real power of globalization is when you combine it with the speed of information over the Internet. It allows anyone, no matter where they are located, even hidden in a small village somewhere in the mountains, to connect and completely change your business, with just one click. It's as simple as that, as fast as you can imagine. There is no extra cost for traveling and opening an office. The world is global, it's even more global than we think, and no borders or regulations can stop it.

Day by day, the world is changing faster and faster and becomes more and more complex.

When I ask participants at my leadership classes what's next, they often say "artificial intelligence," "machine learning," and a return to "individualism." But here is the point: when we talk about it, it's already here, and while we might not see it yet, it's already happening. The truth is, we don't know what's next. But whatever it is, it's going to redesign the game—it will make the impossible possible and will redraw the map of the business world and our lives. No one knows what that is yet. But so far, the trend has always been the same: significantly faster changes and more complexity. The transformation is so fast that products you used five years ago are old now, the lives we lived ten years ago were very different, and everything is changing, which makes planning almost impossible.

It's time to change. Stop creating plans. Inspect and adapt.

All we can do is accept that we don't know what's next. And this time, the change won't be for the next generation—it will happen within the next year or two. In this rapidly evolving world, we need to change the way we work, right now, when there is still time to do it, and we need to inspect and adapt because the traditional plans are changing so fast that it makes no sense to create them.

The world is so different now, and yet we are still trying to use the same way of working as was practiced in the early 1900s. Interesting, right?

Currently, we speak about living in the VUCA world [Bennett14]—the world with high volatility, uncertainty, complexity, and ambiguity. The world that is unpredictable. Now is the time for a change. Agility offers the answer to the current complex problems and allows us to

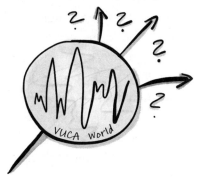

be more adaptive and responsive to change. Inspection and adaptation rather than creating fixed plans seem to be a better fit for our dynamic world.

Companies change not because there is a new method or framework. They change because they have to. Agile is not your goal—it's a necessity to survive and to succeed in today's complex and constantly changing world.

I do an exercise with executives and senior managers who are interested in implementing agile in their organization. I ask them how complex, unpredictable, and fast-changing their business is. Their answers always vary widely, but there are hardly any organizations where the majority of the group would classify the business as predictable. They have different reasons behind the unpredictability: business model disrupters, customers expecting flexibility that is hard to achieve with classical structures, or significant changes in regulations. And most of them are saying, "If we don't start changing now, we might not make it at all."

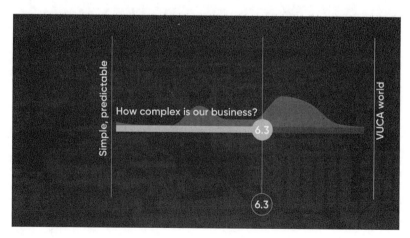

Example of the VUCA exercise

Do this exercise in your organization:

How complex is your business? On a scale of 1 to 10,[2] where do you see your organization?

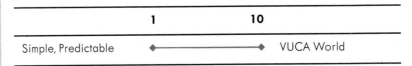

	1	10
Simple, Predictable	◆————————————◆	VUCA World

If the overall results in your organization are

- 1 to 4, there is no need for agility in your business.
- 5 or 6, you should start experimenting with agility; the situation is not yet urgent but might soon be.
- 7 or more, it's high time to change the way you work and become agile now, or you might never make it.

Think about your business. What makes your business model sustainable? What do you need to change so you can address the VUCA challenges?

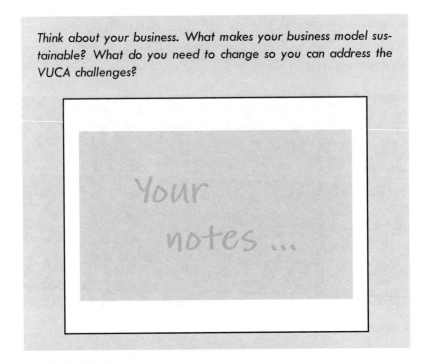

Your
notes ...

---

2. In most of the assessments in this book, we use the scale of 1 to 10. There is no hard measure for the numbers—the numbers are based on your feelings and are subjective, relative to your expectations and circumstances. The scale is often used with coaching questions because, by considering your response along a continuum, you gain new insights (i.e., if your answer is 5, what would 6 look like?).

In our company, when we changed our way of working and started our agile journey, most of our competitors were operating on year plans and fixed budget and scope, and it usually took them a few months to build an up-to-speed team for the customer. We were very well aware of the growing influence of the VUCA challenges, which created a huge pressure for the entire information and communication technology (ICT) business, so we turned the whole business model around. We offered high flexibility as the key differentiator, allowing our customers to add a new team in less than a week, and we allowed flexibility on a Sprint[3] basis in our contracts. In a simple way, with every Sprint, the customers had a chance to experience what we had finished at the Sprint Review,[4] they gave us feedback, and based on the overall value delivered, they could choose to continue investing in the next Sprint or not. Teams were learning new skills much faster as a result of intensive collaboration, and we got an up-to-speed team in less than three Sprints.

I remember one meeting with a new client where we were discussing how we were going to work together. We asked the client if the company had ever outsourced anything. "Yes," the manager said. "So how did it go?" I asked. Long story short, it turned out they were just finalizing one project with a vendor, and literally nothing had gone well. The product was late, it didn't work as they expected, there were many misunderstandings and miscommunications that resulted in a number of bugs being claimed as change requests and therefore cost extra . . . the list went on. We listened carefully to the client's story, and when she finished, all I needed to say was, "Sorry to hear that. It must have been very stressful for you. But that's the reason why we work differently." You could see the surprise in her eyes. "What do you mean by that? Tell us more about it," she said. We got her interest, and linking our way of working to the pains her company had just experienced only increased her curiosity and willingness to give our way a try. But she was still quite hesitant to say yes. "It all sounds very interesting, but can you give us a reference, some company of our size that has worked this way with you?" she asked. We gave her the reference and also offered to start with a low-risk trial project for them to experience how it would be to work this way.

---

3. Sprint is a fixed timebox iteration during which the increment of the product is created. It's part of the Scrum framework. https://www.scrumguides.org
4. Sprint Review is an event in Scrum that allows teams to get feedback from the customers on the value delivered during the Sprint.

It took a while to convince our clients that our way of working was better than what they were used to, but in the long term, we were successful. Interestingly, our flexibility and our radically different approach were tempting enough, so our clients always gave it a try. And once they experienced it, the partnership we built, the transparency we provided, and the working product increments we delivered in every short iteration built high levels of trust in our cooperation. Step by step, we grew our teams at the expense of the competitors, who were pushed to the margins.

What Is Agile Leadership About?

As the world becomes steadily more dynamic and complex, organizations have to change to stay competitive. They must become more flexible, team-oriented, and self-organized. And as a consequence, leaders need to adopt another approach to motivate people and lead the organizations to keep up the speed. We speak about knowledge management, creativity, the need for innovations—and in the past few years about agile leadership—which help leaders to understand the nature of the change that is happening in business right now and prepare them to react effectively to the challenges modern organizations have brought on in all their complexity. The less predictable the business is, the more organizations are failing with traditional leadership approaches, which optimize for repetitive tasks and consistency.

Agile leadership is the leadership of tomorrow.

Agile leadership is not about how to implement agile, Scrum, Kanban, eXtreme Programming, or lean principles. You have people in your organization who can do that. Being an agile leader is a state of mind. We build a world where 1 + 1 = more_than_two, a world that is not divided between winners and losers but where both can win and creativity can make a difference in the equation.

What Is the Difference between Leader and Manager?

First, all managers are leaders; however, leaders don't necessarily need to be managers. Being a leader is not a position. No one can be promoted to be a leader. It's only your own choice if you decide to become one.

Everyone can become a leader, it's only your own decision.

In an agile organization, where hierarchy becomes less important, we put more focus on leadership than on management. There is no positional authority given to a leader. Leaders gain their influence from their actions and behaviors and from their service to the people around them, and their power grows through the respect of others. Traditional managers, on the other hand, are often associated with decision making and certain positional power that must be given to them. Having said that, leadership is a state of mind. Everyone can be a leader. Some of us just might be kind of sleeping, afraid to take over the responsibility and start an initiative. However, there is nothing other than yourself preventing you from becoming a leader.

Leadership is a state of mind, not a position.

You are the leader, so don't wait for anyone else. Agile is not about practices, rules, or processes. Agile is about a different way of thinking, a different way of approaching things, a different mindset. And it's all in your hands. You are the leader, and the only obstacle between the leadership state of mind and the traditional hierarchical mindset are your own mindset and your own habits.

On my agile journey, the most difficult task was to be consistent with the change I intended to create and to be a role model of an agile leader. When I took over the department of 120 people and human resources, I had a vision to build a flexible and fast-learning environment based on the network of the self-organized teams without management. The most important job I had in front of me was to grow leaders who would leverage the power of influence over positional power. Easier to say than do.

I already had my experience with it as a Scrum Master and agile coach, but doing the same at the director level is different. You are fighting not only against your own habits but against the tempting positional power you have, which, if you use it, can temporarily make everything much more efficient and faster. If I could have just told the team what to do on day-to-day tasks, I wouldn't have had to spend hours helping people around me to understand the situation and make their own decisions. It was super time consuming. I spent all my time at work talking to people and helping them to collaborate and take over the initiatives. I spent evenings at home catching up with my work. Telling them exactly what to do was so very tempting. But shortcuts never work well. If I had given up then, they never would have made it. And I would have been stuck as the central decisionmaker and advisor forever—they would never have gotten a chance to come up with innovative and creative solutions, and we would still have been just another ordinary company unable to make a difference for our clients.

Persistence was key. In a few months, it paid off, and I was able to step back and enjoy the power of self-organization. The department was running by itself toward the mission of added-value solutions.

Why Is It Important to Be an Agile Leader?

Agile leaders are key to any agile organization. The more agile leadership exists in the organization, the more likely the overall mindset changes and the agile transformation will be successful. Having a critical mass of agile leadership is crucial for any agile environment; without it, we are only creating another process and adding terminology, and all we get is "fake agile," not business results.

Leaders need to change first. The organization will follow.

Being an agile leader is more important than ever. Nearly every corporation is willing to experiment with at least one agile project. As organizational agility grows, the gap between traditional management and the agile way of working is getting bigger and creates frustration on both sides. The teams are frustrated because management is not supporting them and the organization is not helping them on their agile journey. Management is frustrated because it doesn't know how to produce agile leaders and grow the collaborative team-oriented environment. "When we speak with leaders about this kind of system, most agree intellectually that power, decision making, and resource allocation should be distributed. But making that happen is another matter. Their great fear is that the organization will fall into chaos" [Kerievsky19]. Though that is a common concern, I would argue that agile brings harmony. The well-functioning teams deliver value to the customers regularly, effortlessly, and with joy, which in turn provides motivation and energy within the organization to create innovative solutions and address the day-to-day business challenges.

Agile leadership helps you to face the challenges of the VUCA world.

It's not an easy or a short process—agile is a journey. However, even after just a few iterations, you will see the results. Given the dynamics and complexity of the world today, there is no other way.

Agile leadership helps you to face the challenges of the VUCA world. "Nobody has really recommended command-and-control leadership for a long time. But no fully formed alternative has emerged, either. That's partly because high-level executives are ambivalent about changing their own behavior" [Ancona19].

This book is a great opportunity for change. It brings all the useful agile leadership concepts on a plateau for leaders to sample and decide how they can get closer to becoming agile leaders. Start growing agile leaders today, and the organizational agility will grow along.

Books to Read

- *The Age of Agile: How Smart Companies Are Transforming the Way Work Gets Done*, Stephen Denning (New York: AMACOM, 2018).
- *Managing for Happiness: Games, Tools, and Practices to Motivate Any Team*, Jurgen Appelo (New York: Wiley, 2016).
- *Scrum: The Art of Doing Twice the Work in Half the Time*, Jeff Sutherland and J. J. Sutherland (London: Random House, 2014).
- *Scrum: A Practical Guide to the Most Popular Agile Process*, Kenneth S. Rubin (Upper Saddle River, NJ: Addison-Wesley, 2017).

In a Nutshell

- ☐ Agile is a response to new business realities and challenges of a VUCA world.
- ☐ Agile brings flexible business models and allows organizations to succeed in today's constantly changing world.
- ☐ Being agile is focusing on making people awesome, learning through experiments, delivering value, and making safety a prerequisite.
- ☐ Leadership is a state of mind, not a position.
- ☐ Leaders need to change first. The organization will follow.
- ☐ Agile organizations need a different style of leadership. Agile leaders need to focus on building flexible systems and growing other leaders.
- ☐ Agile leaders don't need to use power but to leverage the power of influence.

3

· · ·

ORGANIZATIONAL EVOLUTION

Organizations are constantly evolving. They transformed significantly in the last century, adapting to the world changes by redesigning the structure, culture, and way of work. There are three different organizational paradigms, and none of them is right or wrong by definition; each of them can be a good fit for a particular time or business reality.

ORGANIZATION 1.0: TRADITIONAL

In the 1970s, the most common organizational structure was the pyramid structure. It was deep, hierarchical, and full of power. Companies had strong bosses who led within that structure. Internally, their approach was based on command and control, bureaucracy, and standardization. The focus was on resources, and each individual had clearly defined roles and responsibilities.

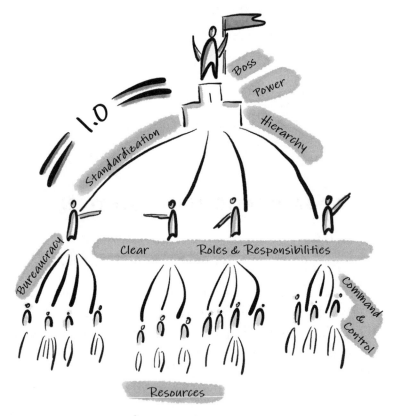

Traditional Organization

Those hierarchical pyramid structures were not wrong in any way. They were the perfect solution for the challenges of the Industrial Age and for the low dynamics of business in that pre-VUCA (volatile, uncertain, complex, and ambiguous) world. Most companies could follow the best practices designed by individuals higher in the company hierarchy, and most of the problems could be analyzed and solved by good processes. A simple structure was needed to address the business challenges, and roles and responsibilities were clearly designed. It worked pretty well. Managers got better results. Companies were successful, they grew, and they became even more successful.

The fundamental belief behind this type of organization was that the boss was always right, there was always some process that could address the situations, and the role of the boss was to improve such processes. Employees were there to follow the processes and not challenge them in any way.

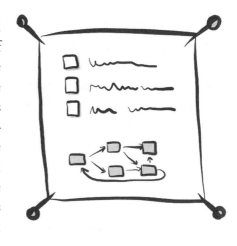

The management believed that the employees, for the most part, were lazy slackers who couldn't work without pressure, so if the results were not satisfactory, the bosses were supposed to add even more pressure. Payment was directly linked to individual performance, and it was considered to be the only motivation for doing work. The bosses also believed that everyone's job needed to be described in a detailed way so that there was no doubt about the role, expectations, and responsibility of each individual. Everyone was expected to do their job and not think about it.

As a consequence, most people were not happy at work. They were demotivated and complained all the time. They took work as a necessary evil. If they could only stay at home and not have to work! The

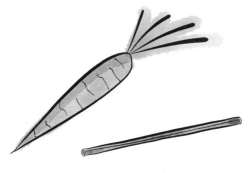

most common management tool was the carrot-and-stick approach: people will do something only if they get a reward—a carrot—or because they are forced to or afraid of the consequences—a stick. The reward needed to be directly linked to the task, and for any mistake, there was a penalty in the form of losing the reward.

The positive side of such an arrangement is that organizations that still hold to the hierarchical structure are fast to solve repetitive problems. In a relatively static environment—such as a production line in a factory—it works pretty well. However, in a VUCA world, such an organization is like a dinosaur who is too slow in responding to changes. The fixed processes are killing any creativity and innovation, and such slow and inflexible organizations will not make it to the next decade.

ORGANIZATION 2.0: KNOWLEDGE

Twenty years later, in the 1990s, the trend in organizational design led to Organization 2.0, which focuses on knowledge. Organizations began trying to adapt to the constantly changing world and the increasing complexity of tasks and to respond with specialization, processes, and structure. Companies realized that the world is no longer simple, and the majority of problems could be classified

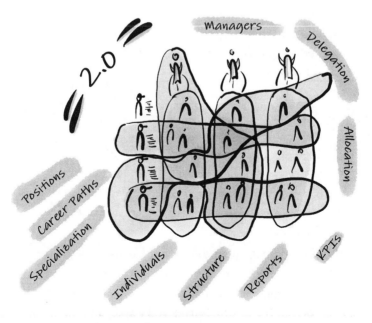

Knowledge Organization

as complicated. As a result, companies adopted complicated processes, focused on deep analysis, and invested in experts. There was a lot of talk about managers, delegation, allocation, positions, career paths, specialization, defined reporting structure, detailed reports, and individual key performance indicators (KPIs).

The fundamental belief behind this type of organization is that complicated problems need detailed analysis and the experience of specialized individuals. As a result, companies invested in learning and specialization. They began to grow. In the Organization 2.0 structure, work that used to be done by one person now needs several specific and dedicated positions, which requires exact synchronization. Specialized departments are created to deal with Java, database, testing, architecture, analysis, documentation, customer segments, accounts, plans, and, last but not least, even chair purchases. Every task needs a detailed description and a process for synchronizing dependencies. And each group of specialists needs a manager. We also believe that if we give individuals the goals and measure their performance against these goals, they will be successful. There is still the belief that the managers make the decisions, and the people below them just do the job. No initiative is expected.

The consequences are that organizations are trying to create processes and specific roles to describe everything, to have every possibility thought over. Companies create career paths to show employees where to grow, and they 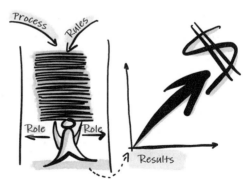 talk about other motivation factors. They spend months describing KPIs, but the more processes and specializations companies have, the less responsibility and initiative individuals take. Management

tries to help employees to value success and to show them opportunities for growth, so practices such as employee of the month,
performance reviews, and evaluations have become the core management tools.

The pressure on individuals to be more successful, better, and
smarter than others is huge. *What if my colleague is going to be rated
better in the performance review? What if I am not promoted in two
years?* It leads to a culture that emphasizes the individual's goals
over the organization's goals. Most managers and experts live with
the belief that they are better than others, which generates a lot of
competitive behavior, blaming, defensiveness, and contempt.

Managers work-
ing in this environment
often micromanage and
treat their employees
and colleagues with
little respect or trust.
People just follow the
process and do what is
specified by their job
description. On the plus
side, the organization is trying to make the world less complex and
deconstruct the difficult tasks into smaller pieces that are easier for
specialists to analyze. These steps make complicated tasks more
interesting, challenging, and manageable. The employees know
what is expected from them and where to focus. They know what
needs to be done. There is room for delegation, which helps people
to take over some task-related responsibility and ownership. As the
organization is individual-, task-, and skill-oriented, it naturally consists of silos, which create a ton of dependencies in a value stream
delivery. The most time-consuming job of a manager is allocations.

The defined positions and roles are not as flexible as is needed
in the modern world, but it's still far better than the fixed hierarchical structures of the traditional Organization 1.0. Organizations

often operate in yearly cycles, with long feedback loops. Creativity is rare. Innovations take time. It's like a slow  whale shark—a great creature living its own life no matter what's around.

Organizations naturally experience a steady need to grow, as each new problem generates a need for new positions. But every now and then, they struggle. They try to cut expenses, but that helps only temporarily and does not bring any long-term success. So management dreams about the previous stage, where it was much easier to manage resources. Back then, managers had real power. They could make decisions. They could force people to work. They could use the carrot and the stick. It was so simple—no need for committees, no need to call a meeting for every single detail. Back then, the allocation of individual resources did not take up most of their time.

ORGANIZATION 3.0: AGILE

The agile organization is a new paradigm, a new form of the organizational design that is flexible and highly adaptive. There is no exact definition of what you need to do to create an agile organization because there is not one specific form that the organization needs to take. It's not about frameworks and practices, as those are too prescriptive. An agile organization addresses VUCA challenges and brings the agile values to the organizational level. In today's world, we need to create organizations that are not afraid of volatility and uncertainty but that are designed for complexity and thrive on ambiguity. And that is not simple. In an agile organization, we build on teams instead of individuals, on different styles of leadership, and on intensive collaboration through the dynamic network structure. We focus on helping others to become leaders and grow emergent leadership over the fixed management positions.

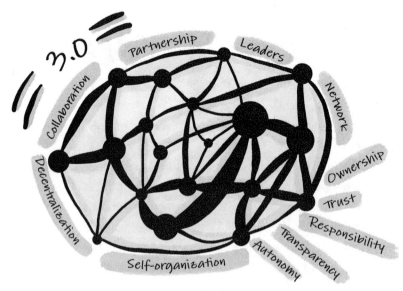

Agile Organization

Instead of seeing the organization as a huge tanker, you can imagine the agile organization as a flotilla of smaller boats going in the same direction, living in the same context, having the same values, but making some decisions differently based on the situation. You can come up with many different metaphors—a colony of ants, a bloom of jellyfish, a chameleon. Or you can simply see the organization as a living organism that, no matter how diverse the different parts of the systems are and how they are distributed, has one goal about which no one has any doubts at all. It experiments and learns from failures, and safety and transparency are hardcoded in the system's DNA. The culture in an agile organization values collaboration and trust, which brings about a higher number of innovative and creative ideas than the hierarchical traditional structures.

The fundamental belief behind this type of organization is that people are naturally creative and intelligent. They will solve any challenge if we create an environment with radical transparency and trust them to do the work. We also believe that the current world of business is too unpre-dictable, and therefore traditional methods are failing. Many compa-

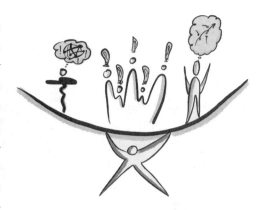

nies feel a strong need for a change: they know they need to be more flexible, more change responsive, simply more adaptive. We believe that if we create good evolutionary purpose, with strong vision, and give people a good environment in which to collaborate and grow, teams will come up with a better solution than any individual alone ever can.

The consequence is that teams are more likely to come up with innovative and creative solutions, breaking the status quo and changing established habits. They put the whole organization into motion and are highly change responsive. As a structured piece, the company is team-oriented, as the complexity of the business must be addressed again by a complex system, and no smart individuals are good enough to crack the challenges of the modern world alone. The leadership is more emergent around challenges that need to be solved, and the structure becomes more flexible and self-organized, self-managed, and sometimes even self-directed. The downside of such an organization is that it needs a strong common goal that everyone believes in. Without it, chaos reigns. Also, the organiza-tion needs enough leaders ready for such a shift. That's what we talk about in this book.

A modern agile organization is built on people and their relationships. It is a collaborative, creative, and adaptive network. It's built from autonomous systems that are connected to each other, so they influence one another but still remain consistent. It's a fundamentally new 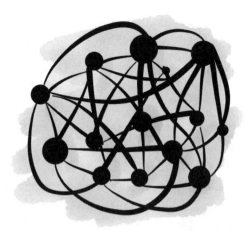 mindset that is a huge mental challenge for most organizations. Be patient: it will take time. Organizations and societies can change, but change never happens overnight. To make the change stick, make the new way of working a habit—it's all relative to the size of the segment we are changing. It takes decades in society at large. It will take years within organizations. It may take months at a team level. Take your time. The push will not solve it. Inspiration will.

REFLECT ON YOUR ORGANIZATION

Every organization is a complex system, and different parts might show some aspects of all organizational paradigms: traditional, knowledge, and agile. However, from a holistic point of view, one model would be the most prominent. Keep in mind that no stage is right or wrong by itself. The organizational design always needs to reflect the overall environment complexity and need for adaptiveness.

Where do you see your organization now? What is the major reason for that classification? Where would you like to see it in the next five years?

Your notes ...

Books to Read

- *The Leader's Guide to Radical Management: Reinventing the Workplace for the 21st Century*, Stephen Denning (San Francisco: Jossey-Bass, 2010).
- *Accelerate: Building Strategic Agility for a Faster-Moving World*, John P. Kotter (Boston: Harvard Business Review Press, 2014).

In a Nutshell

☐ The organizational design needs to match the overall environment complexity and need for adaptiveness.

☐ The agile organization is built on people and their relationships.

☐ The traditional organizations 1.0 and 2.0 optimize for efficiency, dealing with predictable issues.

☐ The agile organization is a collaborative, creative, and adaptive network designed to address VUCA challenges.

4

. . .

THE AGILE LEADER

The agile leader exists in a different dimension than traditional management. It is not a position but a state of mind. Agile leaders do not create any hierarchy or have any given power. Their power grows by the value of their service to the organization.

"It All Starts with a Dream..."

Agile leaders are able to inspire others, can create and communicate an appealing vision or a higher purpose that motivates the organization, and are constantly looking for better ways of working through feedback. Agile leaders need to be inclusive and to support others on their leadership journey. They need to be open to new ideas, experiments, and innovations. They need to support creativity and be able to cultivate the right mindset and a culture of collaboration. An agile leader is a coach, facilitator, and a good listener.

Agile leadership is not about tools, practices, or methodologies. Leadership starts with a dream and a passion for it. It's an ability to look at the organization from the system perspective, understand system dynamics, be aware of what's happening in the system, embrace it, become an integral part of it, and finally be able to act on and influence the system with coaching in order to initiate a change.

The new management paradigm is about collaboration and trust, decentralization, continuous adaptation and flexibility, and cooperation and teamwork.

From the static management prevalent in the Industrial Age, we shifted to strategic management in the last twenty years of the twentieth century, and we quickly moved into the dynamic management that tries to keep up with the modern, constantly changing, complex VUCA world. That's the world that critically needs agile leadership, as anything else is not flexible enough to deal with current challenges.

Leaders Go First

Rickard Jones, Agile Coach, Program Lead, and AgileHR Manifesto Coauthor

Leadership in an organization that is still in transition on its agile journey can be hard. I recall the story of a business leader at one of the major UK retail banks who had to juggle this change along with some serious customer-facing deliveries. It was work that involved reinventing how the customers and staff worked together collaboratively in the bank's bricks-and-mortar branches. If it failed, there would be job losses and customer dissatisfaction. This was not the usual hipster digital journey; it was classic banking with an agile approach. The head of the department started by upskilling not only her people in agile and Scrum but also herself in agile leadership training. This was rare, as most leaders make the classic mistake of assuming they know it all and do not bother to invest in themselves. By taking this training, she inspired her staff to upskill themselves, as they then did. She learned from this experience that when learning is required, leaders go first.

With this training completed, she and her teams could make an informed decision on how they wanted to be agile on their journey. This knowledge allowed them to decide how to restructure the teams. The manager once again cleverly avoided the mistake of assuming that a radical restructuring was not needed. With the set-up capability of all her staff completed, she then exhibited servant leadership by supporting their decisions about the work and growing them to be the best that they could be, even when she did not always agree with them. For her, the benefit was that she was no longer on her own as a leader. The product owners in her team started to go beyond just the product development and into leadership and innovation of the products. One of the team members made the decision to actually stop one of the products, as it was discovered it no longer brought any value to the customers and branch staff. This proactive decision making had been unheard of in the bank before, but it saved the organization millions and allowed that investment to go to other initiatives that would create value. The win-win was only possible because the product owner was empowered to make that decision and the manager supported the decision through servant leadership. Her behaviors changed not only her, not only her direct reports, but also the whole department. As a result, it was possible to see, time and again, teams making fast and valuable decisions. Through the manager's leadership behaviors, she catalyzed the capability within her teams, who now not only self-manage but also self-lead the organization.

Think about your future as an agile leader. What is your dream? What do you want to achieve?

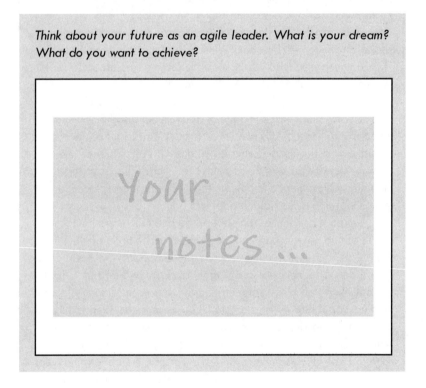

THE SERVANT LEADER

One of the leadership styles that is often mentioned in an agile environment is the servant leader. It is a term coined in the 1970s by Robert K. Greenleaf in "The Servant as Leader" [Greenleaf07]. The term has been revitalized in an agile environment, where the most common reference to the servant leader is regarding the ScrumMaster role [Šochová17a], where the focus is on the community and empathy aspect of the role. Servant leadership is a very useful concept for describing agile leadership. Being a servant leader is the first step on the agile leader journey. It's a simple mental model that often creates the first shift in the leader's mind.

The common misconception is that the servant leader is "serving," or in other words is a "slave" of others, which creates a hierarchical relationship. But that's a misunderstanding. *Servant* is not used in the literal sense but in a highly holistic and philosophical sense. Servant leaders share power and do not consider the hierarchical position as important. Servant leaders are leaders in the first place—they help other people to grow, have vision, and think beyond day-to-day tasks and short-term goals; they are good listeners, have empathy, are aware of the system and their own abilities and limits, focus on good relationships and cultures, are persuasive, form communities, and are inclusive. There is nothing indicating a "slave" position, except the name maybe.

The servant leader is an enabler of the flat(-ter) structure because it removes the hierarchy from leadership. Removing the hierarchy is necessary for agile cultures, which are flatter by definition, as they build on self-organizing teams where the empowerment and autonomy are much higher while the need for traditional management is disappearing. As Patrick Lencioni says, "My dream is that someday people won't talk about servant leadership, because that will be the only type of leadership that exists" [Lencioni19].

Let's imagine you are in the last four months at work before a long holiday of several months. You are going on your dream vacation, a sailing and diving trip where you are going to be in the middle of the ocean, on a boat with no connectivity to the outside world for the entire time. Your hope is that the organization will make it without you. You can't prepare all of the personnel for every decision they will need to take, and you can't let the organization simply carry on, unchanging, until your return, as the business is too dynamic, unpredictable, and complex, and you are facing the challenges of the VUCA world more than ever. There is no single person who can naturally take over for you. You have a flat structure with self-organizing Scrum teams, which are ready to move on to the next level. You feel positive that they can make it and that the organization is ready for the next step.

This scenario is a good example of what is required for mastering servant leadership. It's not about you, but about the others. All you need to do is focus on helping others to become leaders. Create an environment where they can grow, allow them to form communities, and let the leadership be emergent. "The ultimate role of a leader is knowing when to step away and let someone else lead" [Lencioni19]. If you are going to be consistent and suppress the urge to take shortcuts while dealing with challenges, there is enough time to get the team ready. Remember, your goal is not to be efficient, to advise, or to decide. It's to cultivate the teams so they get used to taking ownership and responsibility for organizational challenges without your having to make every decision. After all, in the VUCA world, the collaborating teams are always better than individuals alone at finding optimal creative solutions. If you don't start changing now, next week or next month might be too late.

Think about yourself as a leader in this context. Be honest. The results are not inputs for your evaluation but show some opportunities for your growth as a leader. The assessment is about your feelings and will differ if you do it in different environments.

On a scale of 1 to 10, where do you **focus the most** effort during your day-to-day work?

	1	10	
Advising and deciding	◆————————◆		Listening to others
Tasks	◆————————◆		Relationships
Day-to-day focus	◆————————◆		Long-term focus
Planning	◆————————◆		Learning from feedback
Roles and responsibilities	◆————————◆		Building communities
Efficiency	◆————————◆		Growth of others
Positional authority	◆————————◆		Emergent leadership
Doing the work	◆————————◆		Helping others to do it
Workflow and results	◆————————◆		People and collaboration

As you have most likely realized already, the more on the right you are, the closer you are to the servant leadership mindset. However, the world is not black and white. And neither is this scale. It's not your goal to answer 10 to all questions. The assessment only serves to raise awareness of the issues. The actions follow in the next exercise.

What would need to change so that you feel comfortable moving closer to the servant leader role? What can you change in your focus?

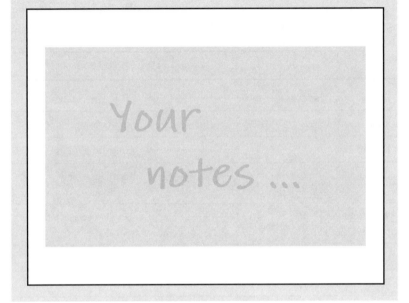

THE LEADER-LEADER

Another useful leadership mental model is described by David Marquet in his book *Turn the Ship Around*, which shows his leadership journey as commander of the nuclear submarine *Santa Fe*, where he realized during a simple drill that giving orders might not always be the best approach. He said, "Leadership should mean giving control rather than taking control and creating leaders rather than forging followers" [Marquet13]. This book presents a practical use case for companies just beginning to transition to agile, because they often struggle with the mindset shift required, believing that their organization is different and that change would not be possible in their context. However, if it was possible on a navy submarine, it is possible anywhere, right?

Marquet's model helps to change the traditional leadership style of leader-follower, in which people are expected to follow orders, into the leader-leader style of servant leadership, in which leaders are there to help other people to grow and become leaders themselves. I personally like this concept better than the servant leader concept, as it focuses on partnership and doesn't have the negative connotation of being a servant.

Acting as a leader-leader is not that simple; it takes a lot of practice and patience. You need to trust in others and be confident that they can come up with a better idea even when you believe that you already know a good solution. You must be able to let it go and trust the system. For simple tasks, it might not be necessary, but the more complex and ambiguous the problem is, the more success you will have with such an approach. The journey from the leader-follower starts with committing yourself to high transparency, being willing to share leadership, giving people autonomy, and trusting that they will make sound decisions.

A good first step is sharing the purpose with everyone so everyone knows where we are heading, increasing transparency so everyone knows what is happening, and creating safety where autonomy can grow. As an example, imag-

ine you have an important customer visit planned next month. A pure leader-follower approach is clear: You are the central decision maker. It's all about you. You come up with a preparation strategy for the visit, and again, it's you who distributes the tasks. The common approach in organizations is to delegate pieces of this process to the team or individuals. Most of us would already be quite happy about it and call it agile. However, the pure leader-leader approach is to create an environment with radical transparency around the situation and together create a purpose and a vision, letting people come up with their intended strategy and tasks. It might sound radical, and indeed, it requires very different skills than traditional leaders need. You must be good at large-group facilitation and system coaching, you must believe in self-organization, and you must trust that others can always come up with a better solution. To rephrase the Agile Manifesto Principles [Beck01a], the best ideas emerge from self-organizing teams. The leader-leader approach tests your agile mindset at the highest level. Try the following check to see how likely you are to act as leader-leader or how deeply the leader-follower model is part of your habits.

Which of the following best describes you? Choose one answer for each topic.

Trust

A. My role is to make decisions; that's why I'm a leader.
B. I can fully delegate clear, well-described tasks.
C. I need to set directions, but the rest can be taken over by the teams.
D. Others can always come up with great ideas, often better than mine.

Transparency

A. People don't need to know everything; too much information creates a mess.
B. Vision, goals, and objectives need to be clearly defined.
C. Information needs to be shared only among people who are in the working group.
D. Everything should be made visible to everyone to support emergent leadership.

Self-organization

A. People need to have defined workflows to be efficient.
B. Self-organization can work only on simple, well-described tasks and with small teams.
C. Self-organization is nice for day-to-day tasks, not for emergent critical issues.
D. Teams can figure it out; they will do their best if they have autonomy.

EVALUATE YOUR ANSWERS

A. You have a pure leader-follower mindset; therefore, the agile leadership concept might be too far away.
B. You still have a mostly leader-follower mindset, and you are entrenched in the traditional way of working.
C. You are taking the first steps toward being a leader-leader. Being an agile leader is a journey, and you are on it.
D. You are fully in the leader-leader mindset; you have internalized the agile leadership principles.

Reflecting on your answers and evaluation, on which area identified by the preceding questions would you like to focus?

What can you do to get closer to the Catalyst leader approach?

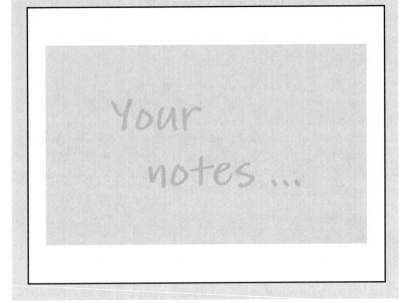

THE LEADERSHIP AGILITY: FROM EXPERT TO CATALYST

The servant leader and leader-leader approaches are simple and sufficient in many cases. Nonetheless, in some situations, it's useful to look at leadership agility from a different perspective, for example, using Bill Joiner's concept described in his book *Leadership Agility* [Joiner06]. It focuses on managers as leaders, showing a journey every manager needs to go through.

The journey from Expert to Catalyst shows a valuable dimension of the management shift in an agile environment. The Expert is a prototype of the manager in the Organization 1.0, where mostly tactical decisions are expected from a manager. The Achiever is a common manager type in the Organization 2.0, focusing on achieving the goals and objectives. The Catalyst is needed to create an effective agile Organization 3.0, where teams self-organize to come up with creative and innovative solutions.

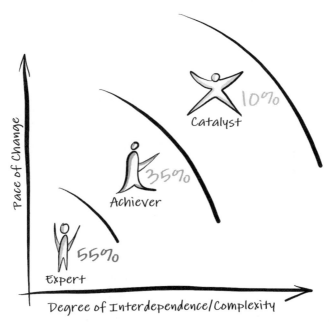

The Expert

This is a classical boss or supervisor—the person who knows best and therefore can advise and lead others by example, using his or her own experiences. Bill Joiner, in his article "Leadership Agility: From Expert to Catalyst," estimates that around 45 percent of managers are currently capable of operating at this level [Joiner11], and around 10 percent are not even there yet. This is frightening. Over half of managers are at Expert level, capable only of leading within the pure leader-follower model. They believe in decision making, and they are task-oriented and tactical, often very directive, even micromanaging. They believe they are the best, they have very high standards, and if it were only possible to clone them, everything would be much easier. They are often hardworking experts and problem solvers. Because of their experiences, people respect them as mentors. They keep one-to-one relationships, focusing on controlling people and increasing individual efficiency.

Trust is usually an issue—Experts dislike giving or receiving feedback. They take care of their part of the organization alone for the most part. They are not agile leaders at all. They are great workers and problem solvers,  though. They are a great match for a simple and predictable environment where automation and optimizing flows are the core part of the leader's work. Being an expert is a valid step on a leadership journey—that's where people gain self-confidence. However, Expert leaders are not the most agile enthusiasts; rather the opposite: an agile journey is usually quite a painful experience for most of them. When they hear about agile leadership and modern organizational design concepts, they usually find them very abstract and hard to understand. They take the entire agile concept as a set of practices, rules, and roles and often turn them into even more intense micromanagement; instances of "Dark Scrum" [Jeffries16] and fake agile are quite common around Expert leaders.

The Achiever

The next level is the Achiever. Bill Joiner estimates that around 35 percent of managers are currently capable of operating at this level [Joiner11]. Achievers are the key people who are already far enough on their agile journey that they can picture agile as a mindset and can feel a need for a leadership style change. Those are the people agile transformation shall focus on, as they are often ready for the next step, and organizations need their support to make the agile transformation successful.

Achievers still believe in their own way of working, but unlike Experts, they can at least operate in one-to-many relationships. They focus on getting buy-in; they are strategic, influential, sometimes even manipulative in order to get their way. They use meetings to sell their points of view and get support for their ideas. Their primary focus is on results. They are very competitive, they like stretch goals and clear objectives, and they believe a good challenge is the best motivator. They think of people as resources for achieving their goals. They are okay with getting feedback as long as it gets faster results. They focus on the stakeholders and customers as well as the employees.

Achievers can handle more complicated environments than Experts can. However, the environment needs to be stable enough so it can be described by processes and outcome measures. As I mentioned, working with Achievers is an important part of your agile journey. They are not agile yet, but they are  open to change. They are capable of embracing the mindset and applying it in their work. They would be zig-zagging there and back, always enthusiastic about any metrics and objectives they can pinpoint, but if you are patient, they will get on board and transform. You often find them "doing" agile instead of "being" agile, but in general they are open to seeing the whole picture.

The Catalyst

Finally, only around 10 percent of managers are currently capable of operating at the Catalyst level [Joiner11]. Those are the agile leaders who have the agile mindset, who understand that agile is deeper and goes beyond practices, roles, and frameworks. These are the leaders who *are* agile, not just doing agile. The central element is the vision and purpose. They believe that if you "articulate an innovative, inspiring vision and bring together the right people they will transform the vision into reality" [Joiner11]. The key focus of a Catalyst leader is to create a space, an environment where people can be successful. They care about the culture where many-to-many relationships emerge, and they focus on collaboration, transparency, and openness.

Catalysts empower people around them and work with teams, not just individuals. They are good at complex situations, seeking different perspectives and diversity, looking for innovative and creative solutions. They are inclusive and don't limit the people they work with by any boundaries. They can be vulnerable themselves, and they emphasize that it's okay to be wrong. However, they make safety a prerequisite and encourage candid feedback and experiments where people can learn from failures. They are good coaches and facilitators, and they help others to grow. It's with Catalysts that the organizational agile journey really begins. The business agility will not emerge without enough leaders with a Catalyst mindset.

Where do you stand as a leader? Choose one answer for each question:

What is most important for you?

A. Tactics
B. Strategy
C. Vision

What is the best description of a leader?

A. Leaders are respected and followed by others.
B. Leaders shall motivate other people.
C. Leaders need to empower others.

What is the most accurate statement about giving and receiving feedback?

A. It's not necessary.
B. Feedback can be useful. I'm open to using it from time to time.
C. I'm proactively looking for opportunities to learn from feedback and help others to learn from it.

Where is your preference?

A. Creating one-to-one relationships (individuals)
B. Forming one-to-many relationships (groups)
C. Facilitating many-to-many relationships (teams and networks)

EVALUATE YOUR ANSWERS

A: Expert; B: Achiever; C: Catalyst.

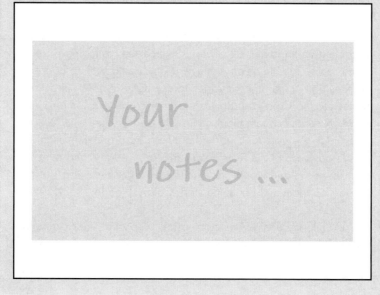

Reflecting on your answers and evaluation, on which area identified by the preceding questions would you like to focus?

What can you do to get closer to the leader-leader approach?

Self-Awareness and Intent

Pete Behrens, Founder and Managing Partner of Trail Ridge

Two of the most difficult aspects of Catalyst leadership that I see in my coaching of leaders as well as in myself are lack of self-awareness and a mismatch of the leaders' desired intent and the perceived intent as seen by others around them. Most Achievers believe they're Catalysts because, in their minds, they are engaging others in the conversation and they are including others in decisions, as a Catalyst would. However, observers of this type of leader may see very different behavior. The leaders' own cognitive bias and blind spots don't let them see themselves as those around them do.

This has recently been a particular focus of my personal leadership practice because of a particularly exposed failure on my part. I learn a lot from failure and feel we need to more readily celebrate failure. Example: This year I hired a new member of our Trail Ridge team—a half-COO and half-executive coach. The candidate was a veteran leader who had engaged in our leadership awareness and practice programs for two years. She had excellent experience as a leader and had proven herself as an effective coach/guide. I knew her well. But my team of managing partners didn't.

I had a choice. I could just hire her (which would mean I would be acting as an Expert). I could convince the managing partners of her value (acting as an Achiever). Or I could seek to cocreate her position in the company (acting as a Catalyst). My intent was to choose the Catalyst path. I posted her credentials on our Slack Workspace and sought input on how to best use her skills to grow Trail Ridge. As we hadn't worked out her package yet, I sought the team's advice on how to structure it. We hired her, and over the next few days and weeks she became an instrumental part of our leadership team and coaching staff. Catalyst leaders rock! Or do they?

While my desire was cocreation, what the other managing partners felt was manipulation. What? One MP said I had already made up my mind to hire her, and they were just along for the ride. They felt their feedback made no difference to the decision. To them, I had played the Achiever. This Catalyst thing is hard. The worst part was that I didn't find this out until weeks later, when I was reviewing feedback from a Leadership Agility 360 Assessment on myself. The partners hadn't shared this with me at the time—it only came out later.

My advice to myself going forward is to be more explicit and break problems down into smaller steps in order to be more transparent. In this case, I should have told the team that I was hiring the new leader (decision made), but that I was not exactly sure how to structure the role (seeking input). Thus, in the future I will evaluate my own thought process better—what I am sure about, what I am open to, and where I stand on the issue at hand.

The following exercise will help you to create awareness of the need for leadership in your organization and a visual map of the leaders you currently have. Based on this exercise, you can think about what needs to change in your leadership style and how you can help others in your organization to grow into the needed leadership style.

Create a visual map of the leadership at your organization. Make marks at the following picture:

1. What is your level of leadership agility? Are you closer to Expert, Achiever, or Catalyst?
2. Where do you see your organization regarding the pace of change and the degree of interdependence and complexity?
3. Where do you see the other leaders in your organization? Are they Expert, Achiever, or Catalyst leaders?
4. What is the required shift of the leaders to match the need of the business complexity and the pace of change? (Draw an arrow.)

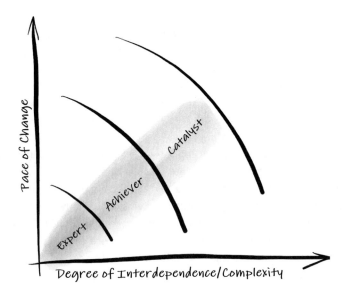

Degree of Interdependence/Complexity

What are you going to do to grow into the required leader style?
How can you help others?

Your
notes ...

The Agile Leader Journey

While all the preceding concepts are useful, they are just mental models helping you to see how you can think about your transition. At different times, a different model might be useful for you to grow toward becoming an agile leader. It's a continuous journey and never-ending personal development.

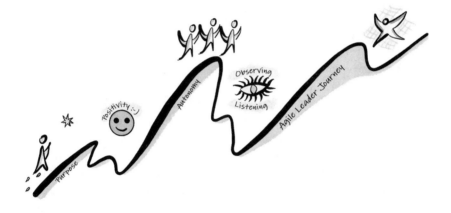

No matter where you are right now, your agile leader journey starts with an understanding of why you are here in the first place. There is a sense of purpose pushing you to go for it and crack any challenges on the way, no matter how hard it is. It requires high integrity, as people will follow you only if they trust you, as well as positivity and great observation and listening skills so you can learn from the feedback and constantly improve. As Robert J. Anderson says in an interview for *Forbes*, "We believe becoming a better leader is exactly the same process as becoming a better person. Both are processes of transformation that enable us to grow beyond the person we are now. Leadership in a VUCA world requires that we evolve into a higher version of ourselves—one that is more competent and conscious, mature and wise, authentic and courageous, relational and purposeful—and that we support others in becoming the same" [Duncan19].

The first time I was trying to be a servant leader and let teams around me figure out their own way of working, I was not ready to let go of my own ideas and give them their space. And they fought back and gave me feedback I was definitely not proud of. It was hard, as my intentions were good. However, it didn't seem that way to the others, and all I could do was to take their feedback and apologize. To my big surprise, they took my apology well, and we were able to continue the next day in a much more collaborative and open way.

Another failure was much harder to overcome, and it took many tries. It always happened when I was not patient enough to listen to all the different perspectives and I tried to take shortcuts. Working with teams and challenging their status quo is never simple, and most of my work is about doing just that. The issues that teams deal with are similar, so sooner or later you fall into the trap of thinking that you'd seen that situation already and you know what needs to be done. And right at that moment, you realize once again how wrong you were to push a certain way without first listening to all points of view. Sometimes I got another chance, sometimes not. And I can continue. Being an agile leader is a journey of continuous learning from feedback and finding better ways of doing things. It will take time; many of the concepts need practice, as they are changing your implicit reactions and habits. I'm far from perfect, but I'm on my journey, learning from feedback and improving my skills.

Purpose

A good purpose gives energy to the system and motivation for others to follow it. The agile leader journey starts with a purpose, a higher sense of value without which the organization would never be as good.

The agile leader journey starts with a purpose.

In the agile leader's world, purpose is not about "how." The steps on the agile journey are flexible, cocreated by the teams around you, and they can change depending on the circumstances and feedback. It's not your role to design those steps nor to set any goals and objectives on the way. It's up to the teams to find the right way, while the leaders' job is to set the environment so everyone else can flourish. Do you find it fascinating? Does it keep you going to work every day? Your internal purpose is the key driver.

I'd never wanted to start my own company, and I'd never planned to become a trainer and coach, either. It just happened to me, and I didn't say no at the time. I don't set any personal goals, so if you ask me what I want to achieve by the end of the year, I don't know. But I was always attracted to helping other people to have a better world of work. Therefore, I spent a lot of time talking to people, introducing coaching to organizations, building the flat structure. I work with clients, and so I joined the Scrum Alliance. The purpose was always the same: *Change the world.* I know how it sounds. Cliché. But that's my only driving force. Can I make an impact? Then I will go for it.

Let me share with you why I decided to write my second book. Yes, people liked the first one. But I felt a strong need to spread the message around. I was teaching many Certified ScrumMaster classes and the feedback I got was, "Wow, I thought I understood it, but now I see it differently. It was eye-opening." It felt great at first, but then it got to me. Even if I taught large classes and managed to do three per week, which was too much already, how many people would I be able to teach? How many ScrumMasters would still struggle and never get a chance to learn what this role is truly about? And I felt down. No matter how great my classes were, I couldn't make a difference. And then I thought, maybe it's time to write a book. That's why *The Great ScrumMaster* [Šochová17a] was born. To make a difference. To change the world. That's why I say yes to certain jobs and no to others. That's why I designed my own agile leadership development program,[1] and last but not least, that's why I'm writing

---

1. The CAL (Certified Agile Leadership) class is followed by a seven-month development program certified by the Scrum Alliance.

this book. It's all about having purpose, because if you don't, you are lost. There are too many opportunities, and it's hard to know how to make the right choice.

How strong is your purpose? Choose one answer for each question.

How engaging is your work?

A. I feel that work belongs to work, and I don't take it home.
B. I'm sometimes enthusiastic about what's happening, but it's not every day.
C. In my free time, I often think about how to improve things at work, and I talk about it with friends and family.

Imagine you got paid the same salary whether you were working for this company or not. Would you still be coming to work?

A. No way. I would never show up again. I have better things to do in my life.
B. I would show up from time to time, when there is a challenge that needs my help.
C. Yes, I need to be there. It is important.

EVALUATE YOUR ANSWERS

You get −1 point for each A, 0 points for each B, and 1 point for each C answer.

If in the evaluation you got 1 or 2 points, spend some time writing down your purpose as a leader. What is your purpose, and what do you want to achieve? Why is it important to you?

If you got 0 points, spend some time thinking about your organization. What specifically makes you enthusiastic at your work? Why is it important that you are there, helping the organization? And then, if you find good enough reasons, think about your purpose as a leader.

What is your purpose as a leader?

Your notes ...

What is important to you in your work?

Your notes ...

Did you get a negative score? Don't worry. Think about aspects of your organization that would need to be changed in order to change your answers. Agile leadership will still be applicable, although it might be hard to apply it at full scale if you don't have a strong enough purpose yourself. Leaders need to start first, and the organization will follow. Having a higher evolutionary purpose is a prerequisite for any agile organization.

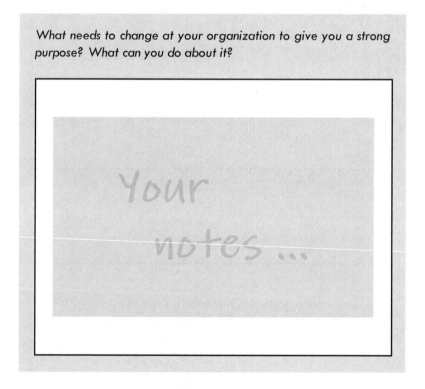

What needs to change at your organization to give you a strong purpose? What can you do about it?

Your notes . . .

Positivity

The agile leader journey needs a lot of positivity. Tell people around you that they are great. Acknowledge their work. Every day, every week, every year. You need to catch them at the moment of greatness and share that. The human brain is more efficient if we focus on successes instead of failures, and you need to switch that pattern in your brain in order to unleash people's potential. In any difficult times—for example, when trying to make significant changes in habits, mindsets, and ways of working—positivity can make a huge difference.

It works like a bank account. If you have high balance and something happens—for example, you get a parking ticket—you might not be super happy about the incident, but you take it as learning, cover the  fine, and move on. However, when your balance is low, the fine is devastating, as you may not have enough to pay for all expenses, and it can mean you can eat only bread for the rest of the month. You perceive the situation as very negative and become defensive or blame others.

The positivity level works similarly at your organization. The more positivity there is, the more likely it is the system will be able to handle any negative issues and learn from them. Celebrate even small achievements, and make people appreciate their own success. Be happy even about small things that went well. In other words, make people awesome, as Modern Agile [Kerievsky19] suggests. Positivity is only a perception. You've most likely heard about the half-empty or half-full glass, right? The more optimistic people see it as half-full, while the pessimists always go for half-empty or even almost empty, as some of my colleagues would call it. However, there is another perspective. I was discussing the concept at one of my classes recently, and one of the agile coaches there said that the glass was full. And when we looked at him with surprise, he said, "It's half full of water and half full of air." Interesting, isn't it? It's just a matter of perspective.

Another example of how to increase positivity is to reconsider how you take failure. Do you think of failure as a bad thing for which you need to find the person responsible, often to assign blame, or as an opportunity to improve and learn? This small perspective change makes a huge difference.

Positivity doesn't cost any extra. It's just a different habit.

Which one best describes your organization? Choose one answer from each section.

When a problem emerges . . .

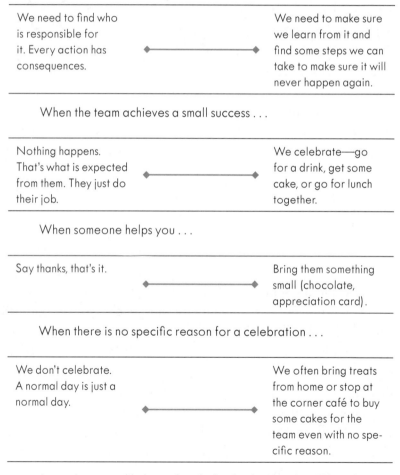

| We need to find who is responsible for it. Every action has consequences. | | We need to make sure we learn from it and find some steps we can take to make sure it will never happen again. |

When the team achieves a small success . . .

| Nothing happens. That's what is expected from them. They just do their job. | | We celebrate—go for a drink, get some cake, or go for lunch together. |

When someone helps you . . .

| Say thanks, that's it. | | Bring them something small (chocolate, appreciation card). |

When there is no specific reason for a celebration . . .

| We don't celebrate. A normal day is just a normal day. | | We often bring treats from home or stop at the corner café to buy some cakes for the team even with no specific reason. |

As you've most likely realized, the farther on the right side your marks are, the more positive the environment is.

How can you increase the positivity at your organization?

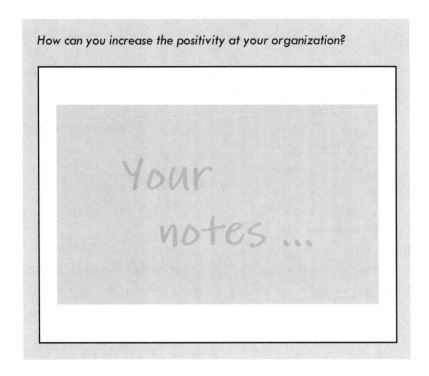

Listening

To be a successful agile leader, you also need to have great self-awareness and awareness of the entire system around you. Listening skills are essential. The concept of the three levels of listening—me, we, and world—describes the different things your mind can focus on during a conversation.

The first level, "me" listening, is the most common one. You listen for your own understanding and learning and so that you know how to react. You let your brain sidetrack and make associations, looking for any personal experience you may be able to share that is related to what you are hearing, any advice you can give, any learning you can take from it. For example: "When it happened to me last year, I . . .," "You have to try this . . .," or you just process it in your mind: *That's interesting—I could use it with my team next time.* It's all about you.

The second level, "we" listening, focuses on the other person or group of people and creates a communication channel between you and the other side where you are a great listener, helping the other side to express their feelings and raise

their awareness about the topic. This listening channel is often used during coaching. You suppress any thoughts about yourself. It's not about you anymore. It's about the other person or the team. It's an active listening where you don't share any advice or thoughts. You try to not even have them—you focus all of your senses on the other people and their thoughts, feelings, and needs. Your role is to help them express their thoughts and ideas.

The third level of listening is the "world" channel: focusing on what is happening around you. It's all about the context and surrounding. At this level, you are aware of the conversation but mostly at the essence level. You feel the energy between people and concentrate on its change. You can hear all the distant voices and sounds, you can feel the air blowing from the air conditioner. The third channel has no limits. It takes in everything. It's very useful during facilitation where, as a facilitator, you need to focus on the flow of the conversation, not influencing the content of it. It's also the level of listening you need while focusing on less tangible things, such as culture, team spirit, and so on.

Try to practice listening at all three levels. Be aware at which level you are listening most frequently and which level is the most comfortable for you. Make notes from the practice. What did you start noticing at the "we" level? What caught your attention at the "world" level?

Your notes ...

If you want to listen at the system level, it is not just about hearing things at all three levels. Listening to the voice of the system requires all your senses. Anything that is happening or not happening is a signal from the system: quietness, frustration, complaining, speaking too much, blaming, supporting each other, laugher, people volunteering, different body language, fear, defensiveness, having fun, and so on.

Examples from a brainstorming session about signals at the system level

There are also those signals that are hard to sense. They are like ghosts. They originate in a different context, driven by some prior experience from another team, a previous job, or childhood, or they can be part of our cultural heritage and society. They are invisible and unpredictable unless you are aware of them.

I remember one situation where the ghost from a bad experience from a previous job completely changed an otherwise healthy conversation. The team had started to implement Scrum. They were at the end of their third Sprint, functioning quite well; the management was supportive and didn't pressure us too much. You would say it was quite a healthy environment. That is, until the conversation at our retrospective touched on fixing bugs, and one experienced developer jumped almost up to the ceiling, saying that we can't track bugs and blame the developers for them. We looked at him with surprise, as blaming was not common at all in the environment. One of his colleagues explained that in his previous job, he had had a very negative experience and that the topic was taboo for the group because of that, as he was unable to talk about it without fear. I remember we approached it with curiosity and respect. We were good listeners, focusing on the "we" level. Through that process, we helped him to speak about it, about the frustration he felt, about his feelings of being betrayed and used. When he was nearly done, he realized that we were all listening, and he paused with a puzzled face. When we asked him about it, he said that this was the first time people hadn't tried to argue with him and had actually listened to him. After a short pause, he added that he was ready to move on.

Ghosts are not rational, and logical argumentation will not help to minimize their impact. Good listening and curiosity are a great start. Ghosts are only powerful when they are hidden and people are afraid to talk about them. Once you help people to air out their frustration, the ghosts usually lose power and become only a funny story.

The ability to let things go is critical for becoming a good listener. It's not about you; no one asked you to judge or to feel compassion for the person and the described situation. You can rarely put yourself in other people's shoes, and most ghosts seem ridiculous to people other than the one carrying them, which is not useful. Remember that everyone is right, but only partially, and that you can never argue with feelings.

Autonomy

Autonomy is one of the core agile concepts. However, most people struggle with it at the beginning of their agile journey. To accept autonomy, you need a high level of trust in the system. You need to believe that teams will always come up with better ideas than any individual alone can generate and that if they figure out a better solution, it has nothing to do with you not being good enough. Quite the opposite—it shows you are a great leader who can create an environment where others can be successful.

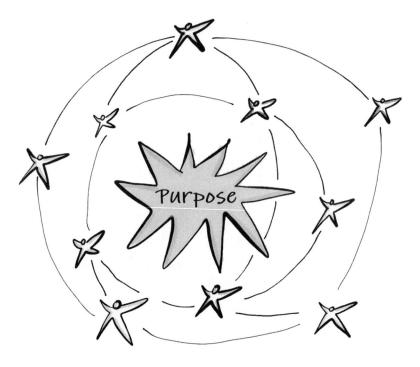

Autonomy is one of the key motivators, together with purpose and mastery [Pink09]. And yet, it is one of the hardest to make an integral part of your culture. Autonomy is the most important ingredient of self-organization and collaboration in general. It requires a lot of self-confidence and readiness to let things go. It also takes courage. It's one of the agile values often missed in organizations. At the end of the day, people don't work for organizations—they work for great leaders. Be one of them. Be brave and let it go. Trust that the teams around you will figure it out.

When I got my new department, I knew I didn't want to build any hierarchy. I felt that if there was one thing I knew how to do better than others in our organization, it was to build self-organizing teams. I trusted that the collaborative team environment can always come up with a better solution than individuals operating in silos. I trusted that decentralized structures are better in change responsiveness than are centralized entities. I saw my role as a leader purely as an environment builder. I had to create a safe space for the teams so they could focus on delivering value to the customer and have the freedom to come up with creative solutions. Indeed, the vision and the organizational purpose were key. Without them, the team would all go in different directions.

I was lucky enough that we had vision and purpose already. We knew who we were as an organization and who we were not. However, this level of autonomy at the organizational level was something new, and many people, especially the other directors, found it hard to digest. And here is what I learned. You can't explain to people from the outside how self-organization works. They need to experience it, which is hard. You would need to deal with all their doubts, such as *How come all those teams don't go in different directions? How does it all stick together?*

I didn't have any data or experience at this level yet. All I could do at the time was to make it purpose-centric. Having a common purpose is key if you give others autonomy. It works like the sun in our solar system, with all the planets circling around. I'd never explained my vision as being flat or agile. I used the vision of who we needed to be to stay competitive and mapped what was happening or could have happened through that lens. I intentionally shared stories of greatness where the teams did something spectacular, like giving outstanding service to our customers or creating something unique, something that had not been done before. I guess I was lucky, as it didn't take long before we were all able to see the impact of working in this way. The doubts disappeared, and trust grew that teams can have a higher level of autonomy.

Think about your team. On a scale of 1 to 10, where do you see the autonomy level?

	1	10	
We wait until someone assigns us a task.	●————————●		We define our own tasks (self-directed).
We follow the rules and processes while working together.	●————————●		We decide how we work together (self-organized).
We need a detailed specification for our work.	●————————●		We figure out the missing things when needed.
Processes shall describe all possible cases to create safety.	●————————●		We are not afraid to take over ownership and responsibility.

The farther on the right you are, the more autonomy there is in the environment.

How can you increase the level of autonomy in your environment?

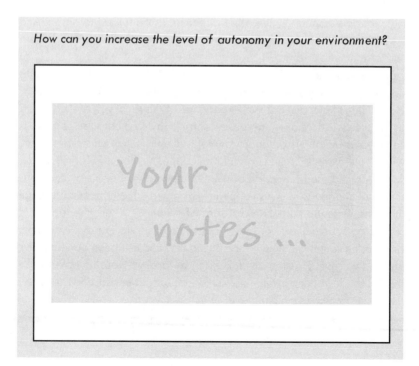

Books to Read

- *The Motive: Why So Many Leaders Abdicate Their Most Important Responsibilities*, Patrick Lencioni (Hoboken, NJ: Wiley, 2020).
- *Leadership Agility: Five Levels of Mastery for Anticipating and Initiating Change*, Bill Joiner, Stephen Josephs (San Francisco: Jossey-Bass, 2007).
- *Turn the Ship Around!: A True Story of Turning Followers into Leaders*, David Marquet (New York: Portfolio/Penguin, 2013).

In a Nutshell

- ☐ Being an agile leader is not a position but a state of mind.
- ☐ Agile leaders don't need positional power but leverage the power of influence.
- ☐ The agile leader journey starts with a purpose.
- ☐ Organizational purpose is critical for autonomous teams.

5

. . .

THE AGILE LEADERSHIP MODEL

The agile leadership model is the guiding mental model for agile leaders based on the ORCS.[1] The core element of the agile leadership model is the system. The system is an invisible part that builds  on the social connectedness and the relationships among people and teams. It's what happens between people, not what happens *to* people. It's intangible and hard to measure, but you can still see it, hear it, feel it, sense it, and work with it. It's like snowboarding— or skiing if you like that better—in a white cloud where you can't see anything. You know you're going downhill, but you can't see it. Sometimes your eyes can even trick you and you go the wrong way,

---

1. Organization and Relationship Systems Coaching: https://www.crrglobal.com/orsc.html.

only to stop and find yourself facing uphill. In the end, all you can do is rely on your feelings and instincts. Feel the slope, and use all your other senses to figure out your next move.

It's similar to what agile leadership is about. You need to train your brain to change your old habits. Don't let yourself be guided only by data; go far beyond them and train your other senses to be aware of the relationships and energy in the team, the department, and the organization. Be able to leverage the Relationship Systems Intelligence where "beyond Emotional Intelligence (relationship with oneself) and Social Intelligence (relationship with other) is the realm of Relationship Systems Intelligence where one's focus shifts to the relationship with the group, team or system" [CRR_nd].

Agile organizations focus more on the soft part, the people aspect, where healthy relationships are critically important. Many organizations are failing their agile transformations just because they don't have a system that is ready for such a change. The system is the magical glue that makes teams and organizations stick together and form one whole, but it also gives them any flexibility they need.

The agile leadership model helps leaders to see the organization from a different perspective, to stay connected with the system, and to unleash its potential through these three steps: get awareness, embrace it, and act upon it.

Let's look at a very simple example. Let's imagine you have several teams working on one product. From time to time, every few days, the system is broken and doesn't work because someone didn't pay attention to the quality and didn't run all the tests. The teams start to get frustrated. You hear a lot of complaining, you can feel the irritation, and the Four Horsemen of Toxic Behavior (or toxins)—criticism/blaming, defensiveness, contempt, and stonewalling [Lisitsa13]—become all too common. If you start listening, you realize there are many different voices and perspectives that often disagree with each other. When you're looking at things from so many different angles, it's hard to see a clear way out of it—that's a typical complex problem. This is the getting awareness step.

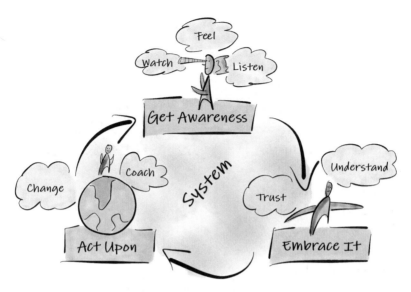

The second step, embracing it, happens the moment you realize that this is a complex system problem and so there is no way to evaluate it, and there is no right or wrong answer either. They are just different perspectives. And you have to accept it. Only then can you act upon it at the system level and tap the system to initiate a change. For example, you can call an Open Space or World Café workshop (see Chapter 11) and let the creativity of the system do the work. Both of these large-scale facilitation techniques are based on system self-organization and as such have great potential to help teams find alignment and figure out some experiments to try. As you might see, it is a very agile way of working. And it all starts with a leader who is ready to start his or her agile leader journey and move from a centralized, individual-focused mindset to the decentralized, self-organized world.

GET AWARENESS

The first step of the agile leadership model is to "get awareness" of what's going on in the system. You learn how to listen to the voice of the system [Fridjhon14] and how to see the current reality in all its diversity and colorfulness.

Every organization is a system that constantly sends out signals. All you have to do is be aware of them, notice them, and listen to them. This first step helps you to choose a good viewpoint so you can see the entire system from the top. It's  like being on an observation tower and watching what's going on all around you from a distance. From such a vantage point, you are in a way separating yourself from the day-to-day operations, you can't see details about the individuals, and you don't hear them clearly either. But you have a good outlook to gain awareness of all the different perspectives, trends, emotions, and levels of energy in the organization.

At this stage, you need to be a good listener and observer. Suppress any urge for action. Acknowledge that you have enough time. It's almost a Zen attitude that you need to cultivate—mitigate your own thoughts, have a calm mind, be ready to let things go, and make yourself open for hearing a new voice from the system.

EMBRACE IT

The second step helps you to "embrace it" and accept that whatever is happening in the system is what should be happening at the moment. Do that without an urge to evaluate the situation or solve any problems immediately. After all, who knows what is right and what is not? Events that look very bad at the moment might actually end up being good. For example, the bug that cost us a lot of stress and some revenue as the system was down for a day happened to be a good thing, as it helped us to improve our system and our products. The conflict that started by blaming one of the designers in the team was not good at the time, but eventually it made us stronger than other teams in the organization, and now we use our bond to prevent such situations. I could list many other examples.

From the system perspective, there is no right or wrong. At any given time, many things are happening at once, and when you postpone your judgment for just a minute, you realize that "everyone is right, but only partially" [Šochová17a]. Your power at this stage comes from your ability to gain enough clarity, which builds your trust in the whole system. To revisit the metaphor from the previous section, standing at the top of the observation tower prevents you from taking sides, so you can easily say, "It is what it is. It's neither right nor wrong. It's just happening," and be okay with it. Accept it, embrace it, and don't judge it.

Act Upon

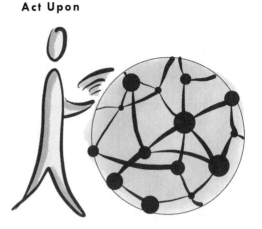

The third step is to "act upon." It's about using the power gained in the previous step to influence things and change the system dynamics and behavior. It doesn't have to be any significant change—a small impulse in the form of a coaching question or a small change in the environment may be enough. It's like tapping the wheel to spin it just a little more: you can do it by visualizing an issue, facilitating a conversation about a certain topic, focusing on hearing more perspectives and being more curious about them, having a deeper debate on ideas, organizing a workshop, running an experiment, coaching, mentoring, trying a specific practice, avoiding another practice, changing a process or a guideline, implementing a method or framework, initializing a structure change—the list never ends. There is an unlimited number of actions on the menu to choose from. As there is no right no wrong action to try, no matter what you choose, the system is constantly on the move. You might impact it in a certain way; however, every system is naturally creative and intelligent [Rød15] and will react in its own way. The next step is to get you back to the observation tower to get awareness of what's happening now, embrace the changes, and become ready for another tap.

Integrate It in a Circle

To give you a small example of the whole process, let's say you've just started the agile journey. The teams have had their training and have started working; some teams are better than the others, but they

are all trying. You still hear a few voices from here and there that the old way of working was better, but most people are investing a lot of energy in the new way. The biggest issue you are facing is the dependency on local vendors. An external vendor's quality is questionable, it lacks the business understanding, and it is often late. If you don't do something, you will miss the next release.

The typical reaction is an evaluation of the situation, followed by an escalation, which rarely solves things on time for the actual release. If you are ready to approach this problem as an agile leader, you are aware that the evaluation will not help. It only creates wrong expectations and frustration from not being even close to meeting expectations. The agile leader would look at it from the system point of view, where there is no right or wrong—there are just different perspectives:

- From the purchasing perspective, the vendor gives us flexibility, and in some cases even the ability to do some work, as we don't have such skills in-house, so there is no issue there.
- From the team's perspective, the vendor is terrible, and we need to fire the vendor and do it ourselves.
- From the vendor's perspective, we need to provide better specifications.
- From the management perspective, it's fine as at the end of the day the product is released so we can ignore the issue.

I can continue, but you get the idea.

The agile leader is aware of all the different perspectives and their influence on the organization. It's not that different from what most people will do, but when this awareness becomes intentional, you see many more angles. It helps you with the next step of embracing it, which, on the other hand, is very different from most people's habits.

The change happens when you learn how to stop evaluating the situation and to trust the system.

The quality of awareness actually predetermines your ability to embrace the situation. This has a lot to do with complexity, which is why agile was born. If you care about only a few perspectives, you don't see the whole system with its interactions, and it's easy to make judgments about what's going on, evaluate the options, and choose what needs to be done. This mental process is very effective in a simple or a predictable world, but the closer we get to the VUCA world, the more options there are, and any accurate evaluation becomes extremely hard, if not impossible. The more flexible and changing the business is, the more flexible the organizational structure and culture need to be, which creates the conditions for agile leadership to take over from traditional management.

Complexity can be addressed only by complexity, so it makes sense to work with the entire system rather than with individuals alone. In our example with the external vendor, the actions taken can be as small as these (see Chapter 11):

- Raise everyone's awareness of different perspectives by facilitating a World Café workshop.

- Run an overall retrospective.[2]
- *Coach* teams on the situation.
- Initiate a *community* focused on improving collaboration with external vendors.
- Organize an Open Space session to find out some creative solutions.

And the circle continues. . . .

The agile leader is not the one who makes all the decisions or who knows what needs to be done in every situation, but he or she is someone who creates a good environment and trusts the system to find the optimal solution.

Let me share a story from one of the companies I've been working with. The company is on its agile journey—it started with a single Scrum team, and a few years after that, word of the success of this team spread, so the company implemented Scrum in all teams, incorporated the business side, and increased the number of both ScrumMasters and product owners (POs). The executive team had seen the impact on the business and customers and started to look at different ways of leading the organization to support agility. Interestingly, they started with a bonus to the POs, saying that as they were a team, they should be able to take the money and agree on the split themselves. Can you guess what happened? Yes, you're right. They were not a team yet, so they acted more as individuals and fought for their own gain, which resulted in an interesting situation. On Friday, they all agreed to split the bonus equally, as that was the only way they could possibly reach an agreement. On Monday, two of them came back and challenged the agreement, saying that they had worked harder than other people and so others should not get the same amount. As a solution, they offered to return the remaining money to the organization rather than split it, as they insisted that it was not fair for everyone to receive an equal bonus. As you might guess, it got personal and ugly. Applying the traditional leadership model, you might say the leadership team used poor judgment and that the whole thing was just a disaster.

---

2. Retrospective focused on cross-team collaboration: https://less.works/less/framework/overall-retrospective.html.

But if we apply the agile leadership model we've just talked about, there is no right or wrong, only different perspectives. So, let's see a few of them:

- The underlying problem of POs not helping each other surfaced, and conflicts that were hidden for years were discussed.
- The leadership team learned something about the difference between a team and a group of individuals.
- The affected parties were healing from the conflict for more than a year. It was quite damaging; however, in the long term, you might say that it made them stronger and it brought them together.
- The people who were accused of not performing got valuable feedback, and even if they were not able to see it that day, in the long term, they learned that they also needed to show their value to the rest of the team.
- The neutral POs started to challenge the way they worked as a team and started to look for ways to become closer.
- The executive team was able to identify and address an issue that had been destroying this group of POs for a long time.
- The organization shifted toward broader product (not system-oriented) and applied scaling frameworks to deliver overall value and minimize silos.

Those are just a few observations. Was what happened a bad thing? Maybe, maybe not. Who knows, right? In the short term, it may look that way. In the long term, maybe not as much. And that's the core of agile leadership.

Books to Read

- *The Responsibility Process: Unlocking Your Natural Ability to Live and Lead with Power*, Christopher Avery (Pflugerville, TX : Partnerwerks, 2016).
- *Mastering Leadership: An Integrated Framework for Breakthrough Performance and Extraordinary Business Result*, Robert J. Anderson and William A. Adams (Hoboken, NJ: Wiley, 2015).

In a Nutshell

☐ The system is an invisible part that builds on the social connectedness and relationships among people and teams.

☐ Agile leaders need to grow their Relationship Systems Intelligence, focusing on the group as an integrated whole.

☐ The agile leadership model helps leaders to unleash the organizational potential through the three steps of getting awareness, embracing it, and acting upon it.

☐ In a complex system, it's hard to know what is right and what is not. Everyone is right, but only partially.

6

. . .

COMPETENCIES

Great agile leaders have four core competencies: they can create a vision, enhance motivation, get feedback, and implement change. They also need to have the supporting competencies of decision making, collaboration, facilitation, and coaching. However, great agile leaders are not born this way—they are constantly developing these competencies. Being an agile leader is a journey, and no matter how great you are now, there is always a better way.

The Agile Leader Competencies Map is a good visualization tool that helps agile leaders to understand what they are good at and what they might need to improve.

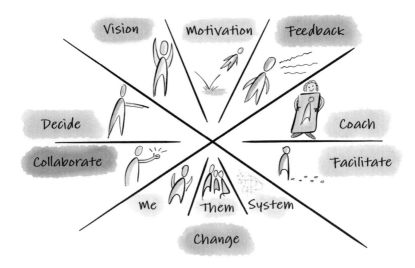

VISION AND PURPOSE

The vision is the driving engine for success. It's not necessarily related to the products but to the organization itself. You can start by asking these questions: *What is my dream? Who are we, and who are we not? Where do we want to go, and why? What would happen if we get there? How would it feel? What would be different? What would happen if we don't make it—would anyone miss it?* Those are just a few coaching questions that can help you articulate your vision.

You might argue that there are thousands of theories and articles written on how to come up with a great vision. However, most of them start from a very traditional mindset and are not very helpful in an agile space. They are too focused on measures and hard goals, missing the essence of necessity and emotional intelligence, and they often lead to a generic vision that everyone ignores and no one really understands or feels inspired by. Maybe that's the reason I'd rather use the word *dream* instead of *vision*. A dream has an essence of unknown mystery, there is positivity hardcoded inside it, and it's inspiring. Don't be afraid to approach the visioning process differently. Be creative. You can start by drawing a picture or coming up with a metaphor. Make it a team effort. Refining the vision for the whole team or organization is never a task for one individual. The whole team needs to own it, they need to believe it, they need to want to be a part of it. That's the energy you need to generate. It brings innovative thinking, creativity, and empowerment when people start offering help and ideas and are ready to sacrifice personal goals in exchange for being a part of something bigger.

I remember the time at my organization when we were trying to re-create the purpose of the organization, to revitalize its spirit. We looked again and again at the empty slogans framed on the walls and featured on our website: "Added value solutions." But no one had ever explained the mission statement to us. We even went back to our founders and asked them. They felt confused. "Why are you asking? Isn't that clear from what we do?" they asked. No, it was not clear, at least not to us. We realized we needed to re-create it and make it come alive, so that people would feel motivated and inspired by it and live and work in accordance with it. That shift was interesting, as I would have thought at that time that someone needed to explain to us what the original purpose was. But there was no need—it was in the air, hidden in the roots of who we were, and all we had to do was pay attention, be good listeners and observers. We had to connect the dots and listen to stories. It didn't even take long. All we did was talk about it and ask why.

Don't be afraid to look to dreams and metaphors when creating a vision. There was no magic in our pursuit of the organizational purpose, no exact process—only constant focus on what connected us and the essence of the value we created together. The organizational purpose is not created in any presentation; it's not about hard measures either. It's melted through the three levels of reality: from the sentient essence level to the dreaming level and back to the consensus reality. In about a month, we had come up with a solid explanation for the employees, tested on several occasions and in conversations. We had a great story to tell new people, a story attractive enough that they wanted to join us and solid enough that it led their first steps as employees. We didn't change the original vision statement—we just reinvented it, woke it from a deep sleep, and made it live again. The "Added value solution" statement became meaningful after all. It stirred up new energy, and we changed the way the company operated. We put the focus on being proactive, on creativity, and on strong customer focus. Rather than just delivering, we worked to help our customers as our partners. By reconnecting to our purpose, we reenergized the organization and set it on track for a better future. It was quite magical.

A good purpose balances the needs of customers, employees, and shareholders. The great agile leaders are never focused on only one group of people in this virtuous circle—they all need to be in balance. Some people can argue

that agile focuses on customers first, and by doing so, it defines the value employees need to deliver, get paid for, and thus satisfy the shareholders. Others would say that Agile focuses on employees first and motivates them to come up with creative and innovative solutions to satisfy customers, get paid for, and make shareholders happy. It's a bit like a chicken-and-egg problem. As usual, all of those questions are wrong from a holistic perspective and can only help in the short term. In other words, focusing on the nodes in a virtuous circle can only address the symptoms of a bigger problem in the middle. With a strong purpose, the debate about where to focus is gone. Indeed—we focus on the purpose. The rest will sort itself out.

Which statement best describes the current situation at your company?

When you share with others what the purpose of your company is, . . .

A. They are not very enthusiastic about it; they ask you if yours is a good job and move the conversation elsewhere.

B. They are very attracted to the idea, want to know more about it, and feel you are lucky to work there.

If the company were to close tomorrow, . . .

A. Customers would move on to a different product or service and forget about it.

B. Customers would miss it.

When you ask employees what they are doing in the organization, . . .

A. They focus on their role and siloed work (e.g., writing code, testing, creating a design).

B. They refer to the value and to the business or organizational purpose (e.g., to help people to invest better, to connect organizations, to help cure cancer).

Evaluate your answers. You get one point for each B answer.

If you got zero points in the preceding exercise, your organization is starving for purpose clarity and is waiting for someone to pull it out of thin air. I strongly believe there is no organization without a purpose. In most cases, it was simply forgotten, lost in the piles of day-to-day tasks and issues, the processes, the change initiatives, the acquisitions. And time plays a role too—it could be that today no one knows anymore what the purpose used to be when the organization started. It's good to go back in time and understand our roots. *What is our legacy? Who are our founders, and what kind of dreams*

inspired the foundation of our organization? What is the organiza-
tional myth? When you start asking those questions in such organizations, you might get responses like, "Here is the vision and mission
statement; you can find it in this presentation" or "We don't have time
for this. There is a lot of work to be done." No one feels motivated by the
purpose, so people turn their attention toward their tasks, which at least
are clear, and toward the job that needs to be done.

On the other end of the spectrum, if you get all three points, you
are lucky, as you work for one of the very few organizations that actually have a purpose. People feel strong energy and fulfillment. Such
organizations are more focused, more creative, more innovative—
and they are ready for organizational agility at the full scale.

THREE LEVELS OF REALITY

The three levels of reality [Mindell_nd] describe what the visioning process should cover. In order to create an appealing vision,
you need to go through all three levels of reality: sentient essence
level, dreaming level, and consensus reality level. It's a very powerful
concept, as it opens a whole new world and brings creativity and
emotions into the visioning process. Traditional organizations were
focused on goals and objectives and hard metrics: "Become a leader
on the marker" or "Be the best retail service" or "Provide high-quality
products while doing our business in a socially responsible and envi-
ronmentally sustainable manner." The real organizational purpose
is more than that: It has authenticity. It brings emotions. It's a heart-
beat of the organization, and it gives organizations a reason why it
exists. We keep ourselves too much in the consensus reality level,
trying to make everything predictable, measurable, and exact.

The three levels of reality model help us to do the exact opposite and start in the sentient essence, where it's all about feelings,
energy, and spirit. That's where the culture is born, that's where the
vision generates emotions and develops its own soul. It's a level of

describing metaphors, hopes, and desires. Don't rush it. Stay here exploring this level for a while. As an example, you can ask some of these questions[1] to explore the sentient essence bit more: *What attracted you in the very first moments? What did you first notice/ feel/experience?* and *What are the metaphors describing your early connection?*

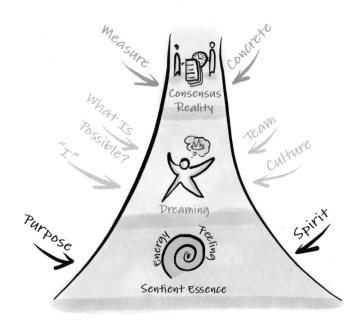

Only when you've spent a lot of time here does the essence create enough inputs for the dreaming level. The dreaming level is all about exploring possibilities and options. As the name suggests, it's about what you want, your desires and dreams. As an example, you can ask some of these questions: *What actual dreams do you have? What are your fantasies or hopes?* and *What are your fears?* It's where the team and collaboration are grounded. It's the level where the essence is transformed and acquires more factual characteristics. It's still quite abstract, but it gradually becomes more tangible.

---

1. Questions are based on the Original Myth exercise from the ORSC program.

Finally, the consensus reality makes the purpose real and brings it back to our day-to-day reality. As an example, you can ask some of these questions: *Who are we? What do we want to achieve? What are our values?* and *What are the circumstances?* The answers will be very different if you let them emerge organically by going from sentient essence through dreaming. It is more encouraging, more challenging, more motivating than the traditional process of staying only in the consensus reality. We are going to use the three levels of reality in some of the techniques described in the following sections, so you can see how to navigate through them and how this concept can be useful in creating a purpose.

HIGH DREAM AND LOW DREAM

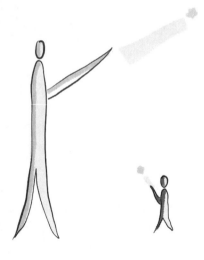

One of the techniques that helps to raise your awareness of your dreams is a High Dream/ Low Dream exercise [CRR19]. High dreams are your purest wishes, when all of your secret hopes come true, while low dreams are limited by your fears. Low dreams are not necessarily bad—they just reflect some of your fears. In this concept, we focus on raising awareness of both kinds of dreams by using the three levels of reality.

To put it another way, the high dreams and the low dreams are a good platform for you to rethink where you are and where you want to be and to create a list of actions you can take to help the organization to live its highest dream.

Using the three levels of reality as a landscape to navigate through, do the following:

- First focus on your high dream for the organization. What is it? What does it look like? What makes it important? Make a few notes.
- Then turn your attention toward your low dream and think about what it may look like if things go wrong. What does it look like? How does it feel? Make a few notes.
- Then think about the factors that might contribute to making the low dream a reality and note them.
- Finally, think about what supports your high dream and what actions you can take so that the organization moves closer to that high dream.

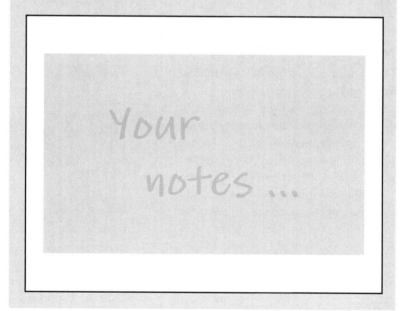

BRINGING DOWN THE VISION

One of my favorite tools for helping an organization to re-create or reconnect with the original organization vision is based on the ORSC exercise Bringing Down the Vision. It's a method of facilitating a large group visioning process that uses the three levels of reality model [CRR19]. It expects you to have decent experience with system coaching and facilitation of large groups, but the results are outstanding. I use this tool for product visions, organization visions, alignment around roles and expectations, and also for communities that need to find alignment around their vision. You can give it a timeframe and ask where participants want to be in five or ten years from now, or just make it about the ideal organization, product, or situation.

Let me share an example of what the process can look like.[2] This example is from a community meetup where we searched for alignment around our vision and wanted to activate the community. The leading question was *What is the future of Agile—where do you see Agile in five years from now?*

Phase 1: My Metaphor

The whole process starts at the individual level, where every person is guided by the facilitator through the three levels of reality and creates a metaphoric image of the organization step by step. Always give people enough time to create that image in their heads and to reproduce it on paper. For example, you can start with the following coaching questions to explore the sentient essence level [CRR19]: *Imagine your organization as a*  *real or imaginary creature. What does it feel? What is it like? What are its needs and challenges? In what ways is it healthy and thriving?* Always give people some time to consider their imaginary visualization and to make a few notes and create drawings. Pictures are always better than text, so encourage people to draw their images. There is no need for perfection. Actually, the simplest images are usually the best.

---

2. You can check out my workshop recording from a community event in London: https://www.youtube.com/watch?v=Sc3aXdefa8A&t=10s.

Phase 2: Metaphor Sharing

When people are done with their individual metaphors, they form small teams and share what kind of visualization they created and explain what it means to them. Teams need to be as cross-functional and diverse as possible to see different perspectives. Facilitators should make sure that the conversation is respectful to the different angles and that participants are good listeners.

Curiosity is the best friend here. The more curious people are about others' metaphors, the easier the next steps will be and the better results they will achieve from the whole exercise.

Phase 3: Team Metaphor

Now, once people have introduced their images to one other, they start to see if there are any similarities or differences and to identify the organization's strengths, challenges, and needs. From their conversations, they search for alignment. They try to create another metaphor that  embraces important aspects from all of their individual creatures. They visualize, investigate it, describe it, and are ready to share the outcome with the other teams so they can merge the essences of all the metaphors and dreams. There is no hurry to finalize the description. This may come later. But this process feeds the organizational vision like nothing else.

The phase could be repeated in a World Café format (see Chapter 11) with the intention of getting alignment from the larger group, to make it visual on a wall, and for the group to vote on the different aspects. There is no limit to the creativity. However, the basic agile values of respect, openness, focus, commitment, and courage are crucial to the success of the exercise.

Phase 4: Actions

This phase brings the whole conversation back to the consensus reality. First the teams brainstorm steps they can take to help the organization to get closer to the dream they've identified, and then they agree on a couple of actions they are taking back. As in the retrospective, we are not looking

for any huge items; instead we care about small actionable items we can take as a next iteration of experiments.

Phase 5: Sharing

The last step is sharing. At the very end, all of the teams share their outcomes from the steps with the whole group in order to merge the essences of all the metaphors and dreams. The entire process is finished by sharing the actions and commitments with everybody to promote transparency and manage the expectations of what's next.

As you might see, the entire process uses the power of metaphor and guides you through the three levels of reality. It is very different from the typical corporate conversations about vision, strategic plans, and goals and objectives. It uses the right brain to generate creativity in the sentient essence level. It is inspirational at the dreaming level and helps people to reconnect with the values and emotional relationships. Finally, it allows you to melt down all that inspiration into a consensus reality and to create tangible outcomes.

MOTIVATION

The second segment of the Agile Leader Competencies Map is motivation. The nature of motivation is different in an agile world. It relies on the power of motivation driven by autonomy and a sense of purpose. "Most people are not inspired by logic alone but rather by fundamental desire to contribute to a larger case" [Kotter_nd]. The key part of motivation is related to the overall purpose. If you do the vision right and create

Example of the motivation factors brainstorming and evaluation

an emotional connection to the purpose, the energy will emerge by itself and you won't need to do much more to increase motivation. Teams will live by the vision and do their best to achieve it. On the other hand, if the vision is unclear, otherwise creative and intelligent people turn their focus toward delivering isolated micro tasks, as those are the only clear points in a very unpredictable, unclear world, and they become demotivated or at least quite disengaged. In such an environment, some would say, "People need clear KPIs, so they know what to do," "We need to track what everyone is doing to make sure they are working," "Bonuses are the key motivation factor," and so on.

The other part of motivation is related to the environment and culture. Agile leaders favor intrinsic motivation factors, as they are more aligned with the team spirit that agile culture is built around. In the environment, people are motivated by a safe-to-fail culture, where failure is taken as an opportunity to learn and improve things, not to blame or punish people. They are also motivated by having the autonomy to come up with their own ideas for how to address the challenges they are facing, by working in a learning environment where they can grow and their contributions are recognized, and last but not least, by an open and transparent environment with a high level of trust. Those factors always win in organizations.

Just for the record, based on several types of research, money is not considered a motivating factor. "There is little evidence to show that money motivates us and a great deal of evidence to suggest that it actually demotivates us. Once the basic needs are covered, the psychological benefits of money are questionable" [Chamorro13]. In other words, people need to get paid "enough"—they need to feel their salary is fair and that they are valued. And here is the problem. This value is very personal, and it doesn't necessarily correlate with the actual amount they are paid. You might be super happy about your salary until you open the newspaper and read the average salary of your position: "Look at that, this is what's common, I need to get a raise." And you might feel your salary is fair until you accidentally learn about your colleague's salary: "He is five years younger, has less experience, and he doesn't even work as much as I do. That's not fair." Surprisingly, if you overpay people, it creates a similar effect: "Guess how much I got for just doing my regular job. Next time I will ask for twice as much."

In agile, we invest in building social capital. Interestingly, money erodes it. Chamorro-Premuzic reports that the results of a meta-analysis[3] "highlighted consistent negative effects of incentives—from marshmallows to dollars—on intrinsic motivation" [Chamorro13]. On one side, we are trying our best to create an engaging environment that would motivate people by intrinsic factors of motivation, and on the other side, we are destroying or lowering the effect by extrinsic factors of motivation (i.e., incentives). That's quite a disconnect.

As in many organizations, ours has some motivated and engaged groups and some very demotivated ones. One of the most difficult cases we needed to solve was a team that was traveling to the customer site every week. It was a long drive, they stayed in a hotel they didn't like, and from a technical standpoint the work was boring. They were getting extra money to compensate for the extra effort, but that money didn't bring the expected motivation, and one day the entire team almost left

---

3. E. L. Deci, R. Koestner, & R. M. Ryan, "A Meta-Analytic Review of Experiments Examining the Effect of Extrinsic Rewards on Intrinsic Motivation," *Psychological Bulletin* 125(6):627–668, 1999.

the company. At the end of the day, they stayed, except for their team lead. We couldn't change the technical part of the work, and we actually couldn't give them more money either. However, what we did was to carefully listen, for the first time ever, to what they were complaining about. We were also fully transparent about the finances and gave them significantly higher autonomy to decide where they spent the budget and on what basis they were rotating to travel. As a result, they changed the hotel and the cars, as well as the system of who was traveling and who was staying at our offices. It was interesting that a small change can make a huge impact. In a couple of months, this was the product everyone was proud of working on, and people were asking to be assigned to that team.

Theory X and Theory Y

One of the most famous theories about motivation, described by Douglas McGregor in 1960, is called theory X and theory Y [McGregor60]. Theory X defines people as lazy slackers who dislike working, avoid responsibility, need to be directed and controlled, and whose actions need to be traced. You often need to threaten them in order for them to deliver any work at all, and,

on the opposite side, their direct reward must be linked to the outcomes. This is where classical micromanagement comes from. All the detailed timesheets, task assignments, and performance reviews are grounded in the theory X beliefs.

In contrast, theory Y defines people as enthusiasts who consider work as a natural part of their life, are motivated, always take ownership and responsibility, enjoy working in the company, don't need many directions, are self-directed and self-controlled. That's where agile was born, based on self-organization, autonomy, and empowerment.

Keep in mind that nothing is black and white. Companies will use a mixture of techniques based on which theory is closer to their beliefs.

Try the following assessment. Make a mark somewhere on the scale from X to Y.

What best describes you?

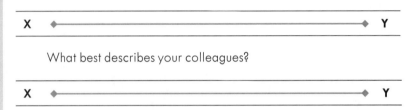

Here is the interesting paradox. I've run this experiment many times in my classes, and 95 percent of people who do this exercise would rate themselves to be more Y than their colleagues. Once I question them, they find different excuses for why that is (e.g., "I'm the manager, so I'm better than the others, that's why I've got promoted"; "That's why I'm here, learning about agile leadership"; or "That's because we care about agile and they don't"). In other words, about half the people believe that they are better than others. They don't need the carrot and stick in order to work, but they don't have that trust and confidence in their colleagues, so they feel others need that control.

Niels Pflaeging has been running this experiment at conferences for years.[4] And it's pretty eye-opening. Imagine the whole conference room, about a thousand people, answering the first question: "What kind of person are you? Write X or Y on a pink Post-it Note, and exchange it with your neighbor." No one believes himself or herself to be an X theory person. Pflaeging then asks them to answer the second question: "Think about all the people in your organization—what percentage of theory X people are there? Write it on a yellow Post-it and exchange it with your neighbor." Now here comes the interesting point: the vast majority of people believe that theory X people exist, and that's very dangerous. As Pflaeging said, this belief that other people can be theory X is a self-fulfilling prophecy, a terrible prejudice and judgment. We are responsible for creating the environment that generates theory X behavior, not theory X people; we do it through the way we work and through the tools we use [Pflaeging14].

Along with McGregor and Pflaeging, I believe that theory X people don't exist, have never existed, and that there is not a single theory X person in the world [Pflaeging18]. It's only our having treated people that way for ages that has created this kind of behavior. All those timesheets, performance reviews, estimates, roadmaps, and velocity charts—they show our lack of trust in people, trust that they will do their best even without pressure and control mechanisms. Trust. It's so simple to say it and so hard to build it. At the end of the day, that's what agile leadership is about. Trust that there are no X theory people in this world, and if there is X theory behavior, it's our role to work on it and change the environment, culture, and tools we use so it disappears.

---

4. You can see one of his keynotes here: https://www.youtube.com/watch?v= NAvVZlhrbig.

What practices that stimulate theory X behavior do you have at your organization?

Your notes ...

What practices that stimulate theory Y behavior do you have at your organization?

Your notes ...

What can you do to improve the ratio between the practices that stimulate theory X and those that stimulate theory Y behavior?

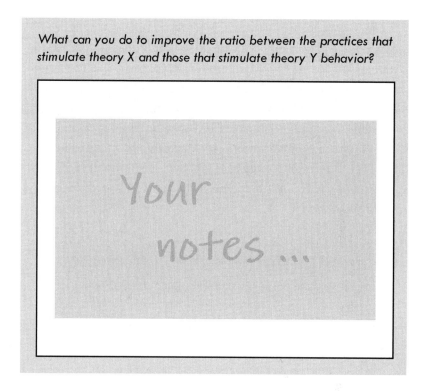

ENGAGEMENT

Engagement is a very important part of motivation. The ADP Research Institute's Global Study of Engagement is pretty pessimistic: "Only 15.9 percent of employees worldwide are Fully Engaged. . . . This means that almost 84 percent of workers are merely Coming to Work, and are not contributing all they could to their organizations" [Hayes19]. Considering the study reports on almost twenty thousand workers in different industries and countries, it is concerning. What is also interesting in this report is the finding that "workers who say they are on a team are 2.3 times more likely to be fully engaged than those who are not" [Hayes19]. We can say that "when organizations make great teams their primary focus, we expect to see more significant rises in global engagement" [Hayes19].

Focusing on teams over individuals is one way agile leaders increase the engagement in the organization. The first step is always raising awareness. If you are interested in your team's engagement, you can give them the following assessment. The assessment statements are from ADP's Global Study of Engagement, where "the eight items are designed to measure specific aspects of employee Engagement that organizations and team leaders can influence" [Hayes19]. However, before you do that, think about your own answers and what could help you to be more engaged. It's always good inspiration.

On a scale of 1 to 10, where 1 means "not at all" and 10 means "completely," mark your agreement with the following statements:[5]

I am really enthusiastic about the mission of the company.

1   10

At work, I clearly understand what is expected of me.

1   10

In my team, I am surrounded by people who share my values.

1   10

I have the chance to use my strengths every day at work.

1   10

My teammates have my back.

1   10

I know I will be recognized for excellent work.

1   10

---

5. Statements are used from ADP's Global Study of Engagement report [Hayes19].

I have great confidence in my company's future.

1   10

In my work, I am always challenged to grow.

1   10

You can call yourself "fully engaged" if your answer is at least 7 for each of these questions.

Full engagement is an important part of the leadership journey. If in the previous exercise you didn't end up at "fully engaged," don't worry. It doesn't mean you are disengaged or demotivated— you are just not working at your highest potential as a leader, and you might have some opportunities to improve your leadership skills in this area. For your score, you can always blame others for not creating a good environment for you to flourish in. For your teams, it's all in your hands. You can make it happen and help your teams to feel the power of being fully engaged. "Workers are twelve times more likely to be fully engaged if they trust the team leader" [Hayes19]. The initial engagement feedback from your teams might be frustrating and harsh, but at least you know what they are missing and can work on it. The good news is that leaders can make a big difference in engagement levels by creating the right environment and building mutual trust.

SUPER-CHICKENS

Margaret Heffernan presented an awesome talk at TEDWomen 2015 about motivation. At the beginning of her talk, she refers to the research done by William Muir from Purdue University about the productivity of chickens. "Chickens live in groups, so first of all, he selected just an average flock, and he let it alone for six generations. But then he created a second group of the individually most

productive chickens, you could call them super-chickens, and he put them together in a super-flock, and each generation, he selected only the most productive for breeding" [Heffernan15]. Isn't that what we do with each evaluation review and each layoff? It makes sense, right? Those people with low productivity only demotivate others and lower the quality, decreasing the overall productivity of the entire group. That's what most organizations would say, right? So, let's have a look at the results of the research: "After six generations had passed, he found that the first group, the average group, was doing just fine. They were all plump and fully feathered and egg production had increased dramatically. When you look to the second group, all but three were dead. They'd pecked the rest to death. The individually productive chickens had only achieved their success by suppressing the productivity of the rest" [Heffernan15].

That shouldn't be so surprising for anyone who has ever experienced being part of a great team. Great teams are not successful because they consist of super-chickens, though both the individuals' skills and diversity are important; the most important factor that drives their success is social connectedness. Agile organizations have found that out, so they support relationships, team spirit, and various communities that connect teams across the organization. They design their offices so that people can collaborate. They have the magic walls all around, which people can use as a whiteboard. They have movable furniture so teams can create space in a flexible way, depending on the needs of the team, and can change it when the team grows. They invest in many different informal chat areas that are colorful, comfortable, and enjoyable—unlike the traditional cold meeting rooms with U-shaped tables.

Agile organizations don't see the coffee machine as an expense but as an investment in social connectedness. They often invest in much more than coffee, and employees either have substantial discounts in their cafeteria or eat there completely for free. They create space for games where people can meet and play together and relax. It doesn't stop with one foosball table in the kitchen area. They realize that investing in people's relationships brings them quite significant value not only in motivation, engagement, and ownership but also in creativity, innovation, and, last but not least, performance.

Quite different from the traditional carrot-and-stick approach, right? Don't get me wrong, all those practices such as employee of the month, the career path hierarchy, and performance reviews were implemented in organizations in good faith. However, they are coming from the false belief that only highly specialized, skillful, and high-performing individuals can make the organizations successful. Companies have been investing in super-chicken employees hoping for a super-flock to appear for the past fifty years, and it's time to change that approach. Instead, practices such as having self-organized, cross-functional teams and investing in their collaboration and social skills seem to be much more successful.

Which practices are you using?

☐ An employee of the month	☐ Cross-functional teams
☐ Career path hierarchy	☐ No positions
☐ Performance review and KPIs	☐ Emergent leadership
☐ Defining goals and objectives	☐ Self-organization
☐ Individual bonuses	☐ Peer feedback

For your result, count −1 point for each checked box from the left column and +1 point for each checked box from the right column. The result will give you a feeling of how agile you are considering practices. The negative score is undermining agile culture and mindset, the positive one is supporting it.

Which practices would you like to try? Which would you like to avoid?

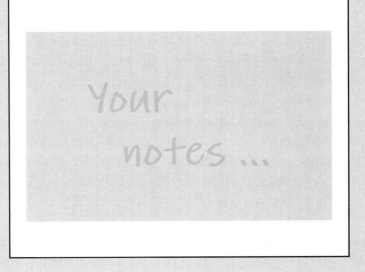

Relax area at Avast Prague

Movable space for conversation at Avast Prague

FEEDBACK

The third segment in the top section of the Agile Leader Competencies Map is feedback. For any agile team, feedback is crucial: it's part of their DNA and an integral part of the culture, as it gives the team an opportunity to inspect and adapt their way of working and continuously be looking for possibilities for improvement. The same applies for agile leaders, for whom the regular feedback flow is an important prerequisite for improving their leadership style. Giving feedback is only one part of the feedback flow, but receiving it is even more important. So how many times have you changed your way of working based on feedback from your peers? And how many times did you reject it in your mind, thinking, *They don't see the whole picture, it's not relevant?* Indeed, you don't have to agree with everything people say, but if there is even just 2 percent of truth in the feedback, what does it mean to you? How can that part be useful? If you think about any feedback from the system perspective, where "everyone is right, but only partially," your ability to learn from feedback increases significantly.

In general, when it comes to feedback, there is never enough of it. The more frequently you exchange it, the less nervous you and others feel about it. Agile leaders make feedback a routine, so it becomes a habit and they don't even notice it. If you ask for feedback only once per year, it's a big thing. It becomes something out of the ordinary, and that's stressful. Thoughts such as *What if they are not happy with me?* and *What if they don't see the value of my work at all?* occupy people's minds and promote defensiveness and blaming as a response.

> Trust, transparency, openness, and regularity create good feedback.

As an example, the Retrospective in Scrum[6] creates a regular habit of giving and receiving team feedback in an actionable form

---

6. Scrum Guides: https://www.scrumguides.org.

so often that people take it as
an integral part of their lives.
Similarly, the Overall Retrospective,[7] as it is designed
in LeSS [LeSS19a], creates
a habit of regular feedback
exchanges at the larger organizational scale, and there is
no limit to where you can use
the concept of the retrospec-

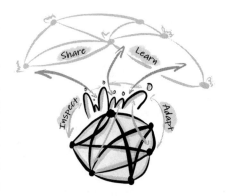

tive. Feedback doesn't stop at the individual, team, or organization
level. The great agile organizations are searching for feedback from
the outside world, opening up by sharing their way of working for
inspiration through blogging, by inviting others to see what they do,
and also by looking for how to learn from other organizations.

Opening up for feedback is a long journey. In our case, it started with
small steps. First, we opened up for honest and candid feedback internally,
inside of small teams, by running regular retrospectives and making them
private to increase the feeling of safety. It took time. Once the trust at the
team level was established and people got used to it, they relied less on
retrospectives and were able to give each other feedback on the spot.
They were collaborating more and becoming great teams, and feedback
became part of their everyday work. The teams were strong and internal
facing. However, anything coming from the outside was taken as a potential threat.

At a certain point, the teams started to feel comfortable with
cross-team sharing and learning from each other. They started to feel
comfortable opening up and hearing the feedback from the other
teams as well. That was when we started the communities[8] and discussed
cross-organizational issues there. The point wasn't to assign blame and
focus on who did what, but to learn together and prevent those issues

---

7. Overall Retrospective is part of the Large-Scale Scrum (LeSS) Framework:
   https://less.works.
8. A community of practice is a group of people who share a concern or a passion
   for something they do, and learn how to do it better as they interact regularly.

from happening again. That's when we became more of a network than individual teams. Our interconnectedness became stronger, and we aligned as an organization.

Finally, when we became strong internally as an organization, open to speaking up and giving each other feedback as we went, we were ready to share our way of working with the outside world. We started inviting other people to see our way of working and give us feedback, speaking about it at conferences, organizing workshops for students in order to attract them, inviting candidates who were deciding if they wanted to work for us or to join us for a day to see who we were. Not only were we sharing, but we were also curious about what other people saw, what they found interesting, important, and difficult. We opened up to receiving feedback because there is always a better way of doing things. It was hard at the beginning not to reject their perspective by saying they didn't get it. But at the end of the day, once we embraced the fact that everyone is right but only partially, we were able to improve in much more effective ways.

Think about feedback in your team within the last few months.

How many times have I given my peers honest and open feedback that they could learn from?

A. Never
B. Rarely
C. Sometimes
D. Often
E. Regularly

How many times have I learned and changed the way I do things based on the feedback from my peers or employees?

A. Never
B. Rarely
C. Sometimes
D. Often
E. Regularly

What can you change so that you give and get actionable feedback more often?

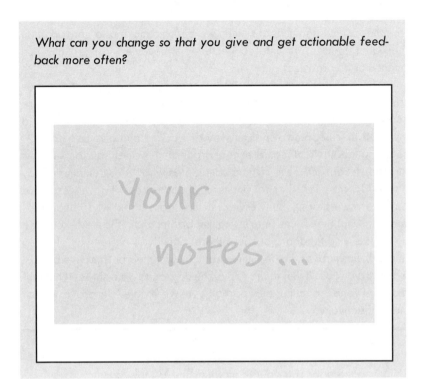

GIVING FEEDBACK

Sometimes, when your culture is not quite where you'd like it to be yet and a lot of toxic behavior exists, you might still need feedback, but the environment makes it hard to give and receive it. If people have little trust in each other, you need to be more careful about what you say and how you say it. In such environments, the COIN conversation model is a good way to get the message across.
Similar to other coaching tools, such as the GROW model, it guides you through the conversation and raises awareness. COIN stands for context/connection, observation, impact, and next.

Context/Connect: We start with context to connect with a specific time, event, or situation that happened in the past. When did it happen? What was the situation? What were the circumstances? Be positive, expect that everything was done with a good intention.

Observation: The observation must be specific but neutral. Don't take sides. Just describe what happened. Don't evaluate, as evaluation in such situations usually comes across as blaming. Observation requires you to be able to keep a distance and apply the agile leadership model. There are no right or wrong situations, just different angles and viewpoints.

Impact: The impact is very personal. It's about your feelings, not about what is or isn't right. How do you feel about it? What does it look like to you? What impact did it have on the team, department, and organization?

Next: Finally, the next step brings us back to the action. Help people to see there was, and is, another way to react. What could have been done instead? How can they handle it next time? Make your requests clear. What do you want them to change?

Imagine a situation where one of your colleagues, the most experienced person, was constantly sending text messages during a workshop and not collaborating with the team. The other team members say, in private after the meeting, that they felt discouraged, as they were afraid that he disagreed.

Context

"I know that you care about this product a lot, and you spend a lot of time helping this team to make it great."

Observation

"I noticed yesterday in the workshop that you were on your phone quite often and didn't engage much with the group. It felt like you were not engaged and were mentally out of the meeting."

Impact

"The impact to the team was that they felt discouraged. They were afraid that you disliked what they are doing and just not saying that openly to them."

Next

"I understand that things can happen, and I would request that you to step away if you need to solve other things and be open about it with the team. It will send a signal that you trust them with their work, and they would feel supported."

Think about a recent situation for which you'd like to give feedback and phrase it in the COIN way to practice:

Your

notes ...

LEARN FROM FEEDBACK

The ability to learn from feedback is crucial on the leadership journey. Though there are many ways to reflect on the feedback, the Leadership Circle Profile [Lead19] is a great 360° profile focused on individual leader development. It compares your results with the norm base of 100,000+ leaders worldwide. It's usu-

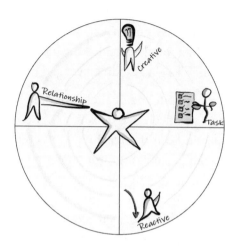

ally eye-opening, as we tend to see ourselves differently than others see us.

The Leadership Circle Profile combines the four dimensions of the leader personality: it compares their *creative* competencies (which are highly correlated with the leader's effectiveness) with their *reactive* tendencies (which get more short-term results) and their people and *relationship* orientation versus *task* orientation. Knowing yourself well and getting holistic feedback as input for improving your leadership style are important steps in your agile leader journey.

When I did my assessment, I was hoping to be more on the creative side than on the reactive side. Looking at the results, creativity was definitely strong, even stronger than I had expected. However, there were some surprising segments in the reactive hemisphere, which told me things about myself I was not ready to hear, so I started making excuses for the assessment results—but the reality was different. On the reactive hemisphere, I hadn't thought I would score high at controlling and protecting either. In retrospect, I can clearly see those aspects of my behavior, and while I believe I have improved, these traits are still stronger than I would wish for. I've made a big step forward because of my coaches, who, without judging me, helped me to see and accept those tendencies in myself. Get awareness, embrace it, and act upon it. I'm far from being done with it, but I've made huge progress on my leadership journey, and I'm glad I didn't give up when I heard that feedback.

Despite the challenges of the VUCA world, most leaders still lead reactively [Anderson15a]. Research shows that leaders who operate from the reactive mindset are able to achieve results only to some extent, and from a certain stage forward, they are unable to generate high performance. "Reactive leaders typically emphasize caution over creating results, self-protection over productive engagement, and aggression over building alignment" [Duncan19]. In contrast, leaders who develop a creative mindset are open to new potential.

To understand a bit more about reactive leaders, let's look at the three types of leaders and their natural tendencies [Anderson15a]:

- **Heart types** are people who form relationships around themselves and are satisfied if people like them and accept them. They care about relationships, and when they are afraid people might reject them, they avoid conflicts and become quite passive. When they are on their reactive side, they are seen as compliant. Their relationship focus makes them aligned with agile principles.

- **Will types** are trying to win by any means necessary. They are competitive, they want to have results and accomplish what needs to be done. They are anything but compliant. They care about being in charge, getting promoted, controlling things. They neither delegate nor collaborate. They hate failure, as they are afraid it will make them look weak. No matter what, they need to be the best. They are perfectionists, often micromanagers. When they are on their reactive side, they are seen as controlling, and it's super hard for them to embrace the agile way of working.

- **Head types** are smart and analytical. They are rational thinkers, able to keep distance even in conflicting, complex situations.

Their inner motivation comes from others seeing them as knowledgeable, as brilliant thinkers with great ideas. They are seen as cold, distant, overanalytical, and critical. When they are on their reactive side, they are seen as protective. When they are in an agile environment, they often tend to overanalyze.

Creative competencies open new opportunities. They multiply the impact you would create through leading just from the reactive mindset. "Transitioning to the Creative Self is the major transition of life and leadership" [Anderson15b]. Leaders with a creative mindset often start with a vision and purpose that generate passion and faith, which in turn translate into a clear picture that helps teams to skyrocket to their success. "Creative leadership is about creating a team and organization that we believe in, creating outcomes that matter most, and enhancing our capacity to create a desired future" [WPAH16]. Creative leadership is key for fostering collaborative, agile organizations and cultures.

Creative leadership is key to agile cultures.

Leadership Growth as a Core Element to Agility

Kay Harper, Leadership and Relationship System Coach

The complexity and pace of change in the twenty-first century are creating a widening gap for all leaders in terms of their effectiveness. Data show that as the world is now more interconnected and the business environment is more volatile and complex, the definition of effective leadership is changing. Data also exist showing that leadership effectiveness is directly correlated to business performance. As a coach, I work with people to help them understand their current leadership competency, how the experiences they've had influence their approach to leadership, to gain awareness of their impact as a leader. When leaders have awareness, they can make conscious choices about how they are impacting their organization's bottom line.

I remember working with a leadership team in a division of a larger company. The leadership team wanted to understand how to work with their teams and team members to help them take on more decision-making responsibility so that they could deliver value more quickly. Knowing that the leadership style of senior leaders is what creates (or prohibits) an environment in which decentralized decision making is possible, we started working with this senior leadership team. Through the combination of Leadership Circle Profile and associated coaching, the leaders each received data that provided insights into how they show up when working with teams, peers, stakeholders, and the executive team of the broader organization. The leaders each gained a better understanding of their strengths, creative competencies, reactive tendencies, and areas they could improve to directly impact their effectiveness. They each created their own action plan, and coaching was provided one-on-one and at the leadership team level. The leaders began to hold each other accountable for making the shifts to which they'd committed. Through time (and team coaching), the delivery teams learned that they had the leaders' support as they took on more decision making. Silos broke down as more collaboration occurred within and across teams. Positivity increased when team members felt more autonomy in delivery. Eventually, the company saw an increase in both the rate of delivery and employee satisfaction. As someone who partners with organizations to help them on their path to agility, I have a hope that more leaders at all levels of organizations will see the need to lead differently and take action to further deepen these new capacities.

DECISION

Even in an agile environment, you need to make a decision from time to time. Agile is not about voting or about never-ending conversations. It's always a tradeoff: let people collaborate and figure it out, or decide yourself.

The ability to make a decision empowers. It brings energy and motivates. In traditional Organizations 1.0, the boss is there to decide. In knowledge Organizations 2.0, the manager is expected to delegate, while at agile Organizations 3.0, the leader empowers others to step in and take over the responsibility for day-to-day decisions and rely on influence over power.

As always, it's good to know where you stand. Do you have enough trust in the system to delegate? Can you imagine letting it go? Those are just a few questions you can ask yourself to start thinking of where you are regarding the decision-making process.

Think about your organization. On a scale of 1 to 10, where 1 means "not at all" and 10 means "completely," rate the following statements [Bockelbrink17]:

We approach challenges by experiments.

We are continuously looking for improvements.

We make all information transparent and accessible to everyone.

We focus on achieving the goal.

We always speak up when we disagree with the decision or action.

We are inclusive and always involve people who are affected by the decision.

We take over ownership and responsibility when needed.

The more on the right side you are, the more effective the decision-making process is going to be when you let it go and empower teams to make the decisions.

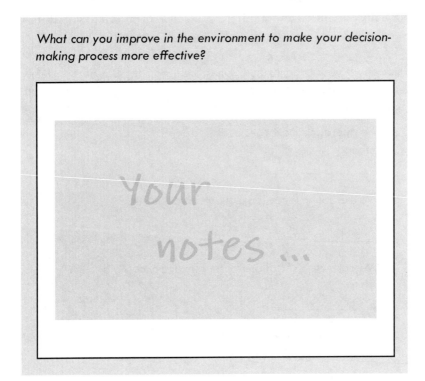

What can you improve in the environment to make your decision-making process more effective?

Your notes ...

SOCIOCRACY

Traditional organizations run a decision followed by a compliance process, while in an agile space, the decision needs to be created in a collaborative way. It's relatively easy to imagine a small team making decisions, but would it work at a large scale? Sociocracy 3.0 brings a framework allowing you to start with alignment via double-linking, which leads to consent [Esser_nd]. In a nutshell, we speak about a fully cross-functional team that always contains the so-called double-linking—

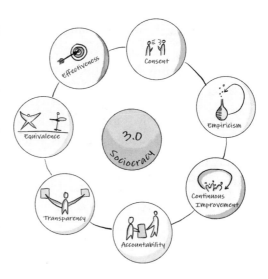

team members as well as management representatives—in order to be able to create a high-level alignment, not just local optimization. This Sociocratic Circle Organization Method was created by Gerard Endenburg[9] in 1980 and developed through the years to a whole framework often used in agile space: Sociocracy 3.0,[10] which defines seven principles and a series of patterns [Bockelbrink17] on how the organization can operate and make decisions leading to the autonomous, tolerant execution.

The principles of *empiricism, continuous improvement,* and *high transparency* are not anything new for the typical agile environment. The *effectiveness* principle, which says you shall "devote time only to what brings you closer toward achieving your objectives" [Bockelbrink17], can be reframed as another agile value: focus. Finally, the remaining three principles are specifically important in the context of decision making:

- **Consent** creates openness around any objections and disagreements.

9. Gerard Endenburg: The Sociocratic Circle-Organization Method: https://www.sociocracy.info/gerard-endenburg.
10. Sociocracy 3.0: https://sociocracy30.org.

- **Equivalence** promotes inclusivity and involves all people affected by the decision in the decision-making process.
- **Accountability** brings the ownership and responsibility to act when needed.

A collaborative approach to agreements, together with the high transparency and continuous evaluation from Sociocracy 3.0, results in solid decisions and makes the organization very flexible when reacting to issues.

POWER AND CONTROL CYCLES

Now let's take a closer look at what is happening in your brain when you are facing a problem and what kind of reactions you have. Christopher Avery describes it in his program The Leadership Gift[11] and in more detail in his book [Avery16]. The concept goes deep into your mind, uncovering your internal processes, feelings, and reactions. Why do you often react a certain way? As Avery says, "The scary part is the need to give up control to increase power and freedom" [Partner17]. It all starts with fear. Fear of failure. Fear of losing control.

When you face a problematic situation, your brain guides you either through the Power Cycle or the Control Cycle. The Control Cycle is a reflection of the fear of losing control—it's grounded in traditional management, where control is all that matters; otherwise you might look weak and unimportant and won't be promoted or won't deserve your job. Whenever a problem emerges, fear starts to take over and you try to get your control back. You evaluate the situation, weighing thoroughly all pluses and minuses, and look for advice on how to solve it by creating yet another rule that would prevent such things from happening or for any process that can help you to regain control. And the mental trap is in motion. With every evaluation followed by advice, you make a decision on what is right

---

11. The Leadership Gift: https://christopheravery.com/the-leadership-gift.

and what is not, and then expect compliance. When that's not happening, you feel an even greater fear of losing control, and that fear is strengthened by the feeling of betrayal. You evaluate the new situation, decide whether or not this should happen, search for ways to regain control, and so on. The fear of losing control grows and generates wider and stronger frustration, which puts increasing pressure on the environment.

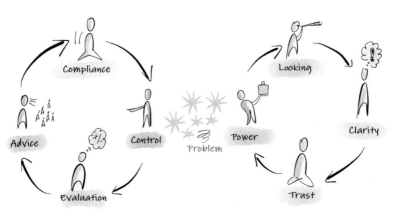

Alternatively, you can choose to follow the Power Cycle. It's not hard, but you must break your current habits and react in a different way than what you are used to. When a problem emerges, instead of evaluating it, you start looking for reasons why it is happening, finding the root cause, trying to see it from a system perspective. The process of looking for reasons brings more clarity to the issue. It shows you different perspectives, makes you curious. Clarity brings quietness and relief to your mind, which eventually creates trust in yourself and in others, which closes the circle and brings you more power than you felt before. "The Power Cycle is not an easy choice at first; however, it is a self-reinforcing dynamic that we can rapidly learn to trust" [Partner10].

To get into the Power Cycle, the first step is to recognize which path you are used to taking. Once you have enough awareness to recognize the pattern before you react in the usual way, you can intentionally choose to look for understanding, take a system view, and apply the agile leadership model instead of going to the evaluation and searching for what is right and what is wrong. Like every change, it takes time, but it is worth it.

COLLABORATION

Agile is all about teams and collaboration. Individuals are not that important. There is nothing magical in this concept—it's just that people got so used to working as individuals that they forgot what collaboration is about. However, collaboration is the key aspect of the agile environment, and if you can't collaborate, there is no way you can become an agile leader.

The traditional organizations are all about processes, rules, and delegation. All we need to do is analyze the situation, decide how we want to handle it, describe it in a process, and follow that process. It shall be enough. It's a world where we rely on processes in our day-to-day decision making. "The process will solve it," people say. In simple situations, it works well, and the transparency and predictability of the situation are an advantage. In complicated situations, this model might not be flexible enough, and people and organizations will struggle to react properly. In a complex situation when it's hard to predict what will happen, this method usually fails.

Process Solves It

> *Tight processes are killing creativity and work only in simple and predictable situations.*

The more compli-
cated the situation a company faces on a day-to-day
basis, the harder it is to
describe the process to be
followed. It seems to be
unavoidable that rules and
practices are not enough
for success; delegation
comes into play, and new
roles and positions are created for those responsible
for a certain part of the process. It's the world of individual responsibility, where
we create a single point
of contact who takes care
of things and whom we
can blame when things go
wrong. You can volunteer
and say, "I'll do it," or you
can assign it to someone

I Do It

else and say, "You do it." In any case, there is no real collaboration. Such role-splitting allows more flexibility because, unlike in
the process-solves-it approach, people can make a judgment based

You Do It

on the particular situation
and solve it more effec-
tively than if they strictly
followed processes.

> *Individual responsibility
> kills collaboration and
> team spirit.*

By starting to help
each other, we cross the

You Help Me

line of collaboration. People start working together, offering help to others and asking for help themselves, which starts to feel like a collaboration, at least at first glance, as more people are working together.

I Help You

However, there is still one person responsible, and the other is just the helper. It's a good first step, but at the end of the day, it's closer to delegation than collaboration, as the unequal ownership makes one side more invested in the results than the other; the owner usually makes the plans and decisions and feels responsibility, while the other person supports the owner with the inputs. It's still more likely to create blaming than a sense of shared ownership and responsibility. It's a start, but it's not collaboration as we understand it in an agile environment.

> *Helping one another with certain tasks is not collaboration. Collaboration requires equal ownership.*

Finally, where there is real collaboration, people have shared responsibility, shared ownership, and one goal. "We do it together," they say. It's not important who does what, and there is no task assignment up front—they all just do what is

We Do It

needed and make their decisions as the need arises. This is the type of collaboration that makes teams in agile and Scrum great and creates high-performing environments. If you truly want to be agile, and not just pretend that following some practices is enough, it's time to get rid of individual responsibility—which is often grounded in your org chart, position schemes, and career paths—and learn how to create a real collaborative environment with shared responsibility and ownership. Learn how "We can do it **together**."

What can you do at your organization to enhance true collaboration?

Your notes ...

The Importance of Pair Work

Yves Hanoulle, Creative Collaboration Agent

We all know that, in theory, two pairs of eyes see better than one. Yet when I'm facilitating an exercise in a pair and my partner interrupts me to talk about something I missed, I'm always flabbergasted. For me, feedback in the moment is the best kind of feedback. It does not make that particular training better, but it improves all my future workshops.

In 2009, I started asking the organizers of my international workshops to put me in contact with someone else who is interested in and knowledgeable on the topic. This person and I prepare the workshop remotely and run it as a pair. Most of the time, we have never physically met before the workshop. Yet we have built trust in each other. We always discuss how we will interrupt each other and other ways to send each other signals. A technique I like is to use is color-coded Post-it Notes that we post on the computer we use to present:

- Green: We are ahead of schedule. You can take your time to talk a little longer, add an extra story.
- Yellow: We are on schedule. Keep talking as we rehearsed.
- Red: We are behind schedule. We need to speed up and drop some stories.

There is another use for pair-coaching: when I start working for a company, I'm hired for my knowledge and my experience. Yet that experience has also taught me that I can't use my knowledge without knowing or better understanding the company that hires me. For that, I prefer to pair up with a person who knows the company. I channel my experience and in return I learn about the company.

FACILITATION

On the right side of the Agile Leader Competencies Map are the facilitation and coaching skills. Until team collaboration becomes the natural way you work, facilitation is a crucial skill that enables effective communication. "In the new knowledge-based, networked economy, the ability to talk and think together well is a vital source of competitive advantage and organizational effectiveness" [Isaacs99].

In the agile world, we rely on facilitation as a core competence. It's all about the ability to talk with each other in an effective way. It's a place where creativity and innovations emerge. The ability to read the room and understand the different communication modes is the starting point in forming collaborative structures. It starts with teams, but eventually you need to be able to scale it to the organizational level of communities and networks of teams and to create an environment where they can all collaborate together even outside of the organizational borders.

Facilitation, a Key Agile Leadership Skill

Marsha Acker, author of The Art and Science of Facilitation: How to Lead Effective Collaboration with Agile Teams

When done well, facilitation is a skill that is not very visible. I was a trained facilitator before I discovered the mindset of agility. Skillful facilitators know how to be present with what's happening in a meeting, aware of both what's being said and what's not being said. In my own experience of leadership, facilitation has served me well. Early in my career, I remember feeling almost paralyzed when disagreements broke out in meetings. I would become silent, unable to find my voice. But in the silence, I realized that I could often see what others couldn't: both sides of the argument. Yet I was afraid to say anything for fear that it would mean taking one side over the other or that it would help one person "win" the argument when I thought they both had valid points.

Deepening my practice of facilitation skills—along with building a richer understanding of group dynamics and being able to read the room—helped me shift my thinking. Rather than believing that disagreements should be avoided in order to have a productive outcome to a meeting, I began to realize that different perspectives are necessary in order to move a group forward. I learned that naming the patterns I could see in group dynamics was sometimes more important than making suggestions for new solutions. I went from facilitating meetings where I would do everything I could to avoid surfacing conflict or differing points of view to viewing them as necessary to group conversation and dialogue. I began designing ways to surface different points of view in order to create an environment where people could voice their perspectives in a constructive manner.

In *The Advantage*, Patrick Lencioni writes, "There is no greater way to change the culture of an organization than by changing the way it does meetings." I've watched this truth play out in client organizations time and time again. We spend so many hours in meetings each week, and yet there are often lost opportunities for greater dialogue of the sort that leads toward more innovation and new thinking.

FOUR-PLAYER MODEL

One very interesting concept describing communication is the Four-Player model created by system therapist David Kantor [Kantor12]. It's an interesting mental map for a facilitator to see where all different actors—or players, as he calls them—stand. In every conversation, you can choose from four different approaches: Move, Follow, Oppose, and Bystand.

The move starts a conversation around a certain topic. At some point, it generates a new idea, then jumps to a different topic. Once that happens, some people follow and support what was said. Others may oppose the idea and disagree through their own argumentation. Finally, the last group of people may bystand and provide a different perspective on what is happening in the conversation. Any healthy conversation needs balanced approaches, and very often the bystand is what is missing the most in the system. It brings the high-level nonjudgmental perspective that creates new options and allows people to look at the situation through different lenses.

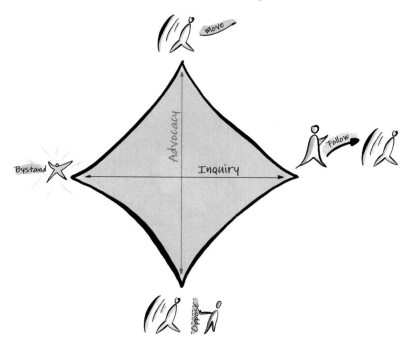

If there are only movers, no one listens to each other, and no real conversation occurs; people don't search for understanding. With no one opposing, the conversation might lack depth, but when people are mostly opposing, they usually shut down the others, and the conversation lacks variety.

The Move–Oppose line is about advocacy, while the Bystand–Follow line is about inquiry [Isaacs99]. Any healthy environment needs both lines in balance; otherwise, collaboration suffers from lack of perspectives.

This example demonstrates the differences between an unbalanced and a balanced conversation around deciding where to go for lunch.

MOVE ONLY

John: Let's go to Taco Taco. They have great food there. (Move)

Maria: I would like to go to Fresh for a salad. (Move)

Fred: It's Friday, so we should go to the Four Stars Pizza at the corner. (Move)

Jenny: The Tri-Tri has great sandwiches, and it's nearby. (Move)

The speakers are not even close to agreement. They each are pushing their favorite solution, and it seems they are not even listening to one another.

ADVOCACY LINE TOO STRONG

John: Let's go to Taco Taco. They have great food there. (Move)

Maria: Mexican food is not healthy. (Oppose) Fred: It's too far away, and it always takes too long to get service. (Oppose)

John: Taking a short walk there is healthy, and we can order online before we go to make it faster. (Move)

Jenny: It is too far, and I need to be back for the meeting. (Oppose)

Again, agreement is no closer. It even creates friction, as the Oppose arguments feel more like pushing. Such communication usually creates defensive behavior, which is not helpful in any conversation.

HOW THE INQUIRY HELPS

John: Let's go to Taco Taco. They have great food there. (Move)

Maria: Mexican food is not healthy. I would prefer to go to Fresh for a salad. They have a Caribbean week right now, plus it's nearby. (Oppose, followed by Move)

Jenny: I would definitely prefer to go somewhere nearby. I need to get back in time for a meeting. We can also try Tri-Tri. It is nearby, and they have healthy options on the menu. (Follow, Move, Follow)

Fred: It seems we are looking for somewhere with tasty food, within walking distance, and with some healthy options. Any other ideas where we can go? (Bystand)

Such a conversation already feels quite healthy. People not only are listening to each other but also are aware of the overall situation.

Talking about lunch is a very simple conversation example in a small-team context. You might ask why we even need a model to agree on lunch. However, the same conversation patterns are happening at a large scale at the organizational level, and you need to be aware of them so you can re-create the balance.

When communicating, everyone has preferred modes where they feel comfortable. What is your most common communication mode?

☐ Move

☐ Follow

☐ Oppose

☐ Bystand

From a supporting skills perspective, a facilitator needs to practice voicing, listening, respecting, and suspending. "Four practices can enhance the quality of conversation: speaking your true voice and encouraging others to do the same; listening as a participant; respecting the coherence of others' views; and suspending your certainties" [Isaacs99]. To refer back to the agile leadership model, listening helps you to *get awareness*. By hearing all the voices in the system and seeking all the perspectives, you bring diversity and more color to the conversation, while the suspending practice helps you to *embrace* it and let it go. *Act upon* is happening on the advocacy line between the move and oppose, using voicing and respecting. Voicing is the most courageous and hardest to achieve as you need to express your own feelings and show them in a broader context. "When we move by speaking our authentic voice, we set up a new order of things, open new possibilities, and create" [Isaacs99].

When used well, voicing has the potential to bring the conversation to a new horizon, to create a new quality of dialog. Finally, respecting is the practice that brings trust. It encourages others to engage in the conversation and actively participate. Everyone is right, but only partially.

As a servant leader, you need not only to practice those skills yourself but to help others become great at voicing, listening, respecting, and suspending as well. The more you invest in that, the better and more effective conversations they will have, and the more likely they are to be successful at collaborating and being a great team.

Which skill is your strength?

☐ Voicing

☐ Listening

☐ Respecting

☐ Suspending

Which skill (voicing, listening, respecting, suspending) do you most need to improve? What can you do about it?

Your

notes ...

COACHING

Coaching is another soft skill that agile leaders critically need for their success. The International Coaching Federation[12] defines coaching as "partnering with clients in a thought-provoking and creative process that inspires them to maximize their personal and professional potential" [ICF20], which is a very different skill than most people are used to applying in an organization. It's all about raising awareness and letting people figure out their own way instead of telling them what to do, explaining, advising, or sharing your own experience. In the context of this book, we are not speaking about one-on-one coaching. Great agile leaders use coaching to address the complexity at the system level and to coach organizations as a whole system.

Let's think about coaching from the perspective of the leadership agility model (see Chapter 4). For the Expert leader, coaching feels like it's from a different planet. "How can I help people if I don't tell them what to do?" they often ask, and they end up disappointed, as coaching doesn't solve any of their problems.

From the Achiever perspective, coaching can be useful, but only from time to time, as the results are more important, and those talks take too much time. They prefer to focus on the work and flow, and they use coaching only accidentally and in rare cases.

Finally, from the Catalyst perspective, coaching is crucial. It helps leaders to keep their relationships healthy and creates a space where people can be successful. Coaching

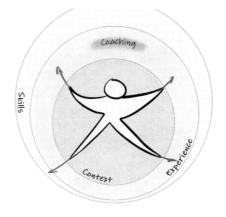

---

12. International Coaching Federation (ICF) is a global organization dedicated to advancing the coaching profession: https://coachfederation.org.

is the key to the next level. The more you believe in people, the more you know that the people around you are smart and creative, they figure out things you might never understand, and they have brilliant ideas. Still, from time to time, they get stuck in their own worlds, seeing only one angle of the situation; they can't take a step back to see the big picture. Their previous experience is limiting them and closing them into a certain layer. Every now and then, no matter how great they are, they don't see the obvious. Coaching is the right tool that helps teams to search for new perspectives and raises their awareness of the system. Everyone is living in their own bubble created by context, previous experience, and the situation at hand. Coaching breaks those boundaries and allows them to step out of the bubble and extend the boundaries of the current reality.

People often ask me how they should start with coaching, so let me share what I did. I have a technical background, so learning soft skills was not natural for me. Many years back, I started as a developer, writing rather low-level software in C++. It was quite a predictable world. A few years later, I became a ScrumMaster and heard for the first time about facilitation and coaching. My reaction was simple—I rejected the idea. It just didn't fit my world. I saw people as smart experts, so why would they need facilitation? They could handle a conversation themselves. And coaching? How could just asking questions possibly be helpful? So I rejected the idea and focused on other things.

Time went by, and the topic of facilitation and coaching kept coming up on different occasions. The change came after a talk I attended. Through the way he gave his talk, Radovan Bahbouh, a psychologist and coach, managed to change my belief that coaching didn't make any sense. I could not get it out of my head and started talking about it with friends and colleagues. Soon after that, I went on a weekend snowboarding trip. I'd seen those other snowboarders going down the hill smoothly, without any effort, and I felt desperate. I had been trying to learn snowboarding for a few years already, and the previous year I'd even signed up for a private lesson. It didn't improve my style at all. I was sharing this concern with my friend, and he asked if I'd like to try to get some coaching. I looked at him with a mix of surprise and disbelief. "You said earlier that you want to try it, so this is an opportunity, if you'd like to take it," he said. Long story short, later that day, I was able to do the curves without any effort, like the other snowboarders I'd seen from the lift. And I've never forgotten that feeling.

When I got back, I went to a bookstore and bought a book about coaching and started practicing. Later, I joined classes from the Agile Coaching Institute[13] to practice the agile coaching and facilitation basics, and then the Organizational Relationship System Coaching (ORSC)[14] to deep-dive into the system coaching domain. It has been a long journey, but I can say that the most important thing that made me believe in coaching was experiencing it firsthand. When I faced an issue and everything else was failing, coaching made a difference. So if you are reluctant to put your faith in coaching, find a coach and let him or her help you with an issue.

CHANGE

The last piece on the Agile Leader Competencies Map focuses on our ability to implement change. Change happens at three levels. First, there is a change in yourself, your beliefs, reactions, approaches, behaviors, and habits—the way you work. Through that change, you become a role model of an agile leader, and people will follow. "Use Your Self: You are your most important tool for change, using your skills of empathy, curiosity, patience and observation" [Derby19]. Every change is difficult, and personal change is usually the toughest. However, the result will definitely pay off. Leaders need to change first. The organization will follow.

Start with yourself: be a model of an agile leader.

---

13. Agile Coaching Institute: https://agilecoachinginstitute.com.
14. ORSC: https://www.crrglobal.com.

Second, there is the ability to influence others. Make them part of the team, create an environment where they become the first supporters, and together create a snowball effect and change the organization together.

Finally, the third level of change is change at the system level. Focus on the entire organization, have the system perspective, and internalize the agile leadership model: listen to the voices of the system, get awareness of them, embrace them, and act upon them. From this viewpoint, the individuals are not important, and neither are the teams. The system level focuses on the overall harmony of the organization, the level of energy, the culture and mindset.

THE CHANGE DYNAMIC

Changing an organization is a long-term task. Most people focus on the beginning. They make an enormous effort to plan it and prepare the first steps. They give special attention to the initial impetus that would overcome resistance. They are careful to guide people in their first steps. And then, when it all starts moving, they get distracted by other tasks and refocus on other issues.

At first, everything goes well, so the change seems to have been a smart move. Give people space, let them move ahead, allow them to find their own way of overcoming the obstacles. Isn't that what self-organization is about in the first place? But things are never that simple.

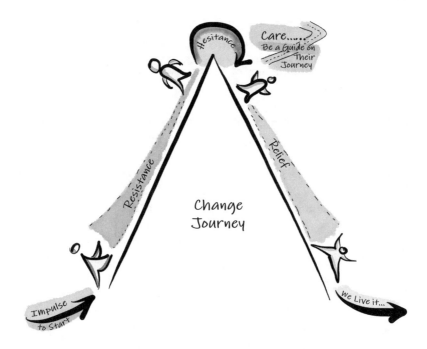

Daniel Pink, author of *When: The Scientific Secrets of Perfect Timing* [Pink18a], describes in examples from various research the importance of the midpoint: "Midpoints are really interesting, sometimes they fire us up, other times they drag us down and simply being aware of midpoints can help you navigate them more effectively" [Pink18b]. Being mindful of where you are in the process of change is the most important part of being an agile leader. Midpoints are hard. Psychologically, you need to make a step toward a new way of working, a new mindset. People are hesitant. At the midpoint, they no longer feel resistance, but they are lacking the passion for a new way of working as well. They are balanced in the middle and looking for assurance, support, and encouragement. They are looking for a guide to help them step over the edge, find relief, and embrace the new way of working.

Put Down Your Sword and Just Listen

By Linda Rising, co-author of Fearless Change *and* More Fearless Change

I was an unofficial "change leader" for Scrum in a medium-sized telecom company. I was enthusiastic but just learning how to involve others in something I thought was important as a way of developing products. I had easily identified a few older guys, resisters, who would not come to my informal Brown Bag lunchtime sessions to learn a bit about Scrum. They didn't seem interested in trying some small experiments to see if the new approach would work for them. They only seemed interested in pointing out what they thought wouldn't work and constantly pushing back whenever anyone talked about it. I thought they were hopeless. As a result, I tried to avoid them, and when I could see they were headed my way, I ducked around a corner and waited for them to pass. One day, as I was coming out of the cafeteria, I saw, too late, that one of the most resistant guys was just a few feet in front of me, walking straight for me. I was caught. I looked around for an escape but saw none. He came up to me and started in—a litany of the problems with Scrum, why it wouldn't work for our teams, how I didn't know anything about "real" product development, how he and other older guys had lots of experience but no one really listened. He went on and on. I stood there, frozen in my tracks, reduced to nodding and replying in monosyllables, "Oh? Really? I didn't know that. Thanks for telling me. That's interesting. I can see how you would feel that way." It was lame, but all I had in the moment. Then a strange thing happened. I will never forget it. At the end of his angry outburst, he paused and said, "Okay. I guess my team could try it." I was dumbfounded. I realized I hadn't argued with him. I never laid out the facts to show him where he was wrong. I had simply kept my mouth shut except for a few nods and short responses to his statements. In retrospect, I see now that I "listened" him into agreeing to try Scrum. I allowed him to have his say. I was polite, respectful, really listening.

I have since learned that many resisters are deep-down looking for someone who will care about their point of view. Once they
have that and the attention and respect of the change leader, they
are usually okay with getting on board. They are, after all, smart
people who want to do a good job. Give them a chance—that's
what I learned. It might help all our organizations move forward.

FORCE FIELDS

Change is a complex process, but sometimes a very simple visual
tool makes it easier. One of my favorite tools in this space is force
field analysis.[15] I found it especially useful for visualizing in a picture the driving and restricting forces on the edge of change, where
you can clearly see what is influencing the system.

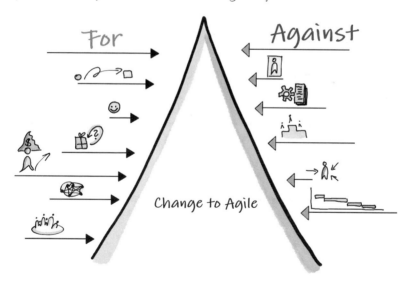

For example, the organizational change to agile can be supported by several driving forces, such as change responsiveness,
higher employee motivation, ability to inspect and adapt on the
basis of feedback, customer satisfaction, flexibility, and team

---

15. The principle was developed in the 1940s by psychologist Kurt Lewin.

collaboration; restraining forces might be silos skills, restricting processes, culture of individual competition, individual focus, and fixed planning and budgeting processes.

As a next step, you need to assess the forces and calculate the result for each side. We usually use the relative coaching scale of 0 to 5, where 0 means there is no impact of this indicator and 5 means the impact is significant. The summary of the relative weights is a good indicator of how difficult such a change is going to be, not a calculation of the decision.

Once you have the assessment, the next step is to change the ratio of the forces to make the change more favorable. That's where coaching is very useful, as you need to get into the creative space and unleash the potential of the innovative solutions. There are two ways to change the scores of the forces and increase the chance for success: strengthen the forces for the change, and mitigate the forces against the change. Though you can use this tool individually, it's even better in a workshop setting, which helps people to be part of it and address the situation leveraging the wisdom and creativity of a system.

Example of a Facilitation Script for the Force Field Analysis Workshop

- As a preparation, draw a peak (as illustrated) and write a topic in the middle of it.
- Ask people to brainstorm supporting forces on green Post-it Notes and opposing forces on orange Post-it Notes.
- Let the team assign the Post-it Notes to each side of the edge, group similar items to narrow them down, and simplify the visualization. Review the groupings to check there are no items missing or overleaping.
- Let the team assign relative weights. You can use simple dot voting; color-coding where everyone gets different-colored stickers to classify a force as red, yellow, or green; or play Planning Poker.[16] There is

---

16. Planning Poker is an agile estimating and planning technique.

no one method for how to do it. It's all about the conversation, not the tool.

- Review the results for each side and compare them.
- Now the real work starts: discuss how you can strengthen the forces for the change and how you can mitigate the forces against the change in order to shift the ratio.

Facilitating such a workshop is simple if you are used to coaching and facilitation, and it's a very powerful tool that shows creative options for how to address the change and, through collaboration, get real buy-in.

Think about a situation your organization is currently struggling with and draw the force fields for and against the change. Once you are done, assign relative weights to the forces.

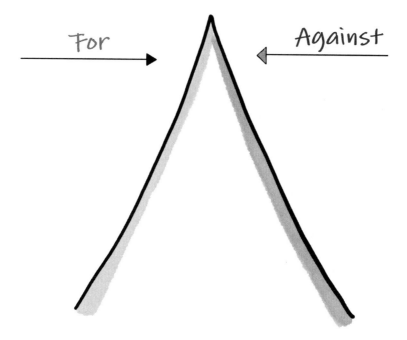

How can you strengthen the forces for a change? How can you mitigate the forces against the change?

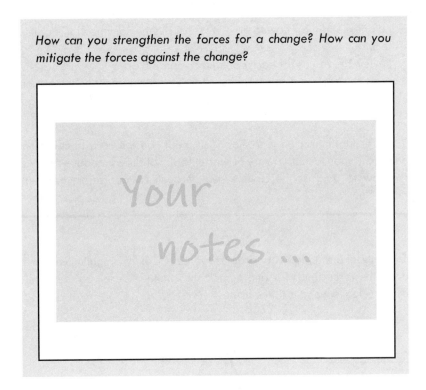

COMPETENCIES SELF-EVALUATION

This evaluation is a good reflection of your agile leader competencies. Agile leadership is a journey, and this map is a guide, pointing toward the next steps. No one is perfect, and there is always a better way of doing things.

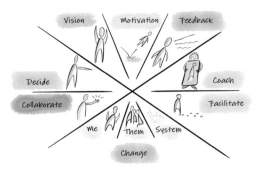

Spend some time reflecting on the Agile Leader Competencies Map. What are your strengths as a leader?

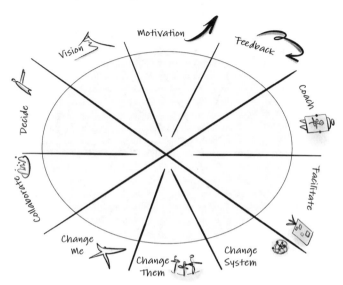

Based on the map, think about the Agile Leader Competencies Map a little more deeply.

What are those competencies allowing you to do? Why are they important?

What are your weaknesses as a leader?

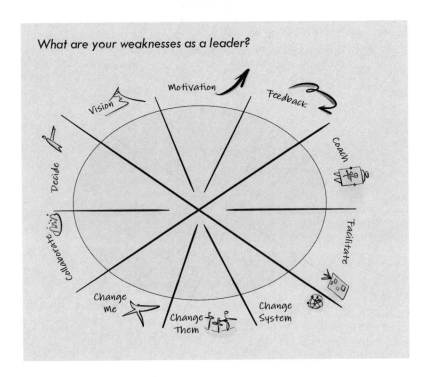

What would those competencies allow you to do if you were great at them?

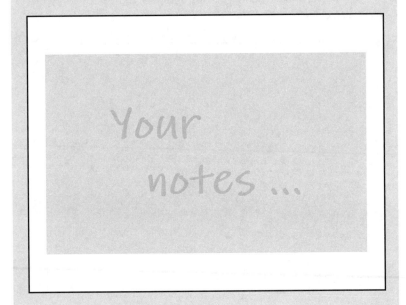

What is missing the most in your organization?

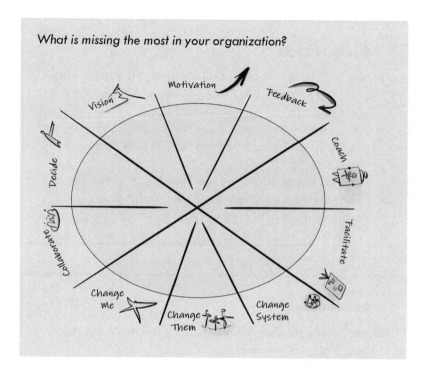

What would be different if those competencies were present in your organization?

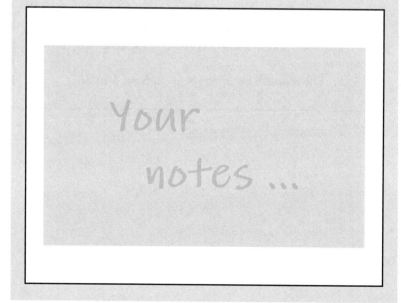

Books to Read

- *Fearless Change: Patterns for Introducing New Ideas*, Mary Lynn Manns and Linda Rising (Boston: Addison-Wesley, 2005).
- *7 Rules for Positive, Productive Change: Micro Shifts, Macro Results*, Esther Derby (Oakland, CA: Berrett-Koehler Publishers, 2019).
- *Leading Change: An Action Plan from The World's Foremost Expert on Business Leadership*, John Kotter (Boston: Harvard Business School Press, 1996).

In a Nutshell

- ☐ Metaphors stimulate the vision; don't be afraid to explore your high and low dreams.
- ☐ Great visions are created by walking through all three levels of reality: the sentient essence, the dreaming level, and the consensus reality.
- ☐ People are naturally creative, take ownership and responsibility, and are self-directed and self-controlled.
- ☐ The only true collaboration starts with shared responsibility and ownership where we can all work together.
- ☐ Facilitation and coaching are critical skills for agile leaders.
- ☐ Start with yourself: be a model of an agile leader.

7

. . .

META-SKILLS

Sometimes it's good to take a high-level look at your skills. Compared with competencies, which are precise and specialized, meta-skills are more abstract—they have a broader reach, are generalizable to nearly every aspect of work and personal life, and are accessible at the system level. Meta-skills fall into three domains: Me, We, and the World.

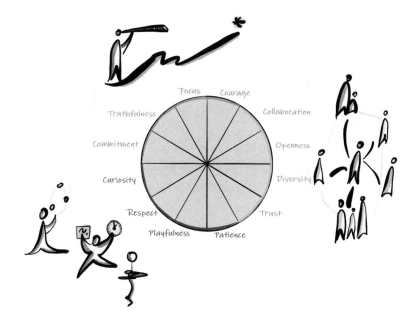

THE ME DOMAIN

The Me domain is internally driven. It allows you to choose a stance and decide whether you want to approach the situation with *curiosity, playfulness, respect,* or *patience.*

Curiosity is the key ingredient of the get-awareness step of the agile leadership model. It stimulates you to search for different perspectives and listen to the voice of the system [Fridjhon14]. It's one of the core meta-skills for system thinking (see Chapter 11 for more details).

Playfulness comes into the picture when you start enjoying the agile leadership model and start looking for innovative ways to understand the system. It makes the second step of the model—embrace it—enjoyable, and everything you do is more fun.

Respect is the core ingredient of the embrace-it step. It helps people to internalize the situation and accept that the voices of the system are diverse, neither right nor wrong, just different. Keeping in mind that everyone is right, but only partially, cultivates true democracy and helps you to let go of the fear of being wrong, which allows you to be playful and curious again.

Finally, patience is needed to avoid rushing through the steps of the agile leadership model and to take your time to embrace the situation. At the system level, you have unlimited time. There is no rush. There is no perfection, there is no end state, just the certainty that in a complex system, there is always a better way of doing things. Internalizing this unlimited-time concept is the first step of mastering patience.

Some time ago, I became part of a very dysfunctional team with a low level of trust, lack of transparency, and a lot of politics going on. It was so hard to be patient. It seemed we were not moving anywhere. It was so frustrating that I was even thinking about giving up and resigning. But I rarely give up. I complain, I'm frustrated, but I always somehow recover and find another way to deal with the situation. This time it was this meta-skill exercise that came to my mind. I thought, if I can't make a difference and change the team spirit, maybe it has something to say about my skills and abilities. I decided to work on my curiosity and patience, and I attended every session with those two meta-skills in mind. I tried to speak less, listen first, ask more questions to understand the intent of all the team members, and be curious about what their stand was. Surprisingly, this exercise helped me in many different situations—I started reacting differently and let things go more often than I used to. It turned out that sometimes very interesting things happen when you focus on your own change instead of trying to change others. In less than a year, this team became one of my closest ones, free of all the dysfunctions we had been dealing with. I would not say it was just because of what I did, but I'm quite sure the two meta-skills helped me to better influence the team and make it healthier.

THE WE DOMAIN

The We domain comes from the environment and drives the way we work together. As you can in the Me domain, you can choose to focus on the meta-skills *collaboration, trust, openness,* or *diversity.*

Collaboration is the core agile meta-skill for every team, as without it, the team becomes

just a group of individuals. The other aspect is that leaders often forget to be part of the team and to do things together. Collaboration enables the cocreation spirit, and it nurtures innovations and creativity. Leaders are an integral part of the team. The stronger the collaboration is, the higher the team quality. Close collaboration enhances the relationships, builds social interconnectedness, empowers, and helps define autonomy.

Trust is a prerequisite of any collaboration. If there is no trust, there are just individuals protecting their own positions. No one would make themselves vulnerable, no one would openly share their ideas, and the entire environment becomes overly self-protective. Lack of trust kills any team spirit and it can lead to toxic behavior and politics.

Finally, just as spices add wonderful aromas, zest, and flavor to your meal, openness and diversity add variety, energy, and depth to the environment. An open environment shows much higher responsibility and faster learning than closed environments with a lack of transparency. Diverse teams tend to be more creative and innovative than homogeneous teams. Nevertheless, diversity is much more than taking care of team composition. It's a diversity of perspectives. Are we proactively searching for diverse views, or are we instead clustering toward the perspectives that support each other? The diversity meta-skill helps us to focus on searching for a variety of angles to raise awareness about the system.

THE WORLD DOMAIN

Last but not least, there is the World domain, focusing on what attitude we show to the world: *commitment*, *focus*, *truthfulness*, or *courage*.

Commitment is the driving force behind an agile transformation. Without it, no change will happen, no issue will be solved, no case will be closed.

Focus is an enhancement of that driving force. It has the potential to create the flow, a state where things are happening almost seamlessly. Context switching kills productivity, while focusing on business value feeds the motivation.

Truthfulness creates integrity. Are we truthful in what we say? Do we also act that way? Or are we pretending and hiding things to make the current situation easier?

Finally, courage is a game changer. Are we courageous enough to experiment? Are we changing the game, or do we prefer to follow the established practices and processes? People will react differently, but there is no leadership without courage, and there is no agile without courage either.

With your organization in mind, choose one meta-skill from each domain that is significant in your organizational culture.

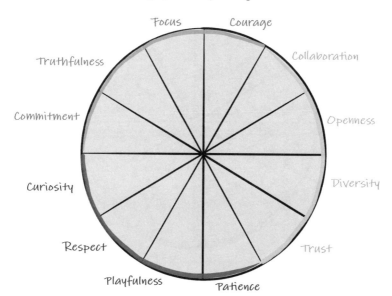

What does that meta-skill mean to you? Why is it important?

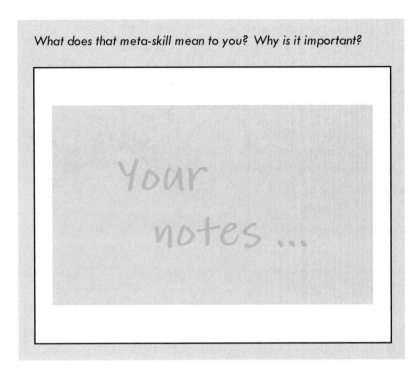

As a second step, choose one meta-skill from each domain that is missing or marginal in your organizational culture.

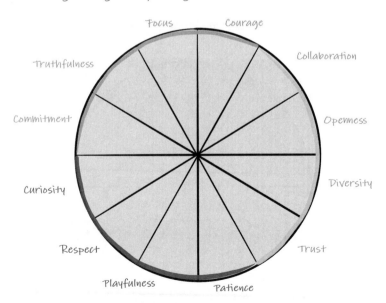

What does that meta-skill mean to you? How do you know it is missing, and what would be different if it were significant instead?

Your notes ...

Books to Read

- *Creating Intelligent Teams: Leading with Relationship Systems Intelligence*, Anne Rød and Marita Fridjhon (Randburg, South Africa: KR Publishing, 2016).

In a Nutshell

☐ Curiosity is the key ingredient in searching for different perspectives.

☐ There is no perfection, no end state, just the certainty that in a complex system, there is always a better way of doing things.

☐ Trust is a prerequisite for collaboration.

☐ Diverse teams are more creative and innovative than homogeneous teams.

☐ There is no leadership without courage, and there is no agile without courage either.

8

• • •

BUILDING AN AGILE ORGANIZATION

Once they have embraced
agility and a new leader-
ship style, agile leaders
naturally help the organization to embrace the same
values and principles. An
agile organization is agile
to begin with. There is no
specific framework needed

to make an organization agile: all you need is to practice the agility
at all organizational levels. Experiment and, through frequent feedback, find your own way of doing things. You can never be finished
in that effort, as there is always a better way of doing things. It's like
a star on the horizon—you can never touch it, but step by step, in
short iterations, you can get closer.

> *The agile organization is like a star on the horizon—you can
> never reach it, but you can come closer, step by step.*

All you need to bring along is courage, commitment, focus, openness, and respect.[1] "Being agile" is not the same as "doing agile." The frameworks, methods, and practices are just tools that can make the journey faster, more enjoyable, and more efficient, but the tools alone will not change the mindset. Nonetheless, there are some concepts that will help you to understand how to be successful in building an agile organization.

INSIDE OUT

Most agile transformations start from the outside in, as a process or structural change where management pushes a new framework to the organization but without real values or culture change. It looks like a good start, as it is simple and practical. However, it usually results in just doing agile, not being agile. The expected organizational success is not any closer, and all you get is "fake agile" and "Dark Scrum" [Jeffries16] implementing practices without any meaning.

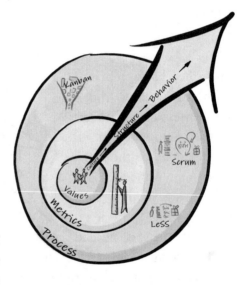

> *Any sustainable change needs to start from the inside out, with a change in values.*

If you care for sustainable agility, the only way to achieve it is to go from the inside out—start changing the values, and build that shift of the mindset from the inside. Do we care about

---

1. Courage, commitment, focus, openness, and respect are the five Scrum values.

learning through experiments, team collaboration, value delivery, and responding to changes? Do we live according to those values? That's where we need to start. Without changing those values, no frameworks will help us.

The most common reason for failure that I see in the organizations implementing agile is having agile as another process and a goal by itself, which almost never works. It usually starts with the same request: "We need to train X number of people in agile." And when everybody is trained, the "agile transformation" is done. Simple and straightforward. But there is no change of structure, culture, or values, nor is there any clear expectation of the outcome. I have been in many organizations that approach agile in this way, and I learned that this shortcut never works.

Let's look at one failure story as an example. Once, I was asked to facilitate an introduction to agile and Scrum training in a very small software organization. Those are usually easy to switch to the agile way of working, as they tend to be flexible and collaborative. In the beginning, we were talking with one particular team—it seemed quite simple. The participants were curious and interested in the content; the managing director and his management seemed supportive. However, one warning that this was not going to be a smooth transition came as we were finishing on day one of the two-day introduction, and the group mentioned that they were not done yet—they still had to finish their work planned for that day. They worked until midnight both days. They all repeatedly agreed that staying late to meet a rigid quota was an exception to the norm and that they should have more time in two weeks when the project was delivered. We always offer ongoing coaching support, but they were positive they didn't need anyone.

In roughly six months, we were called back for a one-day review, and it became clear that the organization hadn't changed much except for holding a few unproductive meetings. The team members were still assigned individual tasks and were still too busy. It didn't take me long to figure out that they hadn't stopped even for a few hours to discuss how they were going to change the way they worked. The only change that had happened was in terminology, and not surprisingly, that change was not enough to get any result. We talked about the need to start from the inside out with the team and management, but unfortunately, the same thing happened—only this time, the organization added more processes and hired an inexperienced ScrumMaster to implement Scrum. As before, the organization refused any agile coaching, as agile was now clear to all concerned, and they were fine. It was no surprise that eight months later, I was there again, this time to train new team members because many people had left. Their ScrumMaster was completely burned out, due to leave at the end of the month as well. This time, everyone was ready to listen and change their way of working. We did a one-day workshop after the training in order to start changes. They also articulated a strong strategic reason for the change and eventually managed to give the team time and support to change the way they work. This time, the change started from the inside and moved outward. It was harder than the previous terminology and process changes, but it worked out and paid off.

List at least three strategic reasons for the change to agile:

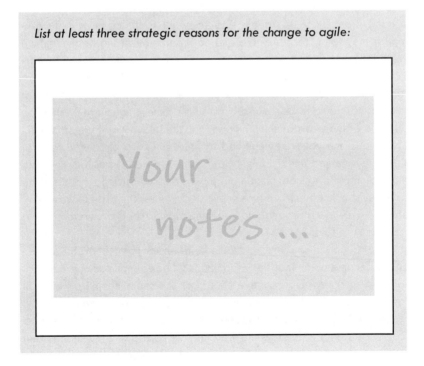

Which values need to change first in your organization for it to become agile?

Your notes ...

How do you know you are getting there?

Your notes ...

What processes, practices, or frameworks can help you to achieve agile?

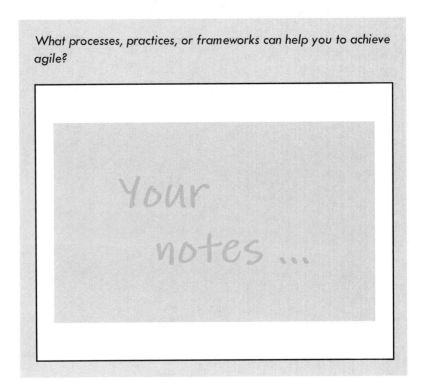

EVOLUTIONARY PURPOSE

The more self-organized and decentralized the organization, the higher the need for a strong and clear purpose, so that the people will show up for the all-important reason that they believe in it. Startups are usually driven by such evolutionary purpose. A good evolutionary purpose shows the direction,

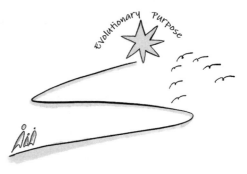

gives people the goal, and is unifying. It defines who we are and who we are not. "The evolutionary purpose reflects the deeper reason the organization exists. It relates to the difference it wants to make in the community it operates in, as well as in the marketplace it serves. It is not concerned with the competition or outperforming others; it is serving the 'greater good' that matters" [Reinvent_nd].

For traditional organizations, such a purpose is very distant and hard to imagine. They live in a world of hard metrics, goals, and objectives. They live in a world where employees need to be told what to do and are measured accordingly (theory X). With a good evolutionary purpose, the world becomes a place where people are naturally motivated (theory Y) and aligned by the purpose—all you need to do is give them autonomy and trust that they are going to make it.

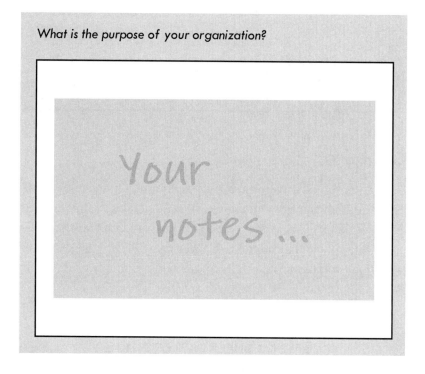

What is the purpose of your organization?

Your notes ...

Which of the following statements best describes your organizational purpose?

	1	10	
The purpose is mostly unknown to employees. It is here, but we don't care about it much.	◆━━━━━━━◆		The purpose gives the deeper reasons why the organization exists; we live by it.
The purpose shows what the organization wants to be internally. There is no clear outside-facing direction.	◆━━━━━━━◆		The purpose shows the difference the organization wants to make in the community or marketplace.
It's all about competition. We must perform better than other companies, grow the market share, and grow the business at the expense of others.	◆━━━━━━━◆		Serving the greater good matters. We are finding allies to amplify it. Profit is just a side effect of delivered value.

The farther on the right you are, the higher evolutionary purpose your organization has.

The evolutionary purpose is a prerequisite for an agile organization. Without it, full autonomy will create chaos. If the previous exercise didn't show a strong enough purpose, don't worry. Agile organizations don't become agile overnight. Having a good purpose is an evolutionary effort. It will happen eventually, and usually much sooner than you might have expected.

EMERGENT LEADERSHIP

Unlike in traditional organizations, where leadership was mostly positional, in agile organizations we rely more on emergent leadership. In other words, anyone can become a leader if he or she has a strong enough idea and courage to take ownership and go for it. Emergent leadership is the key driving force for any self-organized environment. In a well-functioning agile organization, leadership is spread around and decentralized. Leadership is no longer linked to any position, it's accessible to the teams and to individuals, who are free to create any teams around their ideas. Everyone can become a leader. It's your own choice, as long as you're ready to take responsibility and ownership.

The core prerequisites for emergent leadership are radical transparency and frequent feedback—nothing that wouldn't have been in the agile environments already. Anyone can come up with an idea, share it with everybody and ask for feedback, while the people around them make sure the idea is worth following. In the beginning, you can start with a small initiative. Later the initiatives may grow and become wider. What makes it a game changer is that the leaders don't necessarily report to any manager but to their colleagues, and to some extent to the entire organization. The leadership is emergent. What doesn't make sense in a traditional organization starts to make sense at a small scale, at the level of self-organizing teams, and thrives in flat agile organizational structures.

Emergent leadership is a concept that may be hard to understand, so let's take a look at what Google has to say about the topic, since Google made emergent leadership one of its key principles: "One thing we look for is general cognitive ability, the second is leadership—in particular, emergent leadership as opposed to traditional leadership. Traditional leadership is, were you president of the chess club? Were you vice president of sales? How quickly did you get there? We don't care. What we care about is, when faced with a problem and you're a member of a team, do you, at the appropriate time, step in and lead. And just as critically, do you step back and stop leading, do you let someone else? Because what's critical to be an effective leader in this environment is you have to be willing to relinquish power" [Friedman14].

It makes sense when you read it; however, that doesn't mean it's easy to apply. We are all fighting here with the social and cultural heritage of decades of hierarchical, positional leadership. Only in recent years have we started to hear about companies where emergent leadership has become a core driving force for their success. This reflects the fact that industry has needed to deal with VUCA challenges only in the past few decades. Complexity needs to be addressed by complexity, and emergent leadership is one of the concepts that allows organizations to be more creative and innovative and to better deal with complexity.

Team Forming in a Corporate Environment

Ondrej Benes, Head of Deutsche Telekom IT, Czech Republic

Our international telco corporation was undergoing massive transformation toward becoming an agile organization. Some parts had been using agile for ages; other parts had just started or were about to start sooner or later. We opened the discussion about how to approach forming our future agile teams within the organization. Pretty quickly, we came to the conclusion that we would do an experiment: let our colleagues form teams themselves. What we laid down were some conditions to be met by the to-be-created teams (maximum number of people in a team that a team needs to be cross-functional and able to handle the whole lifecycle from analysis to operations, etc.).

And we did not stop there. We decided to go yet deeper in terms of democratic team forming and let the newly established teams select their ScrumMasters. Also, it was up to Product Owners and these teams to agree on who would perform the Product Owner role toward which teams. We all were very, very curious about what was going to happen. There was no emergency break in terms of sponsor final veto or management right to overrule, so we had no idea of all the paths it may take us on, but we trusted the system to behave with the best intentions.

One day, we met with the team in an offsite session. Participation was on a voluntary basis. Those who decided not to come had prepared their avatar and delegated their vote to someone in attendance. After some initial hesitation, physical moving around started—we could observe how people were grouping with others, how names were being added or crossed out on team flipcharts representing team rosters. The intensity increased as we approached the time limit. Then a feedback round via the thumb up/thumb down sign told us whether we were satisfied with the result or another round was needed. Once teams were created, we jointly reviewed all upfront submitted nominations (ScrumMaster, Product Owners, etc.), modified the list on the basis of ideas from those present, and proceeded further with selection. Within half a day, the teams forming, and the other roles voting experiment was completed in real time, face to face, and transparently involving anybody who decided to participate.

This activity may not sound very dramatic to born-agile startup organizations and in fact may sound like a common sense thing to do, but in the context of our huge international—and, at that point in time, still very hierarchical—corporation, it was at least a bit unusual.

We were glad that we were brave enough to put the program-level roles into the game as well. I still believe that this was a good message for the team. In my view, it was a demonstration of not just spoken but lived transparency, empowerment, and shared leadership. There were certainly also lessons learned about what to do differently next time—one example could be to have given qualification criteria when gathering nominations for roles such as ScrumMaster and Product Owner. We may have been too "liberal" in that the nomination was open to anyone who showed interest in the role and had the ability to convince the team to accept him or her. This may not have been the best approach, as you need to carefully consider here the overall maturity of the environment. It turned out later that the system of self-regulation failed in some regards, and the teams often selected a candidate they knew while knowingly compromising on some qualities rather than choosing somebody they did not know but who might have had higher potential. Yet another confirmation of the fact that human beings naturally tend to avoid the unknown (survival instinct).

If I were faced with the same situation, I would do a similar exercise again. I believe such team forming is the right way to invite everybody who wants to steer things, to influence the environment we work in. It supports engagement and emergent shared leadership.

CULTURE

As Edgar Schein said in one of his books, "The only thing of real importance that leaders do is to create and manage culture. If you do not manage culture, it manages you, and you may not even be aware of the extent to which this is happening" [Schein17]. And yet, many leaders are still focusing on the processes and frameworks, avoiding the topic of culture. I can understand that, as it took me a while as well. Culture is intangible. It's hard to touch. Hard to define, hard to measure. However, it is a critical piece of organizational success. Culture reflects our values and philosophy, the way we are. Being agile is about changing the mindset. If enough people change their mindset, the culture changes, and the organization becomes an agile organization. Simple if you say it this way, hard to make it happen.

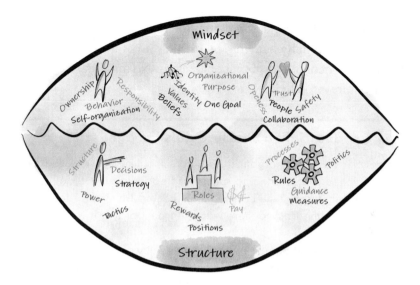

Culture is like a clam. It consists of two parts—mindset and structure—which are connected. You can't separate them from each other. If you do that, the culture dies and the organization will struggle. Similarly, like a clam, those two parts will open farther from each other to accommodate a change, then close when the structure meets the mindset, which creates positive energy and readiness for another change. We may debate whether the mindset follows the structure or vice versa, but I don't think it is important. It's all about the right balance. It's about being aware of both halves and not sacrificing one for the other.

Changing the mindset is harder, but it brings long-term results. Start with a purpose in mind. Come up with a purpose strong enough that it makes you get out of bed every morning and put some energy into achieving it. Something you truly believe in and are willing to take ownership of and responsibility for. Something that makes you collaborate with other people, something that makes your day. When you succeed with the mindset shift, it will create pressure on the existing structure, and you get the energy to change the structure.

On the other hand, sometimes the only way to accommodate a change is through changing the existing structure—for example, from component to cross-functional teams. No mindset will grow if the structure is too tight.

Too Tight a Structure Kills the Mindset

I remember helping an organization where the mindset was killed by a fixed structure that created no space for people to even breathe. The company went through the basic agile and Scrum training for teams, but already during the training there was one indicator that it was going to be hard.

Any conversation about cross-functionality, collaboration, learning, or refactoring ended with the team saying they had no time. When we touched upon the metrics the first day, I mentioned just as a joke that they could measure how many lines of code were written by each developer per day. People usually laugh when I say that, but this time, I got this weird look instead. "That's what we have," they said. "No one will help anyone, as they might not create enough code themselves," they continued. It turned out their pay was based on that metric. New people were leaving because they didn't have enough work they could do without help, and as no one would help them, they couldn't learn fast enough. As a result, they couldn't reach a reasonable salary quickly enough. When I asked how they dealt with this problem, they said that was the reason they were at the training. They felt they needed a change. They had partially started ignoring the metrics and collaborating more.

This example is one of the weirdest ones. This team had micromanaged individual processes, focused on maximizing individual efficiency, and made everyone highly competitive no matter whether the value was there. Their director was often canceling the team's vacation plans at the last minute because they needed to work more or needed to finish something over the weekend. You might ask why the team members didn't leave. I guess they got paid after all, and in that region, there was not much work. They kept getting promises that with the next project it was going to be better. But it never was.

Unfortunately, the organization was unable to shift the mindset. It failed to create any Scrum development teams or even have frequent retrospectives. There was no discussion about the scope or priorities, as "everything" had to be done. In the end, the employees asked me if

I would be willing to talk to their bosses. Sure, anytime. However, it never happened. The management didn't care. They were purely in the achiever mindset, believing that their employees needed the pressure to do any work (theory X), and the organizational design, which was highly hierarchical, was not about to change either, because the managers would take any delegation as a threat to their position.

Unfortunately, there are no magic pills for such organizations. Sorry about that. Some environments are just not ready yet. Agility needs a sense of urgency (which in this case was not there yet) and certain readiness at the management level (not even close), or enough space in the structural part of the culture so the mindset can grow within (not there either). Any agile attempt will fail unless the structure changes a bit to create the space and opportunities for a new mindset.

If you want to change such an environment, agile leadership will help. Look at the organization from the system perspective, applying the agile leadership model and acknowledging that what is described in the scenario is neither wrong nor right. Reading it only gives you one perspective. Stay a bit more on the listening side and *get awareness* by proactively searching for different perspectives. A common understanding is key, and transparency is always a great help. Then, once you manage to let it go and *embrace it* as is, the third step of *act upon* will show you very different opportunities than if you just take sides trying to decide what is right and wrong.

One possibility of how to act upon is to do the previously mentioned force field analysis. It's clear that the forces for and against adopting the agile mindset were not balanced in that organization, not even close; however, the tool helps you to identify where the teams should focus in order to get it into balance and shift forces toward the agile side of the scale.

Another way to approach this from the act-upon stage is to visualize the power or the collaboration and show the results from the different ways of working. When everyone on the team feels that the current state brings too much pressure, they might feel a sense of urgency already. In the preceding scenario, they'd been doing it partially already, and sometimes all that is needed is to have the courage to overcome the first obstacles and not give up. Just keep going.

However, there are so many other options to choose from, so don't overanalyze it. Just give it a try, spin the wheel a bit more, and see what the get-awareness step would bring you. Don't create plans for the future—just stay in the moment.

Too Open a Structure Can Create Chaos

If you open the structure too much while the mindset is not yet firmly in place, all you get is chaos and the failure of otherwise well-working practices. For example, one organization I worked with was going from a hierarchical management that made all decisions without much delegation into very advanced agile practices. The management was struggling to let go. From their traditional mindset, managers didn't even see the different delegation steps. They either decided themselves or let go. For them, it was a black-and-white world. One day, they decided that because they were agile, meaning they had implemented Scrum at the team level, they should delegate the decisions about Product Owner bonuses to the Product Owners team. The problem was that this group of Product Owners was far from being a team, and even worse, the members had different goals and were competing for success. They had no common goal, as the organizational vision was quite abstract and didn't work as a unifying evolutionary purpose. Because individual relationships were very weak, it was a pretty toxic environment where blaming and contempt were part of the day-to-day life.

The freedom to decide on the bonuses is a great practice for well-functioning teams, but here, it only led to a huge fight. The conflict hidden behind the curtain of artificial harmony fired up and was stronger than ever. It was ugly, creating frustration among both Product Owners and management, because there was no clear right or wrong solution.

It gave some feedback to the management, reminding them that teams need to be taken care of, that they are different from a group of individuals, and that to make a team of these employees, management needed to create a team environment. I also gave feedback to the team, showing them honestly where they were. The first few weeks and the early retrospectives were hard, but in the long term, the retrospectives led to more honest and candid feedback and helped the Product Owners to form a better team. Some of the issues they had pretended didn't exist surfaced and were improved—even some things completely unrelated to the current situation. So, who knows what is right and what is not? In a complex system, no evaluation is helpful. Just get awareness, embrace it, and act upon it.

Having a strong purpose, values, and identity are the key to an agile culture. Otherwise, the organization is held together only by artificial rules, regulations, and processes. And when you take away the rules, regulations, and processes, people suddenly don't know what to do, and they end up having individual fights. In a traditional organization, when there is no order or process to follow, very little work gets done. In an agile organization, the direction is defined by the organizational purpose, and the "how" is determined by the values and identity, so things happen naturally even without a push.

The Balance between Mindset and Structure

This example is from a midsize company that let the agile culture grow step by step. Several years ago, the company started with a mindset change. It took one project and tried Scrum at the team level. When I talked to the management, it was clear they had approved the Scrum experiment because the experiment was project-limited and because it tended to be a people-oriented company, management disliked saying no to employees. However, any discussion about self-organization ended immediately, as it created fear of losing control.

At every step, the organization had seen this project as different, weird, awkward, and, perhaps to the surprise of management, successful. Managers started adopting the Scrum terminology and accepting the ScrumMaster role. You could see there was not much happening outside of the project team, but the team members completely turned around the way they worked, and the results were almost instant: better quality, higher motivation, more creativity, and higher value delivered.

The results of this experiment—the one project—were so appealing that eventually one of the managers from a different division tried it with one of her teams. And then, step by step, the mindset part of the culture was on the move, and new teams were picking up and joining. In some teams, there was a structural change needed to allow cross-functionality and close business relationships, while other teams became cross-functional without many structural changes. Eventually, the organization was ready for scaling up. It combined a couple of fragmented projects into broader, business value–driven, customer-centric products under one Product Owner, and the management started to talk about agile leadership, team collaboration, and the agile culture. Then a new CEO was chosen who initiated changes in HR, finance, and the overall way the organization worked, so it became team-oriented, collaborative, and culture-driven.

The entire journey was neither smooth nor short. We are talking about an organization of several hundred people changing over a period of almost a decade from a very traditional mindset, individual-focused structure, and expert leadership into a quite agile organization focused on the value streams, with team collaboration hardcoded in their DNA, and significant presence of agile leadership. However, at every step, they looked into the balance between structure and mindset and used frequent feedback loops to correct the deviances when one part was too far from another. Did they do it perfectly? Not even close, but they made huge progress on their agile journey, which brought tangible and measurable positive outcomes to their business.

An iterative approach whereby you run small experiments and learn through frequent feedback loops is a good way to start the agile journey. There is no right or wrong way to change an organization, and often you won't know the impact of an action until you try it. The company in the preceding example tried many things, often needing to step back, regroup, and give the other half of the culture time to catch up. For agile leaders, the hardest meta-skill is patience. Being patient is the key differentiator between the Achiever and the Catalyst leadership styles. It's the difference between being immediate result oriented and being focused on long-term goals. The culture shift can't be pushed; the right culture needs to grow.

The culture shift can't be pushed; the right culture needs to grow.

What words would you use to describe your current company culture?

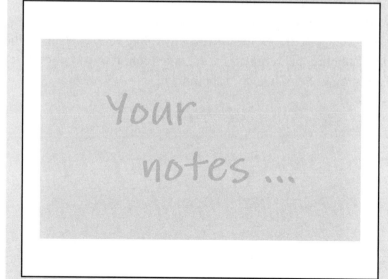

What words would you use to describe your desired company culture?

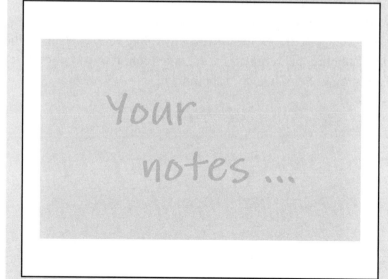

Compare the two lists and think about what actions you can take to support the shift toward the desired state.

Your
notes ...

The preceding exercise is usually done in organizations as a workshop. You can use Post-it Notes and dot-voting, or go digital and leverage some online survey and voting tools that make the data-gathering phase much easier, faster, and transparent even for large groups. See Chapter 11 for more tips.

Which words would you use to describe your desired company culture?

Example of Desired Company Culture assessment results

In my work, most of the time I focus on mindset change, as it has the potential to create the right balance of forces for the change, supporting a change in the structure of the organization. Start with small steps: little by little, start doing things a different way: collaborate; increase transparency, flexibility, and adaptability; and consistently share success stories. Let everyone see the impact, let the organization feel its own experience with agility. You can publish success stories in the internal magazine, organize regular agile meetups, write blogs, create live Facebook videos—no channel is better than the other. Every channel will catch its audience's attention and interest. Don't be too frustrated by processes and guidelines. As the mindset develops and the higher transparency makes things clearer and more tangible, the organization will realize that the current structure is preventing you from accomplishing the desired change, and the entire culture will shift. The culture clam closes up—the mindset and structure parts meet and start a new cycle of moving away from each other, waiting for another change to accommodate.

The good news is that when a mindset receptive to change is achieved, then changing the structure is relatively easy. But it's a never-ending process, a continuous culture ping-pong of mindset, structure, mindset, structure, mindset, structure. . . .

The Power of Culture

Debra Pearce-McCall, Owner and Founder, Prosilient Minds

When I got promoted and made the big decision to move my family cross-country, I never expected the position to last only two years—and teach me a lifetime of lessons in agile leadership. The stakes were high; our focus was our customers' health, well-being, and sometimes even lives. Our corporation measured our performance in everything from seconds (e.g., how long until the telephones are answered?) to cents (rate per covered person per month) to significant health outcomes, to the challenging duo of utilization rates (keep them low) and customer satisfaction ratings (90% or higher). We performed well, but when our contract came up for renewal, the other party decided to take it all in-house instead of outsourcing again. My next big decision was opting for transparency and figuring out how to best inform everyone on staff that we were going out of business—but not until after another year of providing the same levels of service (those life-impacting stakes weren't going away!). My agile intuition to be honest, inclusive, and experimental held up over the next year: we would stay in business, it just would not be business as usual.

Years of experience in psychology and human systems, studying and working with our minds, relating patterns, and the processes of change, had already served me well as a leader. I knew the importance of psychological safety, clear communication, repairing misunderstandings, and other "soft skills" and could integrate those with budgets and meeting agendas, tough decisions, and performance standards. I could be very present, adaptable, and creative, and I encouraged that in everyone around me. This challenge was clear: What changes would motivate folks to remain in these disappearing jobs? In a lovely upward spiral, the numerous agile initiatives I created over that year kept everyone engaged and committed, which then gave me leverage to use when negotiating our severance packages (to be received only if we stayed until the end). Of several, here's one fun example: Too far from "headquarters" to ship back our office equipment, I offered an alternative. We held our own "special sale" where employees bought office furnishings and supplies at amazing discounts, and we then used the money to have a fabulous finale party with families invited. And here is one career transforming example: I developed a program where anyone who was qualified and interested could be cross-trained (e.g., healthcare providers in our clinic could learn care management or utilization review; intake coordinators could learn billing and claims management, and vice versa). Almost every employee took advantage of these opportunities, which contributed to our 100% retention and to how easily folks acquired jobs after we closed. At the end of that final year of unusual business, we even achieved every performance measure, while doing all we could to ensure a smooth transition to the new operation, for all of our customers. In the decades since, I've coached leaders in all kinds of industries and situations, witnessing the power of the same keys I learned to apply that year: life means change and adapting, so open to it with curiosity; be real, as it's a waste of energy not to be; communicate clearly; cocreate whenever possible; intend kindness and inclusion—and much of the rest will take care of itself, often in ways we may not be able to predict!

"WE" CULTURE

An agile organization needs the right culture. At the end of the day, it's all about collaboration: how we work as a team, support each other, and take over the responsibility and ownership for the team. Agile leaders need to create such a culture because, without it, agile can never be successful.

Tribal Leadership: Leveraging Natural Groups to Build a Thriving Organization summarizes the journey the majority of people in the organization need to go through. A *tribe*, according to the book, is quite a natural formation of people. "Birds flock, fish school, people 'tribe'" [Logan11]. In any organization, you can find different kinds of tribes.

The first one Logan describes is "Life Sucks." The good news is that these tribes are not common; only 2 percent of organizations are likely to be dominated by a Life Sucks

tribe. We are talking about prisons, mafias, street gangs. They don't understand how you can be happy about anything. Their mindset is "Life sucks. And you just don't get it: there is no light at the end of the tunnel, no hope that it will ever get better."

If you experience this type of tribal leadership at your organization, be patient. Approaching them with a shiny "Teams are great!" is probably unhelpful, and if you talk to them about moving to agile, you might as well talk about moving to Mars.

The second tribal type is "My Life Sucks." Such tribes are common in the traditional Organization 1.0, where employees feel disrespected and demotivated and complain about everything. The tribes define steps on the mindset journey. In this tribe, you

hear complaints such as "My life sucks because I don't get paid enough," "My life sucks because I have to drive two hours to and from work every day," "My life sucks because I have an incompetent boss," and even complaints about

trivial, easily corrected issues: "My life sucks because we don't have good coffee at the office."

People in the My Life Sucks tribe can at least see the light at the end of the tunnel. Overall, only 25% of organizations are likely to have such a tribe in the majority. These organizations usually treat people according to theory X, and carrot-and-stick practices are the norm. You can see heavy micromanagement, employees trying to game the system, a high percentage of sick days, low retention, and literally no one who would stay if they won even a small lottery.

Let's take a look at how you can help people to move to this level. Although the Life Sucks tribe is not that common, it's important to start there, because for those who are in it, even the My Life Sucks belief represents significant progress. Life has no light at that first stage, so the first step could be to help them find friends from the second tribe. People in the My Life Sucks tribe are not that different—they are still not happy about things, but they already see the light.

The third tribe is "I'm Great (and You Are Not)." At this stage, people finally experience their own success and feel great. "I'm better than others," they say. "I can do this, and they can't. I'm a manager, and they are just employees." "I'm great at my work, and they can never be that good at it." This is one end of the spectrum. Managers at this end often generate employees in the My Life Sucks tribe. On the other end of the spectrum, you can see a good version of this tribal leadership stage: the specialization. "I'm great at visual facilitation," "I'm great at explanatory testing," "I'm great at UX design," "I'm great at selecting chairs for our company." The second part of the sentence ("and you are not") is still there, just not that important, as everyone knows that everybody is great at something, and being great doesn't mean others are not good. This tribe is a majority in about 49 percent of organizations. I'm Great represents the good version of the traditional organization and is typical for Organizations 2.0, which focus on knowledge and specialization.

On the positive end of the spectrum of this tribal leadership stage, we aim for everybody's success. People are different, everyone can be great at something, so let's find it and make it happen. Let's help everyone to be successful. All of the traditional practices, so typical  in our organizations—such as an employee of the month, defined career paths, and detailed position descriptions focused on specialization, but also key performance indicators (KPIs), detailed goals and objectives, bonuses, and performance reviews—were invented to support this tribal leadership stage and help people to experience their individual success and move away from the My Life Sucks tribal leadership stage. In the I'm Great stage, the more individually successful people you can create around yourself, the better.

At this stage, there is a lack of collaboration; individuals feel happy when they are promoted but not particularly enthusiastic about the company as a whole. "It's work like everywhere, I mean it's not bad, I have a good job, they pay me okay, you know, it's fine," they would say when asked how they like their job. They might add a list of benefits the company is providing, but there is no real enthusiasm here either. In general, such employees like to chat with their colleagues, and if they won a small lottery, they might still hang out for a part-time job, as it's a good distraction from being at home. You rarely see I'm Great people working from home or overtime. The work belongs only at work, they say.

The fourth tribal leadership stage is "We Are Great." There is still a tiny bit of "you are not" in the background, but it's not as strong as in the previous stage and not at the individual level. This is the world of teams, the world where agile starts to make sense. It's the beginning of the agile journey. It starts with small teams that

collaborate, help each
other, and become bet-
ter together. For the
first time, it's not about
individuals but about
teams. About 22 per-
cent of organizations
are likely to have this
tribe in the majority.
This is a great achieve-

ment. With the first few teams, the "we culture" starts to emerge. It's
not about individual success but about success as a team: "We are a
great team (better than other teams in the organization)." People in
the teams feel the identity, the belonging.

This stage is also about being proud of your organization: "We
are a great company (and the other organizations are not as good as
we are)." At this side of the tribal leadership stage, we start building
networks of collaborative teams. The "we" is much broader and the
collaboration much stronger. The cross-team collaboration starts
picking up, and teams become less important again. The success of
an individual team means nothing. We need to help each other and
deliver the value together. The stronger we are as an organization,
the better for the customers and the business.

The We Are Great stage is typical for Organizations 3.0, which
embrace agility at the team level and have started their agile transformation by implementing some frameworks, such as Scrum,[2]
LeSS,[3] or Nexus,[4] or that are inspired by the Agile@Spotify[5] example. Companies talk about business agility and agile out of IT. At
the team level, we apply the theory Y—we believe that people don't

---

2. Scrum: https://www.scrumguides.org.
3. Large-Scale Scrum (LeSS): https://less.works.
4. Nexus: https://www.agilest.org/scaled-agile/nexus-framework.
5. Scaling Agile@Spotify: https://blog.crisp.se/wp-content/uploads/2012/11/Spotify
   Scaling.pdf.

need many directions, that they are motivated and will take ownership and responsibility. At the organizational level, it might still be challenging, as organizations have inherited plenty of processes from the traditional world and forget to eliminate them. But in general, you see a trend of focusing on cross-functionality, which results in much broader job descriptions and flatter hierarchies; during their agile transformations, corporations' organization charts typically are reduced from ten or more levels to around three levels. Organizations move from individual KPIs toward team-oriented goals, experiment with OKRs,[6] and last but not least, move away from the variable part of the salary toward the higher base. The transparency is much higher, which results in their willingness to share case studies, blog about their agile journey, and share their stories at conferences. In business, they are still quite protective and focus on competing with other organizations.

Collaboration results in a strong sense of ownership, common identity, and a shared goal. People are motivated, they consider work as an integral part of their lives, and they have no problem doing some work from home or working overtime if necessary. They would recommend working for the company to their

---

6. Objectives and key results (OKR) is a framework for defining and tracking objectives and their outcomes popularized by Google: https://en.wikipedia.org/wiki/OKR.

friends without any hesitation, and were they to win a small lottery, they might take a vacation but would soon be back at work. In general, if you want to shift a major tribe from I'm Great to We Are Great, implement agile.

The final stage of tribal leadership is "Life Is Great." This stage is still quite rare, and only 2 percent of organizations are likely to have such a tribe in the majority. It's a place where you've achieved the agile mindset at the organizational level. There are no competitors—the other organizations in your space are potential partners for alliances and coalitions. They form flexible networks with others on their journey, and the evolutionary purpose is key for organizational success. It's a world where 1 + 1 is more than 2. Radical transparency is a necessity. Such organizations are open to the public, organize tours for visitors, and share their knowledge insights.

This is the real agile organization, which is agile not only at the team level but at the organizational level as well. It's a long journey for most organizations nowadays, but there are great examples already. You don't need to be like them tomorrow, there is no hurry. Any organization needs to grow into that mindset. But already today, you can get inspired and start your journey.

DOING agile is not helping; you must BE agile.

At this level, people are enthusiastic about the purpose, and they do whatever it takes to achieve it. They collaborate and are highly receptive to new ideas from inside and outside. They often take very creative approaches that few have tried before. They have courage, focus, respect, openness, and commitment. They are not doing agile, they are living agile. When people with this mindset win the lottery, they'll still be hanging around helping people to achieve their evolutionary purpose because they believe in it and because it matters to them.

If you want to shift the major tribe at your organization from We Are Great to Life Is Great, become agile at the organizational level. Make transparency and autonomy key organizational values,

be open to experiments, see the organization as a network of collaborative teams, become customer-centric and purpose-driven. There
are no competitors, and there are no boundaries imposed internally
on the emergent leadership. Agile leadership needs to become the
way of working and needs to be spread across the organization. Help
people to grow and become agile leaders and support them on their
journey. Become a role model of an agile organization and an inspiration for the entire industry.

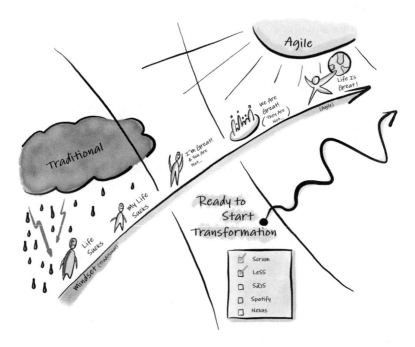

The tribal leadership concept presents an interesting mental
model for visualizing how you can see the mindset part of the culture evolving. No matter how fast you would like your organization
to change, you can't skip steps—you have to go one by one. There
is no way to jump from the major tribe of My Life Sucks to We Are
Great. The mindset doesn't change that fast; however, it doesn't
have to take years—you just follow the journey and be consistent
with following agile practices.

As an example, you can see how I use this model in a workshop setting to start a conversation about different organizations or different parts of one organization. Mapping companies to the tribal leadership model is not a right-or-wrong categorization. Rather, it's a subjective exercise meant to open discussion about certain aspects of the organization. For example, Why do you see the organization there? and Where would you like to see it in the future?

The participants start by writing a Post-it Note with the name of their company or their part of the organization and placing it on the map where they believe the major tribal leadership stage is. Some participants prefer to use a symbol (e.g., star) instead, as they don't feel safe about the map possibly being shared outside of the workshop participants. Then we talk about it, share stories, hear why they feel the major tribe is there. As a next step, they brainstorm other organizations just as an inspiration and to deepen the conversation. Again, it's not about being right about those organizations, as there is no right or wrong anyway; it's just a model to encourage discussion about where they see the different environments and why. The final step is to think about where they would like to see their organization or their individual department in the next year and what they can do about it.

Result of mapping companies to the tribal leadership model

Think about your organization. What is the major tribe at your organization (or your part of the organization)?

- Life Sucks
- My Life Sucks
- I'm Great and You Are Not
- We Are Great
- Life Is Great

Where would you like to see your organization or department in a
year from now?

- Life Sucks
- My Life Sucks
- I'm Great and You Are Not
- We Are Great
- Life Is Great

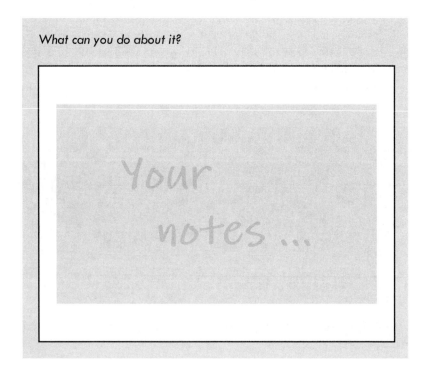

What can you do about it?

Your notes ...

When speaking about partnerships or alliances, the different tribal leadership stages of the parties will create a compatibility or misalignment and can be used to predict the success of such a partnership or alliance. Just imagine the organization in a We Are Great phase trying to build a business relationship with an organization with managers in the I'm Great stage and employees mostly in the My Life Sucks tribe. Their values are neither complementary nor aligned, and such a relationship is most likely going to fail.

As an example, in the organization I worked for, we built balanced partnerships with our customers. In an agile space, we often talk about the customer relationship, trust, and collaboration. It sounds simple. However, the mindset of both the company and the client need to be ready for such a partnership. To support that relationship, we changed the way we wrote contracts to reflect the partnership collaboration. Our contract didn't define scope or timelines, it just reflected the way we intended to work together: use Scrum, collaborate, have a transparent backlog. With every Sprint we delivered value, we got feedback on it at the Sprint Review, and we planned a new Sprint if the value was still needed. There were no fixed deadlines; when the overall delivered value was good enough for the customer, we stopped. In a true agile environment, we don't need that many processes around the business. We just take customers as an integral part of our process, are transparent with them, and collaborate.

Agile works great with such partnerships. However, it requires a certain readiness of the mindset on both sides. If companies with the I'm Great (or lower) mindset doesn't have enough trust in the We Are Great way of working, they will be looking for so many process assurances, regulations, and protection mechanisms that they will eventually kill the spirit of any partnership and will shift the overall mindset toward the lower tribal leadership stage or even one step below it. It's as if they are speaking two different languages. One is looking for what-if scenarios, while the other trusts the collaboration, feedback, and transparency and strives to have the same understanding of the purpose. One side is questioning the motivation, while the other trusts the system and takes all the legal process assurances as redundant: we have the same goal, they say, let's move on and achieve it together.

When you face a significant mindset disconnect, be patient and show the benefits to the other side step by step. Create a safe pilot project for the organization to experience it, and be a good guide for it on the agile journey. Changes take time, and changing the mindset takes twice as much time as changing the structure.

COMPETING VALUES

Culture is a complex system, and another way to look at it is to focus on the relationship of four competing values. The competing values framework[7] is based on research of the major indicators of an effective organization and pro-

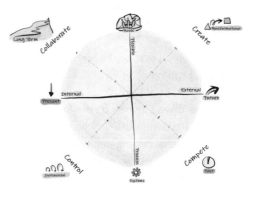

vides a different perspective on agile organizations. The top competing values are (1) present internal versus future external drive and (2) flexible versus fixed processes orientation. The competing values will result in four different culture quadrants—control, compete, collaborate, and create—which quite naturally stretch over the diagonal axes. Do we collaborate or compete? Are we flexible, or do we prefer to build long-term fixed systems within which to operate? In every organization, the culture is a mixture from all four quadrants, but the recipe for that mixture is always unique.

---

7. The framework was originally described by R. E. Quinn and J. Rohrbaugh in "A Spatial Model of Effectiveness Criteria: Towards a Competing Values Approach to Organizational Analysis," *Management Science* 29(3): 363–377, 1983.

The very traditional organizations have a culture mix in which control and compete cultures are dominant, while agile organizations have a mix of mostly create and collaborate cultures. Within the Modern Agile [Kerievsky19] concept, the "make people awesome" and "experiment and learn rapidly" principles shift an organization to the northern hemisphere of the competing values framework. The We Are Great culture moves the organization from the compete to the collaborate segment, first at the team and eventually at the organizational level, while the Life Is Great culture makes the organizational collaboration even broader and spreads across the market, forming wider partnerships and alliances.

EXAMPLE 1: MIDSIZE IT COMPANY

As an example, let's look at the midsize IT company I worked for a few years back, which was struggling with a lack of flexibility. The business demanded highly flexible cross-functional teams, which needed to learn fast. Each customer environment was so different that the pressure was tremendous to learn fast while keeping the focus on high technical excellence. It came to be too much. We were unable to grow people to the expected level, and we were failing to get up to speed fast enough with new customers. We had a traditional structure of functional departments, where most of them were quite hierarchical and process-oriented. We had a few agile team pilots but not organization-wide agile practices. The management was in the competing and protecting mindset, but the organization was collaborating. The innovations were close to zero, limited to the purely technical level.

When we started our journey to become an agile organization, we concentrated on high flexibility, creativity, and overall business focus while not compromising on technical excellence. We were aiming for higher collaboration, and as a result, we shifted to even higher cross-functionality and collaboration across the traditional roles. We decided to take a bold step and unleash the potential of our employees and support their creativity and innovations by moving significantly toward the create culture. The practices followed the vision of the culture shift: we descaled the organization to a very flat structure with only one level of management, based on self-organized teams; we broadened the positions and their descriptions; we got rid of fixed KPIs and moved to frequent peer feedback and coaching employees to grow; we created innovative camps where everyone could join and work on some creative idea and support communities and emergent leadership. This journey to the desired state took a little bit more than a year until it was self-sufficient and growing and improving organically.

EXAMPLE 2: SMALL SERVICE ORGANIZATION

This example describes a small service organization. The organization had very hierarchical management and a toxic culture where people were competing with each other, and their key goal was to show they were better than others so they would get promoted. The situation resulted in huge demotivation. Many people were leaving the organization, and customers complained that the work delivered by the organization was not bringing any value to them because internal fights were more important than the customer-centric approach. The organization claimed it was agile, but "agile" was in name only.

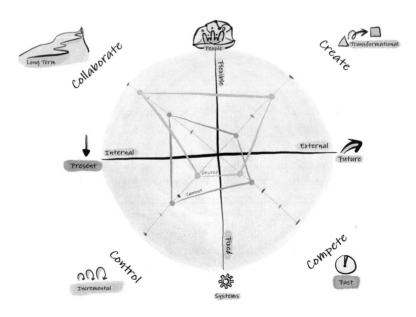

Midsize IT company example

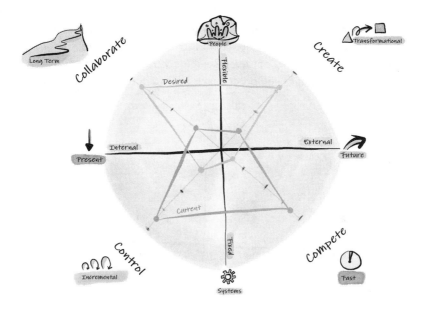

Small service organization example

When the management changed, its vision was very bold: change the organization to a flat structure based on self-organized cross-functional teams. It was a big shift from control and compete to collaborate and create. In one word, it was *agile*. The strong vision and evolutionary purpose made it possible. The transparency about the intended shift and voluntary participation in the new culture shift (stay and help or get a package and go) helped as well.

EXAMPLE 3: LARGE FINANCE CORPORATION

This final example is from a large finance corporation I worked for several years ago. This organization didn't feel as strong a need to change its structure and the way it worked as the organizations in the previous examples. However, it still felt a need to become more agile—in this case, more innovative, adaptive, and flexible. The corporation felt it needed to give people a little bit more space, to flex its processes, and to be more team-oriented at the project level. But there was no intention of changing any of the individual-based practices or the management structure.

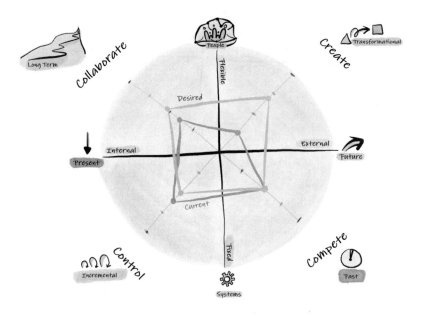

Large finance corporation example

The organization wanted to be more creative and innovative, to unleash the potential of its business and expand beyond banking. It wanted to be different from similar banks and to test prototypes quickly to create new services faster than its competitors. That vision was appealing and motivating and allowed the organization to run a set of experiments as Scrum pilots, Kanban teams, and innovative labs, and a couple of ideas were successfully transformed to the projects and delivered to the market.

Now that you've seen these examples, think about your organization and draw the current and desired stages on the picture. Where are you now? Where would you like to be?

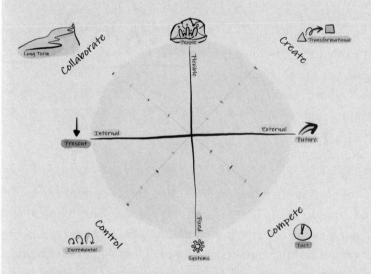

No matter how close or far the desired state of the organizational culture is, think about three actions you can take right now to get closer.

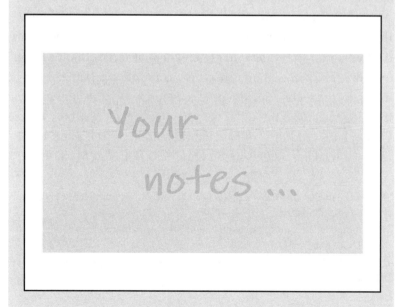

NETWORK STRUCTURE

Some organizations don't have an obvious center. The hierarchical power structure is not the only structure that exists in organizations. There is a social structure, which is built on top of relationships and social interconnectedness, and also a value-creation structure [Pflaeging17].

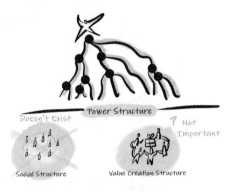

Organizations based on power structures are simple to understand, simple to manage, simple to operate. They simplify the decision-making process and responsibilities. They can also be superefficient if they are designed well. Their biggest disadvantage is that they deal with lack of empowerment, which often causes demotivation and disconnect of the employees from the value they are supposed to deliver, but more important, they lack the flexibility and creativity to deal with VUCA challenges.

Traditional organizations like to avoid complexity. Therefore, they try to simplify the decision-making process by having clearly defined power structures and pretending that social structures don't exist or are not important, since the organization is supposed to be driven by the set of rules and processes and is supposed to use linear thinking to address the value delivery piece by piece. Tools such as Gantt charts[8] and the critical chain method,[9] as well as typical linear issue-tracking systems such as Jira,[10] come from this world.

---

8. Bar chart that illustrates a project schedule. Named after Henry Gantt, who described it in 1910.
9. Method of planning based on theory of constraints described by Eliyahu M. Goldratt in 1997.
10. Issue-tracking system by Atlassian and popularized by software development teams.

If during your agile journey you make the hierarchical power structure less important, organizations don't fall into chaos, as they can still stick together through the social and value-creation structures, which become much more important in such cases. In agile organizations, when people want to exert influence, they need to be part of the community that is responsible for that issue; if they want to work on a certain value, they need to be part of that product team. Agile organizational transformations happen through radically decentralizing decision making and simplifying the organizational structure by "descaling the number of roles, dependencies, architectural complexity, management positions, sites, and a number of people" [Grgi☒15], as it is defined by the LeSS framework, for example.

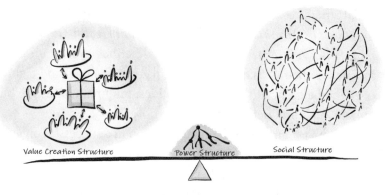

Value Creation Structure   Power Structure   Social Structure

At their core, agile frameworks usually focus on strengthening the value-creation structure and making it the most important part of the organization. We talk about value streams; the customer-centric, value-driven approach; and using the Story Mapping,[11] Impact Mapping,[12] and Lean Startup[13] methods. No matter how strong the focus is on the value structure, it's not enough by itself— the social structure is equally important. At the end of the day, it's all about the mindset.

11. Story Mapping (Jeff Patton): https://www.jpattonassociates.com/user-story-mapping.
12. Impact Mapping (Gojko Adzic): https://www.impactmapping.org.
13. Lean Startup (Eric Ries): http://theleanstartup.com.

SMART VERSUS HEALTHY

Focusing on individuals and interactions, building great teams, and creating an environment where people can collaborate freely are key to organizational success. Frameworks and methods by themselves will not help, and without the right mindset, organizations will fail to implement them no matter how hard they keep trying. That might be the hardest part of agile. Don't take me wrong—tools are handy because they help you to not get lost on a day-to-day basis, frameworks are helpful because they give you some boundaries, and processes are useful because they give you predictability and common ground in the constantly changing world. However, by themselves, they are not enough. In order to be successful with agile, the social structure needs to be supported as well. Patrick Lencioni, in his book *The Advantage: Why Organizational Health Trumps Everything Else in Business* [Lencioni12], describes two requirements for success: being smart (strategy, marketing, finance, and technology) and being healthy (minimal politics, minimal confusion, high morale, high productivity, and low turnover).

"Being smart is only half the equation in a successful organization. Yet it somehow occupies almost all the time, energy, and attention of most leaders. The other half of the equation, the one that is largely neglected, is about being healthy" [Lencioni12]. Organizations spend way too much time on the smart side, focusing on strategy, marketing, finance, and technology, so they have no capacity left to minimize politics, confusion, and turnover while focusing on high morale and productivity. "None of the leaders—even the most cynical ones—deny that their organizations would be transformed if they could achieve the characteristics of a healthy organization. Yet they almost always gravitate to the other side, retreating to the safe, measurable 'smart' side of the equation" [Lencioni12].

How much time do you spend on the smart versus healthy aspects of the organization?

Smart	◆————————————◆	Healthy

What can you do to improve the healthy focus?

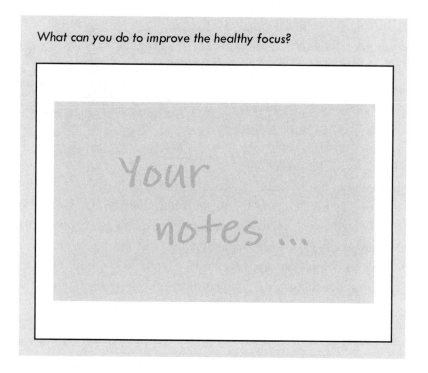

While working with individuals is important, it has only a limited effect on the organization. "What really improves a system as a whole is working not on the parts itself but on the interactions between the parts" [Pflaeging14]. And that is exactly where the agile leadership effort should be focused. Not on how to work with individuals—that was a realm of traditional management—but on how to work with systems, teams, and the relationships among people. It's what happens between people that matters. From such a perspective, the organization can be seen as a network of teams, where the lines are the key point of the focus. "You are not here to solve the issues for them, you are there to help them straighten their relationship so they can work towards the resolution" [Šochová17b].

Even though organizations look different in the agile space, they still have some sort of structure—it's just the power structure that is very limited and not as influential as in traditional organizations. There is no exact model to follow. In fact, there are many examples: organizations based on fully cross-functional teams and

self-management; flat orga-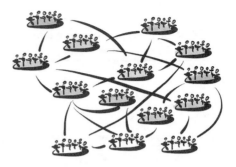
nizations;[14] Spotify[15] and its
tribes, chapters, and squads;
organizations that imple-
ment holocracy;[16] and those
that aim to be teal organizations[17] (see Chapter 1).
There is a lot to choose
from, but in the end, all of them are going to be hard to implement,
as they require changing the organization down to its roots. All of
them are trying to solve the same problem: how to survive in the
VUCA world, how to be super-adaptive and flexible, and how to
deal with complexity and ambiguity. Simple to say, hard to do for
organizations that are used to planning projects, budgets, and goals
in yearly cycles and to optimizing for fixed repetitive tasks.

Cross-functional and Community-centric Teams

Melissa Boggs, Chief ScrumMaster, Scrum Alliance

At Scrum Alliance, we found ourselves at our own crossroads.
When I stepped into my role in January 2019, we were not built in
such a way that we could listen closely or move quickly. Ideas were
often lost in the maze of hierarchy and approval processes. Some
of our team members felt stifled and unable to creatively problem

---

14. For example, Valve (https://www.bbc.com/news/technology-24205497) and
    Morning Star (https://corporate-rebels.com/morning-star).
15. Spotify engineering culture (https://labs.spotify.com/2014/03/27/spotify-
    engineering-culture-part-1).
16. For example, Zappos (https://www.zapposinsights.com/about/holacracy).
17. For example, Buurtzorg (https://www.buurtzorg.com/about-us/buurtzorgmodel)
    and Patagonia (https://www.virgin.com/entrepreneur/how-patagonias-unique-
    leadership-structure-enabled-them-thrive).

solve. We could continue going down the same road and get the same results, or we could choose to rethink our way of working.

In recent months, we have rebuilt our organization into cross-functional and community-centric teams empowered to deliver. We have flattened hierarchy to eliminate red tape and place decision making with those closest to our community. We have embraced agile values and principles wholly and deeply and as an organization. It's been hard work for the entire team, but it's worth it. Slowly, we are starting to see the fruits of our labor, evidenced by candid conversations with each other and with our customers. We've increased our ability to change course on the basis of those conversations. We are buoyed by the laughter and energy in the office as new ideas are introduced and collaborated upon.

We are proud of our commitment to learning what it takes to live out the Scrum values every day, and in doing so, we are joining others leading the agile movement. We understand from experience that it feels risky. We've been trying things we have never tried before and letting go of control in places we've tightly held. The good news is that it's opening doors we never knew existed, and we are thrilled to be sharing what we've learned with you.

We are all at a crossroads. Which path will you choose?

REINVENTING ORGANIZATIONS

One very popular book in the space of agile organizations is *Reinventing Organizations* by Frederic Laloux [Laloux14]. It classifies organizations by color. It starts with the red organization, which is the pure command-and-control organization where hierarchy, power, and fear are key artifacts and no one shall even think about moving a different way; proceeds to the amber organization, which is still heavily reliant on hierarchy, processes, and formal role definitions to bring stability and control; and finally to the orange organization, which is where most of the traditional organizations land, focusing on profit, competition, and clear goals and objectives.

All three categories are just different representations of traditional organizations. They all rely on hierarchy, and they all expect fixed structures to define the decision-making process, responsibilities, and work to be done. In the orange world, we talk about innovations, but they rarely happen, as the organization is so tied to its way of working that there is only limited space to react to new challenges.

The red, amber, and orange structures are often operating with the majority of people from the My Life Sucks and the I'm Great and You Are Not tribes. For example, when the managers are on the left side of the spectrum of I'm Great and You Are Not, most of their employees end up quite naturally at My Life Sucks. Though the two models exist in different dimensions, it's still useful to see how they often overlap.

Example of mapping companies to the Reinventing Organizations *model*

At the agile end of the spectrum, we have green and teal organizations. They no longer have a fixed structure because they have optimized for adaptiveness. The biggest difference between the two is that green organizations still have a defined structure, even though it's a flexible one, while teal organizations have a liquid structure. Green organizations focus on culture: they talk about empowerment, engagement, and shared values. They also focus on delighting the customer, balancing different stakeholders, and delivering value. Teal organizations, with their liquid structure, are driven and interconnected by a higher evolutionary purpose, which creates their wholeness and togetherness. Without it, the teal organization would fall apart, leaving only chaos behind. Teal organizations build on self-organization and emergent leadership, so that the decision making is distributed. Both green and teal organizations are optimized for complexity, give people higher autonomy, experiment with new approaches, and are very much business-value driven.

Think about where your organization or department is right now. From the three options, mark the one that is the closest fit.[18]

Structures and Processes

Structure	Fixed hierarchy	Defined network	Liquid network
Salary based on	Position rank and achievement	Participation-oriented	Opportunity-driven
Information Flow	Formal strategic meetings	Transparently sharing information	Free network peer groups

Knowledge and Skills

Decisions are driven by	Strategy, goals, and objectives	Organizational values	Evolutionary purpose
Leadership	Targets and instructions	Inspiration and empowerment	Space, trust, and autonomy
People development	Training and mentoring	Coaching and networking	Open space (often beyond organizational context)

Values and Culture

Work orientation	Results	Team	Community
Climate and Culture	Pragmatic and result-driven	Friendly and community-related	Open and creative
Customer Relationship	Strategic	Based on partnerships	Cocreative

18. This assessment is based on the Reinventing Organizations Map designed by Emich Szabolcs and Károly Molnár [Szabolcs18]: https://reinvorgmap.com.

Thinking and Feeling

Trust	Process and individual skills	Common values and community	Free will
Fear of	Failure	Rejection	As an informative feeling
Attitude	Strategy and individual benefits	Empathy	Wholeness (complete acceptance of the others)

Items in the first column are characteristic of traditional organizations (red, amber, orange), items in the middle column are characteristic of green organizations, and items in the last column are characteristic of teal organizations.

Organization	Red/Amber/Orange	Green	Teal
TOTAL points			

The assessment will show which type of organization you lean toward.

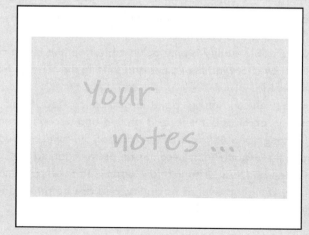

Where would you like to see the organization in the future? What can you change in the organization to get there?

Books to Read

- *Tribal Leadership: Leveraging Natural Groups to Build a Thriving Organization,* Dave Logan, John King, and Halee Fischer-Wright (New York: Harper Business, 2011).
- *Reinventing Organizations: A Guide to Creating Organizations Inspired by the Next Stage of Human Consciousness,* Frédéric Laloux (Brussels, Belgium: Nelson Parker, 2014).
- *The Advantage: Why Organizational Health Trumps Everything Else in Business,* Patrick Lencioni (San Francisco: Jossey-Bass, 2012).
- *Company-wide Agility with Beyond Budgeting, Open Space & Sociocracy, Su: ive & Thrive on Disruption,* Jutta Eckstein and John Buck (Braunschweig, Germany: Verlag nicht ermittelbar, 2018).
- *Organize for Complexity: How to Get Life Back into Work to Build the High-Performance Organization,* Niels Pflaeging (New York: BetaCodex Publishing, 2014).

In a Nutshell

- ☐ The agile organization is like a star on the horizon: you can never reach it, but you can get closer, step by step.
- ☐ There is no specific framework needed to become an agile organization. All you need is to practice agility at all organizational levels.
- ☐ Sustainable agility is only achievable from the inside out. Start by changing the values and shifting the mindset from the inside.
- ☐ In a well-functioning agile organization, leadership is nonhierarchical but is spread around and decentralized.
- ☐ If enough people change their mindset, the culture changes and the organization becomes an agile organization.
- ☐ Green and teal organizations optimize for adaptiveness, have a higher level of flexibility, and are better at dealing with VUCA challenges.

II
• • •
THE DIFFERENT PARTS OF AN AGILE ORGANIZATION

Be open and courageous to experiment with agility at the organizational level

9

• • •

BUSINESS AGILITY

Be open and have courage to experiment with agility at the orga-
nizational level.

Business agility and the agile organization are still very new concepts. "Business agility is not a specific methodology or even a general framework. It's a description of how an organization operates
through embodying an agile mindset" [Agile19]. Nowadays, most
organizations are familiar with agile at the team level. Organizations
from different industries are experimenting with it, implementing
it, and succeeding with it. The level of agility differs by region, but
it's safe to say that most organizations have some experience at the
team level—they have tried agile with at least one pilot project.
Also, most new graduates are leaving universities with some level
of agile understanding and experience, which indicates that agile at
the team level has reached the late majority.[1]

Some organizations are already applying agility at the product level, delivering value end to end, and applying various scaling frameworks and cross-team collaboration models, but we are

---

1. A concept in the diffusion of innovation theory described by Everett M. Rogers
   in 1971.

still at the early adopters stage, and not many organizations have implemented such a level of agility yet. However, many successful case studies have been published in which people talk about the impact of agile on the business, and the term *business agility* is picking up fast. As the *Business Agility Report*[2] states, "Sixty-nine percent of respondents have been on the journey for less than 3 years" [BusAI18].

What is currently a hot topic is the agile organization, and without a doubt, we are still at the innovators' stage — the pioneer green and teal organizations [Laloux14] have experienced amazing success with implementing agility at the organizational level. We talk about different organizational structures and cultures that operate under a different premise. They are value-driven, customer-centric, cross-functional. They care about people and create team-oriented cultures built on self-organization, autonomy, and decentralization. They change the way they work with people and invest in a different leadership style. In these organizations, all functions have become agile — agile finance, agile marketing, agile HR. It's a whole new world.

Which parts of your organization are agile? (If any relevant parts of the organization are missing, add them to the list).

- Agile HR
- Agile Finance
- Agile Executive Team
- Agile Board of Directors
- Agile Development
- Agile Marketing
- Agile Sales
- _____

---

2. The *Business Agility Report* surveyed a diverse range of organizations representing twenty-nine countries, across twenty-four industries, and ranging in size from 4 to 400,000 employees. The only consistent factor among them is a common goal: to become an agile organization. Some have just started the journey, while others have been leaders for nearly a decade [BusAI18].

What benefits would you see if all parts of the organization were operating in an agile way?

Your notes ...

Radical Self-Organization

Pawel Brodzinski, CEO at Lunar Logic

People often ask me how we designed the transformation from a relatively flat but traditionally managed organization to what we call Radical Self-Organization. The interesting thing is that we didn't. Right now, Lunar Logic is a company with no managers, where everything is transparent to all the employees, and everyone can make even the most serious decisions. As an example, anyone can set anyone else's salary, including their own. There isn't a single power reserved for the CEO. If the CEO can do it, everyone can.

And yet it is an accidental, or emergent, outcome. The initial changes we devised were small. Just a bit more transparency here and there. Fewer small decisions made by a manager and more by those who are affected. The big change was, indeed, the persistence and alignment of small changes. We were continuously distributing more and more autonomy across the board.

There were, of course, a few huge steps among many small ones. One of them was introducing a new salary system in which the payroll is transparent, and everyone can influence what anyone earns. Such a move can't be undone. You can't make people forget the data they know. We were preparing for this move for ten months, addressing all the concerns along the way.

Only a couple of years into this continuous experimentation with the organizational model, I started asking the question, *If we keep doing this, what is the end game?* Only then did I envision that, fundamentally, there is no ceiling for embracing autonomy and self-organization in every aspect of the company life. The realization swayed our perspective from thinking of what we wanted to change next toward thinking of what decision-making powers still need to be decentralized. The journey, in fact, never ends. Even once all the formal power has been distributed, we still need to support everyone with embracing and using it.

Of course, it isn't as easy as giving people more autonomy. On the way, we learned the role of accountability, alignment, well-defined constraints, and technical excellence. We keep learning how to balance all the facets of an organization operating without managers. We reinvented hiring, changed how we work, and right now, we are reestablishing our strategy together.

Was it worth it? Totally. And it's not just my subjective opinion that Lunar Logic is a much more humane workplace than the norm. We can measure it too. The average tenure is twice the industry standard. The perceived engagement is 75 percent up. Our financial results skyrocketed. Had someone told me at the beginning that this would happen, I wouldn't have believed it.

AGILE AT THE EXECUTIVE LEVEL

Agile can't stay just at the product development team level. Every agile transformation not only changes the way teams deliver but also creates a disturbance and a gap between management and employees. And the more agile the teams are, the bigger the disconnect that is created. Managers feel lost, forgotten, and they start to fear that those self-organizing teams might eventually not need them. One problem is that they've never been part of any agile or Scrum team themselves. They've seen them working, have joined teams for reviews and listened to their

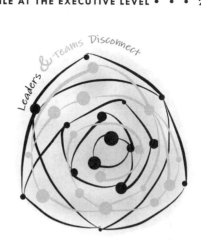

stories, but that's not the same. People need the experience to understand a different way of working. You might still remember your first reaction when someone told you that this agile and Scrum method will be great. *What?* you thought, *this silly process will never work!* Speaking for myself, I still remember how I felt several years ago when we were exposed to agile. I didn't like it, and I was not a supporter of it at all. Many people feel the same way as I did, and the same thing that was beneficial to me can help them as well: experiencing it for themselves.

One important step companies often skip during their agile transformation is getting top management on board. Executives deeply need their own experience with agile and Scrum. They can't just read about it. If you really take the

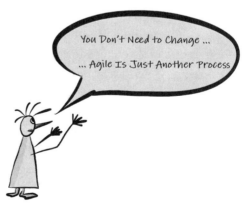

agile transformation seriously, it's time to change the way you implement it. It's not just a different process decided by C-level executives and implemented without their notice. It's a significant change in the culture and mindset that needs us to start from the other side as well, forming self-organizing teams of executives. On your organizational agile journey, executives need to experience agile and Scrum; otherwise, the disconnect becomes bigger and bigger, and the gap between the agile-mindset teams and management grows until the whole organization becomes like a broken washing machine, spinning around in short cycles without delivering any real results.

There is no doubt you need agile team experience at every level. Very often, by design of the roles, a team starts as a group of individuals with their own goals, no common passion, no trust, and no unifying purpose, and then, step by step, they experience what self-organization is about, how cross-functionality works, and how this way of working is different and awesome once they embrace it. Applying Scrum at the executive team level is a great practice that helps people to understand the business value and prioritization and learn how to do refinements, planning, standups, reviews, and retrospectives, just like any other team in the organization. They get used to delivering value regularly, iterating, and getting feedback and collaborating. In the same way that a first pilot project is difficult for a product development team, it is hard—often even harder—for the executives, and without a strong sense of urgency and a strong enough reason for change toward agile, neither the organization nor the executive team can be successful in their agile journey. This hands-on experience is critical for organizational success.

Like any other exercise, getting started is difficult. Most managers at the beginning of the agile journey would say, "Other people need that, not me." But I don't think so. Leaders need to change first. The organization will follow. The first time you experience the power of true team spirit, you never want to go back, no matter where you are in the company org chart. It works the same way across the structure.

If you are ready to try, the first step is to get a real agile coach, not a consultant. Find someone who will guide you on this journey,

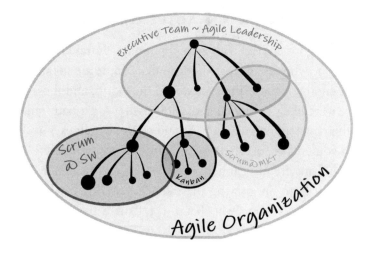

someone who has embraced this way of working and will help you to overcome day-to-day obstacles, who will guide you toward agility without taking the steps for you, and who won't sell you any simple recipe for success. The goal is not a speedy transition to agile; it's to get hands-on experience with this different way of working.

Where on the scale of 1 to 10 would you place the executive team of your organization currently?

Group of individuals	1	10	Team with one goal
Have no own experience with agile	1	10	Acting as an agile team
Decide on agile and leave teams to implement it	1	10	Become agile themselves to help the organization embrace it

The farther on the right you are, the higher chance your organization is going to be successful with agile.

THE CEO IN AN AGILE ORGANIZATION

Searching for a CEO with an agile mindset is frankly a nightmare. Everyone who's tried it can confirm that. There are not many CEOs with enough agile experience yet in the world, and those few who have it are likely not looking for a job, as they are usually quite happy in their current organization. So, no matter which executive search firm you choose, or what you write in the position description, the search firms are no real help here. Unless you've already expended effort up front on growing the talent internally, you'll need huge luck to get someone who has more than a basic understanding of agile.

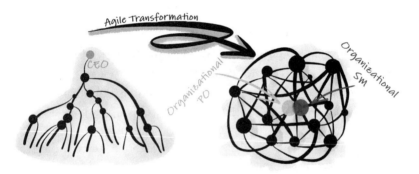

No matter how desperately you are searching for a CEO, this is still just a small obstacle. The real need for change starts only when most of the organization already has an agile mindset. Since organizations have changed and agile is no longer solely the domain of IT, and since business agility has gained acceptance in nearly every department, the need for a change at the top level is inevitable. Why do we need a CEO in the first place? Why don't we go one step further and change the top to become a role model for the entire organization? Shouldn't we change the *entire* way we work? Shouldn't the C-suite apply the same principles the teams do? Sounds like simple logic. And, as usual, it is simple to understand but hard to do because it requires courage—the courage to say, "We are going to be different. We will have an organizational ScrumMaster and an organizational Product Owner instead of a CEO because it is closer to the way we work at this organization, it fits our values, and last but not least, we believe it will help us to be more flexible and adaptive at the organizational level." And that's worth trying.

The organizational ScrumMaster focuses on the right culture, mindset, and structure so that the company becomes a high-performing, innovative organization that embraces agility. The organizational Product Owner focuses externally on the business and shapes the company's purpose so that everyone knows where the company is heading and why and to ensure the organization is business-value driven. Both roles need to respect each other and be open with each other, as is the case in a single Scrum team, because together they will be part of the organizational team and the network structure of self-organizing teams. In Scrum, there are two roles instead of one for a reason. When you ask people if they would recommend combining the two roles, they answer, invariably, that it's not a good idea. The same reasons that make us say it's practical to have two different roles are valid at the executive level as well. When you think about it, having an organizational ScrumMaster and an organizational Product Owner fits the way we work much better than having a single CEO, as it supports the right organizational mindset, transparency, and collaboration, and it is consistent with who we are.

From a legal perspective, it is perfectly possible, and it's not that much work either. You might need to change the bylaws a little, but there is no reason why you can't do it. From a hiring perspective, it's much simpler, as you are not looking for that superhero personality who can effectively interact with both internal and external sides. There is nothing preventing you from doing it. As I said earlier, all you need is courage. And that's one of the Scrum values anyway. Experiment, and then inspect and adapt.

Now, do I believe that the organizational ScrumMaster and the organizational Product Owner will eventually make themselves redundant when the teams become self-organized? No, I don't. It's the same as at the team level. Even if the team is self-organized and knows the business well, there is still work for the ScrumMaster and the Product Owner. Similarly, at the organizational level, there is a need for the organizational ScrumMaster and the organizational Product Owner even after the network of collaborative teams becomes self-organized, business value-driven, and customer-centric. The organizational ScrumMaster and the organizational Product Owner would use the leader-leader style to help other leaders around them to grow, and in due course, the organization would become purpose-driven, with emergent leadership and a liquid organizational structure. Like in a Scrum team, the organizational ScrumMaster and the organizational Product Owner would then progress from explaining, telling, and sharing to coaching, facilitating, and keeping the system spinning [Šochová17a]. And that's what agile leadership is all about.

The Scrum Alliance was looking for a CFO with an agile mindset for almost a year, which seemed like forever. It was a long journey, and no one was living up to the goal of "transforming the world of work" and building "sustainable agility." All the traditional executives lacked a deep understanding of the agile mindset, and all the agilists lacked the executive experience. In the end, the idea of applying Scrum at the organizational level was a game changer. By having an organizational ScrumMaster and an organizational Product Owner instead of a CEO, the entire executive team as well as the entire organization went flat. People always ask what difference agile can make, but in this case, the outcome was almost instant. The organization transformed into several customer-centric, cross-functional, self-organizing teams and started delivering value almost instantly. The focus shifted toward finding alliances rather than competing, and we became the thought leader on the agile space once again. It was a bold experiment, changing the entire way the organization operated and was structured. But so far, so good.

Living up to your values will pay back.

The journey so far of being a PO with a SM in co-leading Scrum Alliance has been great. I cannot imagine now not having a co-leader to do this job. By allowing each of us unique focus areas (myself external customer and on strategy, and Melissa [Boggs] on internal team building and organizational strategic structure) it's allowed us to really play to our strengths. I don't have to be all things to all people, because WE together fill the role of a traditional CEO.
—*Howard Sublett, Chief Product Owner, Scrum Alliance*

AGILE BOARD OF DIRECTORS

Are you wondering why you should be agile while your board of directors is not? There is no reason why the board of directors should not act as an agile team. However, as is true for people at every level contemplating a new way of working, change is scary. Most of the board members would be coming from traditional companies and would have no experience with agile. Governance is important, but the usual committee structure presenting a report to the board each quarter doesn't prepare board members to react to challenges. First, let's start with an overview of what any agile entity needs: the agile values of transparency, trust, respect, collaboration, and a shared understanding of purpose so that people have the same goals. The idea is to be a great team, not just a group of individuals. But applying radical transparency, getting feedback, and collaborating are often very hard at this level. Not that it wouldn't be useful, but it's not easy. Second, the board must be consistent with the organization. If agile stops at the board level, it creates a gap between the organization and its governance, and the whole organization will struggle. Finally, agile boards are not just governance bodies—agile boards of directors create purpose-driven organizations with a sense of belonging, which skyrockets organizational success. It's critical that agile boards collaborate on the key strategic initiatives with the rest of the organization, which, if you think about it, is a huge step away from filtering everything in and out of the board through the CEO. The agile board of directors' focus is on three principles: team, flexibility, and strategy.

Team over Individuals and Hierarchy

While traditional organizations are formed by stable departments and individuals, agile organizations form communities built around the purpose. Internally, there is usually a quite liquid structure to keep adaptivity and strategy focus in our complex world. It embraces the team as the key building unit and forms a collaborative network of teams. Similarly, the board of directors is a team that has one goal. Even if internally there is a structure of committees, each committee is a collaborative team as well, and all committee chairs and the board chair act more like facilitators than managers of the group. The board as a team is just a small part of the whole picture. We use the "team in the team" concept in Scrum—the development team is part of the Scrum team, which is part of the product team once it scales, and the product teams are part of the entire organization, which acts as a team, or collaborative network, in which all those pieces stay together only because of a strong purpose and a common goal. The same way that the board forms a collaborative team with the CEO, the board and the CEO would form a team structure with management and eventually with the entire organization. Too much hierarchy kills the collaborative mindset and team spirit. In the majority of organizations, there is always going to be some hierarchy, but maybe the way of working could be driven not by the hierarchy but by a common purpose and collaboration, with radical transparency as a prerequisite.

Flexibility over Fixed Plans and Budgets

The more we are responsive to changes through collaboration, the higher the need for adaptiveness in the organization. Agile organizations are moving from yearly fixed budgets toward the Beyond

Budgeting principles [Beyond14a] and toward purpose-driven continuous planning over annual top-down fixed goals and plans. You will see more volunteer-based virtual teams over fixed departments and, at the board level, more transparent and collaborative committees. People are grouping around the common cause instead of the fixed plan, while planning itself becomes a continuous inclusive process instead of a top-down annual event. Anyone should be invited to join when they have something to add to the purpose of the event. Keep it transparent, inclusive, open. All you need is an iterative process with regular feedback and an opportunity to inspect and adapt.

Strategic over Operational

A good board of directors should be focused 80 percent on strategy and significant business issues and only 20 percent on reporting. Nothing new, right? It's the same old 80/20 rule we often use in agile product ownership. Agile boards are going through a significant shift, refocusing on the strategic over the operational. Don't get me wrong, governance is important, just as the importance of processes is noted in the Agile Manifesto:[3] "While there is value in the items on the right, we value the items on the left more" [Beck01b]. The same applies here. Reporting is part of transparency—an almost unnecessary part because transparency makes all of the information available to everyone at all times. The board wouldn't have to meet to get a status report. They should be meeting to discuss strategy, understand one other, have creative conversations and visionary sessions, give feedback. The boards should meet frequently, every one or two months (that's their Sprint time), and should focus on communication and work between meetings. There is no need for reporting—all documents should be visible, so the meetings are

---

3. The Agile Manifesto of Software Development consists of four principles we value, the first of which is "Individuals and interactions over processes and tools."

reserved for conversations about the direction. As in the product environment, the shorter Sprints generate better understanding, feedback, and higher delivered value. Finally, keep in mind that the less fixed the structure and the plan, the higher the need for good facilitation, as without it you might end up in chaos.

From Outputs to Outcomes: A Board's Journey with Business Agility

Sandra Davey, Chair, Board of CHOICE, www.choice.com.au

At a company board that I serve on as a professional director, we never decided to "go agile" or do an "agile transformation." That wasn't our language, our plan, our intention. It happened slowly with many triggers, and one of them was a realization of the disconnect between how the board was thinking and responding and how people in the organization were thinking and responding. Staff were working agile; the board's first taste was seeing a shift staff's focus from outputs to outcomes. Our people were rallying around outcomes or goals to achieve the change they wanted, and the challenge we now had was that the information coming to the board hadn't caught up to reflect this fundamental change.

In the context of how the organization planned and allocated resources, there was a disconnect; the board was rallying around information and material in the form of traditional business plans, sixty-five items in this particular year, full of outputs, features, and dates (how and when), and yet the teams had moved to rally around goals and outcomes (why and what).

Here's a typical example: an item on the business plan in the board papers would describe an output: "By Q4, deliver a mobile app to help Australian citizens select the best health insurance plan." This type of information encouraged the board into "telling" or "instructing" mode and into the weeds; we'd soon be scrutinizing the detail with questions such as *When are you delivering the health insurance comparison app?* A board's contribution shouldn't be in the operational detail; it needed to be more strategic. Upon agreement with the Leadership Team, the board started using the OKR framework,[4] liberating us from detailed "how and when output-based" conversations to more strategic discussion focused around outcomes. Instead of demanding that teams build a mobile app for health insurance comparison by Q4, the board focused on discussing the big issues affecting Australian consumers. Instead of asking for a "thing," we began describing problems: *How might we enable Australians to seek out the best health insurance plans for their needs?* Describing outcomes, goals, and problems liberated the board from unnecessary detail but, importantly, left the organization to figure out the best way to get there and by when.

OKRs help us describe outcomes, not outputs. They help us describe outcomes as aspirational goals, leaving the people and teams to describe the key results, or what success might look like. Gone from board papers are detailed business plans, and in their place, three or four key OKRs that teams within the organization can rally around. These OKRs are companywide, thus keeping the board at a strategic level and leaving the organization to the tactical operational detail. OKRs have fundamentally improved the quality of the conversation at board meetings, keeping us focused on strategic outcomes and, importantly, liberating the people and teams to figure out the best way to get there.

Books to Read

- *Evolvagility: Growing an Agile Leadership Culture from the Inside Out*, Michael Hamman (Lopez Island, WA: Agile Leadership Institute, 2019).
- *Outcomes over Output: Why Customer Behavior Is the Key Metric for Business Success*, Joshua Seiden (Brooklyn, NY: Sense & Respond Press, 2019).

---

4. Objectives and key results (OKR) is a goal-setting framework for defining and tracking objectives and their outcomes.

In a Nutshell

☐ In agile organizations, all functions have become agile: agile finance, agile marketing, agile HR. It's a whole new world.

☐ In order to succeed with agile, you need experience with the new way of working at every level, including executives and boards of directors.

☐ Agile organizations work better with organizational ScrumMaster and organizational Product Owner roles than with the traditional CEO role.

10

. . .

AGILE HR AND FINANCE

The more organizations shift toward agile, the more they need to redesign how they work internally. This chapter introduces some of the implications that internal redesign has for an organization's human resources (HR) department (e.g., recruiting employees, creating development programs and career paths) and finance department (e.g., budgeting, financial reporting).

AGILE HR

Let's look at the different functions of HR in an agile organization and explain the fundamental shift HR needs to make in order to support agility in the organization.

Agile HR changes the focus in the agile

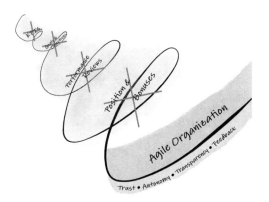

organization to the overall employee experience; it supports the culture shift, choosing the employee-centric approach over the governance role typical of traditional HR departments. Agile HR is responsible for enhancing the agile values and fostering the agile collaborative culture in the organization. To do so, HR needs to gain the trust of the employees, make them the center of HR's focus, enhance their overall experience, and be agile itself. HR staff need to become servant leaders who care deeply about making people awesome so that they can deliver value to the entire organization, are not afraid to experiment and try new practices, and make safety a prerequisite [Kerievsky19].

Agile HR shifts focus to the overall employee experience

Supporting the Culture Shift

To visualize how typical practices align with the expected culture shift in an agile organization, I often use the competing values framework, as it nicely shows the shift from control and compete cultures toward create and collaborate cultures. It's a very thoughtful and interesting exercise because it puts everything in context, since all HR-related practices are connected to the culture.

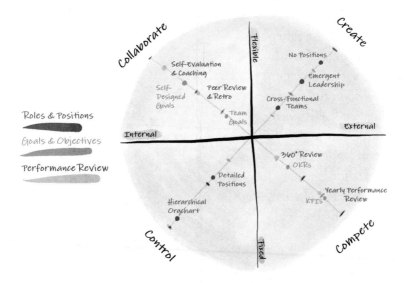

Agile is a journey, represented as a shift from the current culture to the desired culture state. If your current culture is very deep in the control quadrant, then going to an organization with no positions might be too big a step to take in one go. Similarly, going from individual key performance indicators (KPIs) to self-evaluation and coaching might be too much. On the other hand, when you have a mostly agile organization based on self-organized cross-functional teams, neither individual KPIs nor objectives and key results (OKRs) help you on your journey.

Agile HR practices need to be aligned with the culture.

In other words, every practice has its own timeframe when it's useful. If you apply it too early, you only create chaos and fail, and if you apply it too late, people will be frustrated and demotivated by useless processes and you will slow down the entire agile journey.

Recruiting

In an agile organization, knowledge and skills are no longer the key factors we are looking for. The agile organization is built on collaboration, it encourages innovations, and it needs high flexibility. Past experiences are also applicable only to a certain extent. It's more about having an open mind, being able to learn new things, and collaborating with others to deal with complexity and unpre-  dictability than about being an expert with deep but narrow specialization. If you don't think so, think about your own career and that of your colleagues. How many of you are still working in the same specialized field? Most people change their career more than once. Such changes are now required more often than ever before. With that in mind, would you still care about hiring experts with a particular specialization? Not really, as they create silos and prevent your organization from changing the direction of the business. An agile organization needs people who are ready to learn, inspect, and adapt. People who are not afraid to take responsibility and run experiments. People who are not stuck with one way of working (because "we always did it this way") but who are ready to change their way of working as the business needs require.

> *Skills are easier to learn than a mindset.*

Google is a good example of this approach:

> If it's a technical role, we assess your coding ability, and half the roles in the company are technical roles. For every job, though, the No. 1 thing we look for is general cognitive ability, and it's not I.Q. It's learning ability. It's the ability to process on the fly. It's the ability to pull together disparate bits of information. We assess that using structured behavioral interviews that we validate to make sure they're predictive. . . .
>
> What we care about is, when faced with a problem and you're a member of a team, do you, at the appropriate time, step in and lead. . . .
>
> It's feeling the sense of responsibility, the sense of ownership. [Friedman14]

If you think about it, it's very hard to create an agile job description based on skills and experiences, as those are soon to be irrelevant. The new advertisement for an open position might instead say:

> We are looking for an enthusiastic, flexible, and open-minded person who is ready to take over responsibility and collaborate with others on achieving the value. We are a team-oriented organization with a flat structure, which will support you in your personal growth. Join our team for a day to experience our culture. Together we can [achieve the vision].

Quite different from a traditional job description, right? But when you want to try it, you realize that recruiting companies are not yet ready to support such needs. They ask questions such as *How many years of Java experience do the candidates need? What is the position description you are hiring for? Are you looking for developers or searching for a new CEO?* It's quite a mismatch. What we learned in one of the organizations I worked for is that hiring new graduates is easiest for most of the team positions. They are flexible, have interesting ideas, and are eager to learn new things. All we had to do was create a team-learning environment based on pairs and teamwork where they could get up to speed fast. We realized that learning is easier than unlearning old habits, so in most cases, training fresh graduates was easier then hiring senior employees with individualistic habits that were more harmful than helpful for the team environment. It's a hard message for all people who believe years of experience counts and should result in a higher salary. Maybe so if you are working for the government, but in the agile space, not necessarily, as the recruiters in agile companies may not care at all about your years of traditional company experience.

Unfortunately, I've had similar experiences with executive search companies, no matter how big the name of the recruiting company. They often have no idea what agile is, so they are not helpful with assessing the candidates or finding relevant people. If you start looking for a leader with executive experience and an agile mindset, you soon realize they are hard to find. Most executives have the habit of acting as directive managers from traditional hierarchical organizations, so it's easier to grow leaders from your organization than to hire them externally.

If you can't measure experience and skills and you can't count working years, how can you find out if the person is the right match? It's the same as in every other relationship: start "dating." In this case, it's about getting personal experience and starting to build a relationship with the candidate in order to give both sides the opportunity to determine whether they are compatible at the culture level. You don't start a relationship on the basis of what someone writes or says about themselves. You are together because of who both parties are. With hiring, it is similar—mindset and culture are hard to change. Skills can be learned.

Hiring is more about creating relationships than assessing skills

---

Purpose-Culture-Engagement

Ondrej Benes, Director, T-Mobile

Through our experiments, we learned that in the mid- and long-run, it pays off to do more cherry-picking when hiring for any role. Best would be probably to pretend that we are about to build a green-field team. But this is a classic never-ending time vs. quality battle under the delivery pressure. And even (re)hiring tens of internal colleagues, when nothing like the internal labor market was there yet, takes weeks. Only after our experiments did we realize that we had failed to create space for not compromising on the quality and engagement elements. Lay down the purpose, and hire and fire based on the cultural fit and resonance with the purpose—thanks, Zappos guys, for these lessons! Creating purpose-culture-engagement is the key.

The Interview Process

Once we had changed whom we were looking for, we needed to change the interview process as well. As the traditional curricula vitae (CVs) look into years of experience and hard skills, they are not very useful. Companies can get creative here. They can ask candidates to write an essay about why the company should hire them, create a short video on the topic, design comics showing the company how they imagine the work, or write a company press release about hiring them to the position. You would be astounded by the amazing things people create and by how much more you learn about the candidates from such artifacts.

Once they get the basic information about the candidate, companies try to shorten the process and make an offer within a day or two. The long process is often frustrating, and great candidates often don't wait until you finish multistep interviews but instead take a job somewhere else. One good practice is to do behavior interviews and simulate scenarios to see how the candidate would respond. It tells you much more about the candidate than any hard skills tests can tell you.

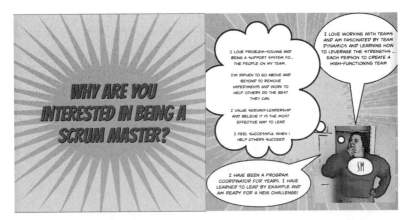

Example comics designed by Kseniya Kreyman as a ScrumMaster submission

Agile companies rely on team interviews. Well-functioning teams will find a good match for the organization while keeping focus on diversity. They will also give the candidate a better feeling for what the organization is like and what kind of challenges they might expect in the job. Another common practice is to have breakfast, lunch, or dinner with candidates, to give both sides the ability to chat about the company and the candidate's expectations in a less formal environment. Informal conversation is critically important for learning about one other. Finally, very often, companies invite candidates to spend a day in the organization. It's a great experience for both sides.

An interesting exercise that helps you to raise awareness about different HR practices and their alignment with the current and desired culture is to run a workshop mapping the practices against the competing values map.

As preparation, you need to create a poster for each category of HR practices you want to discuss (e.g., recruiting, positions and career, rewards, performance review) and explain the competing values framework. Ideally, the workshop defining the current and desired culture would be done beforehand, as it helps people to internalize the concept.

Then the participants brainstorm all practices, processes, and tools the organization is using and can use in the future and map them against the picture.

Finally, it's all about the conversation, so people should talk about the options and their relevance to the desired culture shift.

At the end, you might have several options to try or to investigate further to determine whether they are aligned with the desired culture shift or run against it and need to be discussed further with the larger group. There is no need to make a decision on the spot. This workshop is great for raising awareness about operating high in the create and collaborate hemisphere. It may not solve all problems, but it will definitely generate inspiration and new ideas.

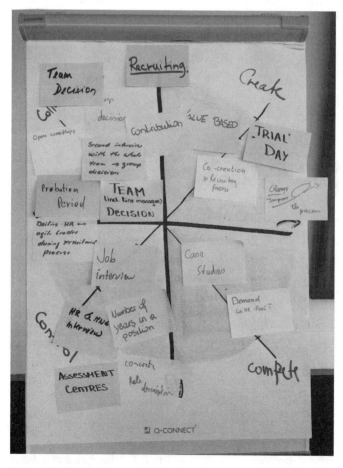

Example of recruiting practices placed on competing values map

Evaluations and Performance Reviews

Once you hire the right person to the team, it's time to start thinking about evaluations and performance reviews. In a traditional organization, it was pretty simple. Each employee was assigned a task, and each task could be evaluated and linked to a particular KPI. In an agile organization, it's not that simple, as multiple people collaborate on the same task, and if you try to set some KPIs at the beginning of the year, they mostly become irrelevant somewhere along the way, so there is nothing to evaluate at the end of the year.

The simplest practice used in agile environments is to set a team goal instead of individual goals. There is still a risk that the goal becomes obsolete during the year, but at least you support the team collaborative culture. A slightly better option is to break the year cadence and create shorter goals. After all, there is nothing magical about the year cadence when we deliver products regularly.

A good practice is to let teams design their own goals. "Research shows that goals are not only more likely to be reached if they are created by the one that should achieve the goals, the goals themselves are actually also set higher" [Whitmore09]. In order to make it work, you need a high level of trust and a 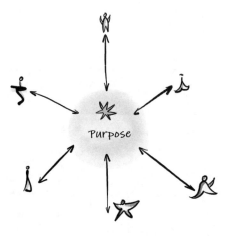 clear shared vision that everyone understands—the evolutionary purpose, which helps you to define areas where different parts of the organization can focus. When we started our agile journey in our company, we needed to enhance the team spirit and enable team collaboration, so the focus area was defined by the question *What did I do the last quarter to help the team?* It's not measurable by itself, so the organization is not imposing goals on people by cascading them but is still influencing the direction by selecting the focus areas. "The overall purpose is not to command and control, it is to create a view for each individual to align their current focus towards current strategy" [Whitmore09].

Coaching for Growth

A good step toward a more agile way of working is to replace performance evaluations by coaching conversations focused on employee development. As with every coaching arrange- 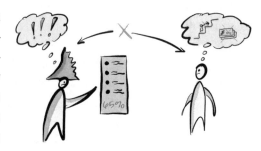 ment, it is not about the coach but about coached (the employees in this case), and the focus should be on raising the employees' awareness of themselves and their abilities and potential. Nor is it not about evaluation, as evaluation is not motivating anyway. It's about helping people grow according to what the organization needs at the moment.

From the organization's side, you only need to decide what competencies are important for achieving the organizational vision and strategic goals and which are critical for supporting the T-shaped skills[1] of the cross-functional teams. The competencies will likely change over time—some may be retired and new ones will emerge. But change is nothing new in agile, right? If you'd like to stress the

---

1. *T-shaped skills* is a metaphor used in agile teams where each person has a deep knowledge of one skill in his or her area of expertise (vertical line of the T letter) along with a broader knowledge of other skills (horizontal line of the letter T) used in the team.

mindset shift on top of the skills, you can also discuss values along with competencies. You can cocreate your own values or use preexisting values that describe the agile mindset, for example, the five Scrum values: courage, commitment, focus, openness, and respect. You can use them the same way as you use competencies. In other words, employees will do their self-assessment of the competencies and values, choosing a few they are good or great at and a couple they'd like to become better at, and the coaching conversation will help them to gain better awareness of their abilities, limitations, and dreams. You can also ask your peers and teams for feedback and support on the selected competencies and values, which can feed the entire process through incorporating diverse perspectives that help people improve. The process is about growth. Employees should be asking themselves, *What competencies am I still learning and need help with to grow? What competencies am I good at that help me be fully effective at my work? What competencies am I great at, so I can mentor others?* There is a limit to the number of the items in each category because one of the agile values is focus; you can't learn too many things at the same time, and you can't actively mentor people in too many different competencies at the top level either.

In my company, we had this coaching conversation each quarter, looking into the different aspects of the organization's needs. At the beginning of our agile organization shift, we looked into four quadrants: technical skills, customer communication, people skills, and languages. It was a big shift, as until then the performance review was all about technical skills and whether employees fulfilled the tasks assigned to them. The shift to agile changed that focus. We explained that if you didn't work according to the team expectations, we would address that at the retrospective and help you learn. We focused those conversations only on the people development aspect. We used a simple coaching scale for each domain, and employees rated their skills on a scale of 1 to 10, where 1 meant "I don't have that skill" and 10 meant "I'm great." All such scales are relative to the environment and other people. It was not about the absolute number but more about wanting the employees to consider questions such as *What would I be able to do if my rating were increased by one or two points? What difference would it make, what abilities would I have, and what would it allow me to do?* In general, we asked coaching questions based on the GROW model [Whitmore09].

When done well, coaching can skyrocket people's performance. But unfortunately, not many managers are good coaches, which is a limitation in most organizations. And here is one very important need that can be easily addressed by agile HR—developing coaching and facilitation skills across teams can make a huge difference to organizational success. More so than any hard skill.

Retrospectives and Peer Feedback

If you are ready to be truly agile, you can run regular and frequent retrospectives instead of using any form of performance evaluation. Together with radical transparency, this will create enough clarity about performance toward the Sprint Goals, product vision, and the entire organizational purpose that people can adapt in a very efficient way. It's simple and powerful. Indeed, you can have not only team retrospectives, which generate powerful feedback from peers, but also an overall retrospective [LeSS19a] at the multiple team level—as it is designed, for example, in LeSS—and an organizational retrospective that can be facilitated by agile HR, for example, in the form of a World Café or Open Space (see Chapter 11).

Together these practices will engage employees in solving team, cross-team, and organizational issues and increase their motivation to come up with creative and innovative ways to be better at delivering value and achieving the organizational purpose.

> *We value regular peer feedback focused on development over evaluation.*

The frequent retrospective cadence provides regular feedback that allows fast changes and small improvements on a day-to-day basis, preventing the big disappointments and surprises of traditional performance reviews, which often cause demotivation and stress. Issues get resolved sooner,  before they become too big and poison the team or department, and people get help to work on those issues early, ideally from their peers. You might not be ready for that change tomorrow if the culture of transparency and trust is not prevalent yet, but you can go step by step until KPIs, performance reviews, and formal evaluations are gone and frequent feedback, inspection, and adaptation become a regular way of work.

At this stage, we often stop using the name agile HR and change it to talent development, and the entire focus of HR changes to support the overall employee journey and growth. Supporting coaching and mentoring programs and creating an environment for effective peer feedback are just two ideas of where to start.

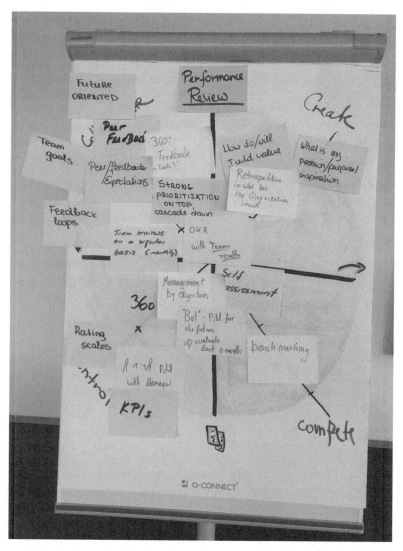

Example of performance review practices on competing values map

Career Paths and Salaries

Now let's take a look at positions, career paths, and salaries. As I mentioned earlier, positions are not that important in agile organizations, as people collaborate, take over responsibility, and become leaders as needed—not because it is in their job description. In traditional organizations, it's all about the position. We hire to fill the empty position, we specify what people do and don't do, and the established hierarchy shows employees what role they might take on if they get a good evaluation and are promoted. The position defines the range of the salary. The whole concept breaks once you stop treating people like individuals and create a team environment where people self-organize their work and collaborate according to their skills and abilities. Such a shift naturally creates the need for fewer positions, and in some Scrum development teams, there are no roles, just team members. Your positions can follow the Scrum organizational design, and, for example, instead of having a software developer, a software tester, and an analyst, you can just have one position, a software engineer, or simply a designated team member. Every defined position potentially creates silos and gaps, dependencies, and the need for synchronization and handover, none of which help you create high-performing teams.

What You Can Do in More Agile Environments

If the previous paragraph didn't give you too big a shock, you are ready for the next step. When team members contribute to the same goals, do frequent peer reviews, and hold each other accountable to improve their skills, the only reason for positions and career paths is the direct correlation with the salary. The solution is obvious: decouple salaries and positions. In this case, you don't need any positions at all, as the team roles are emergent based on what the team currently needs in order to meet its goals. Salary can be linked to peer feedback and the individual value of each team member to the organization.

> *In more agile environments, we decouple salaries and positions and make the roles emergent.*

After all, focusing only on money makes people less productive. "The more people focus on their salaries, the less they will focus on satisfying their intellectual curiosity, learning new skills, or having fun, and those are the very things that make people perform best" [Chamorro13].

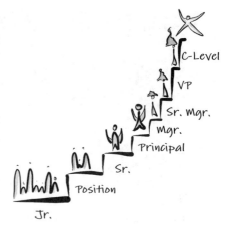

It's a startup mindset. Imagine that you are not an employee but an entrepreneur, and every day you need to prove that you bring enough value to get paid. Stressful? Maybe. Be aware that every practice like this needs a certain culture and organizational agility. I would not start the agile journey with it, but you can take it as a next step and be ready to move there when your organization is ready. However, if you feel you are ready, here are two tips on how to start.

The first choice is a hard change, where employees get two options: stay because you believe in the change and are ready to take ownership and responsibility to succeed and achieve the organizational purpose or take an exit package of x amount and go. The people who stay are those with the right mindset, and any transformation will be met with far less resistance. The second choice is a gradual change. Start with decoupling salaries from positions. Sooner or later, the positions become irrelevant so no one misses them if you remove them. You must have courage if you are to choose the first option. On the other hand, the second option would make your journey longer and more painful. It all depends on what you want and where you are. It doesn't have anything to do with the company size or the industry. However, for a larger corporation, you might start with a pilot division or one geographical location before you implement it throughout the organization. Agile is not about practices, it's about mindset. And this is very true for agile HR and talent management as well.

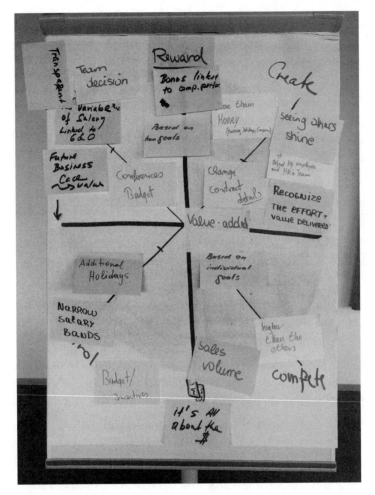

Example of reward practices on competing values map

New Thoughts on Salary Decisions

Jutta Eckstein and John Buck, authors of Company-wide Agility with Beyond Budgeting, Open Space & Sociocracy: Survive & Thrive on Disruption

The director of Mayflower, a German software and consulting company, reports that a small group of employees were dissatisfied with the way their salaries were set because the process didn't adhere to agile values. The employees informally hypothesized that making their salaries transparent among themselves would improve their ability to work in an agile way. They shared their salaries. The resulting openness improved their enjoyment in working together as a team. The group then went a step further and made their salaries transparent to all their colleagues. More and more colleagues followed their example. This triggered the creation of a new process that was tried and modified several times before the group (for the moment) settled on the following policy: An elected person takes part in all salary discussions (salary representative). Before salary discussions start, management calculates how much money is available for increases (increase budget). Management defines a set of vital company interests that every employee should support (e.g., the employee helps to achieve both customer and team satisfaction). In the salary discussion meeting, the following people participate: the person under discussion, two people the person under discussion invites (typically peers), the elected salary representative, and the director of the branch where the person under discussion works. The salary discussion follows a defined process: After an open dialog about the person with the person present that allows for all perspectives on the person's growth, achievements, or underachievements, each participant rates the person's contribution to the company's interests. Knowing the person's actual salary, each participant secretly writes the suggested new salary on a sticky note. After all have shown their suggestions and have provided some rationale, the group develops a suggested new salary for the person. After all salary discussions (with all employees) have taken place, management adds up all the deltas of the suggested salary increases and verifies if the increases are within the increased budget. If the sum of all deltas overruns the increased budget, all deltas are proportionally reduced.

What to Do in an Agile Organization

The more agile you become at the organizational level, the more flexible and dynamic the team structure and the more difficult it is to say what each position or role is. The more agile the way you work becomes, the higher the need for transparency at every level. We can see what every person is doing and can challenge him or her and give feedback. Any employee can join any initiative but with all responsibility toward the organizational purpose. As nothing is hidden, it's in a way controlled by everyone. Emergent servant leadership is the key part that links everything together and makes sure there is harmony instead of chaos. Such environments are ready to make all salaries transparent and let employees be part of the decision. To be fair, not many companies are there yet, so you don't have to do it all tomorrow. However, you can still be inspired by the possibilities.

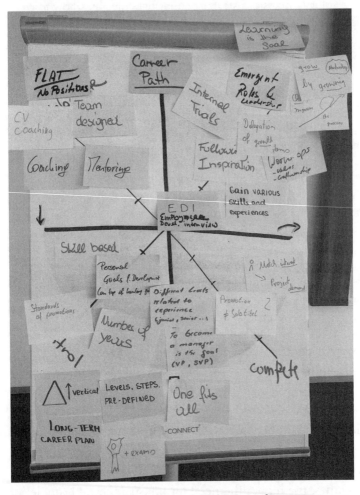

Example of career path practices on competing values map

I've had many conversations with people about their careers and about what comes next, and it felt that the missing ingredient was courage. That's the true agile value we all keep forgetting—the courage to break the position structure and the prescribed career paths and create a brand-new job for yourself. Don't wait until someone opens a position. Design it yourself. Create a need for your skills and the value you can deliver. Defined positions and career paths are over. They belong to the last century. In the modern world, we need more emergent leadership and flexible solutions for actual problems. Fixed roles only keep the status quo. You are a leader. Step out of your position box and create your own role focused on value, one that allows you to satisfy your dreams.

Leadership and Self-Deception

Another interesting concept from the book *Leadership and Self-Deception* [Arbinger12] is looking at our reactions when we see people as positions or roles. Whenever we do that, we mentally close them into a box created by the position description, which immediately creates a certain expectation of the person. "He is a tester, so it's his job to find all the bugs"; "She is a developer, so she should write good quality code"; or "She is a wife, so she is expected to take care of the house."

When those expectations are met, there is no issue, but when they are not, which is actually quite common, they create tension, frustration, and stress, which very often manifest in blaming the other person

for not doing what we expected from him or her.

In agile environments, we are aware of this closing-in-the-box effect, and this whole psychological aspect is another reason we build cross-functional teams and move out of detailed position descriptions and steep career paths. However, don't forget that every practice is linked to a certain culture. In highly individual cultures, steep career paths and detail position descriptions are useful, as they give people some vision for growth. In very collaborative purpose-driven organizations, they become impractical, and it's time to abandon them.

When we first explained the vision of not having detailed positions and career paths in my company, it created a lot of fear. "What will happen to my salary?" "How will I get a raise?" and "Does it mean that we are all the same?" people asked. Not necessarily. People are always different and gain the respect of others by helping them and bringing value to the team. Frankly speaking, we hadn't been using the positions in our Scrum teams for a few years anyway, so why have them when the rest of the organization was about to create cross-functional teams as well? The only reason was that organizations are used to it. It's the comfortable habit. It took courage and a lot of our time to explain why we don't need positions in agile teams and what would happen to each individual person as a consequence. At the same time, we also decoupled salaries from the positions and created team-oriented goals linked to a small bonus, which in turn linked to the overall organization revenue. Not a big deal, you might say, but you should never underestimate the need for overcommunication while doing such radical changes.

Leadership, System Coaching, and Large Groups Facilitation

Finally, let's look at the skills and practices of good agile HR. Primarily, it's about an understanding of the agile mindset and the ability to create an environment where the agile culture can flourish—an environment supporting collaboration, transparency, open peer feedback, trust, team spirit, ownership, empowerment, and responsibility. Agile HR should support the culture shift. The first step is to raise people's awareness of where they are and where they want to be from a culture perspective. The more agile your organization is, the higher the need for coaching and facilitation skills. The role of HR is critically important for growing coaching and facilitation skills in the organization and for supporting individuals and teams on their journey.

> Being a leader is not a position; it is a state of the mind. Anyone can become a leader.

Another fundamental shift needs to come from management and is based on decision making and delegation of leadership, which is not based on position but is a state of mind. Anyone can become a leader. The decision is yours whether you are ready to take over ownership and responsibility and lead an initiative, a team, or a product. Regular, frequent peer feedback will raise enough self-awareness that leaders can emerge through the organization. We often describe emergent leadership as one person acting as a leader of one initiative while at the same time being a team member of another one. As evaluations transform into regular peer feedback and coaching for development, the key goal for leaders is to help other leaders to grow, and here again, good coaching and facilitation skills are indispensable.

> Agile HR = agile leadership + system coaching + large groups facilitation.

The fact that in agile organizations HR changes the focus to the overall employee experience is only the beginning. Let me suggest another idea. Good HR should act as an organizational Scrum-Master, or agile coach if you like, operating at the third level of the #ScrumMasterWay concept [Šochová17a], focusing on the overall system. At this level, it's not so much about coaching individuals as about coaching teams and organizations as a system, leveraging tools from system coaching such as ORSC.[2] It's less about team facilitation than about the ability to facilitate large groups with

---

2. ORSC is Organizational Relationship System Coaching: https://www.crrglobal.com.

hundreds of people, leveraging tools such as the World Café and the Open Space (see Chapter 11). It's about being a model of the agile leader, growing the we culture, and mentoring other leaders to grow into agile leaders. In short, agile HR supports the growth of the agile culture.

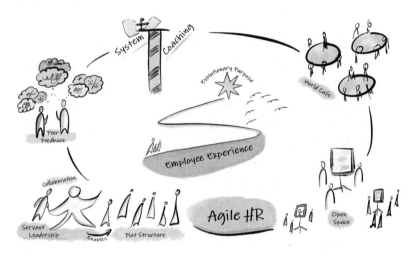

I kept the most radical idea for last. At the end of the day, in a very agile flat organization, there is no need to have any formal HR roles. We have self-organizing teams formed around any issue that needs to be solved. We have radical transparency to identify problems early and regular feedback and coaching to support growth. It's straightforward and simple if you have the compatible culture. If not, the lawyers will jump in and say you can't do this, that the organization can't fire people easily if there are no detailed positions, that you wouldn't know how much to pay people if there is no evaluation, that people will not do their best work if there are no KPIs—I can go on and on. The entire HR function fits the knowledge Organization 2.0 with an orange structure. The more you shift toward dynamic organizational design and toward agile, the less need there is for fixed HR processes and for HR overall.

AGILE FINANCE

Like agile HR, agile finance is crucial for organizational agility. "When examining specific divisions, while there are fewer organizations transforming Finance and HR, those that do have higher outcomes" [BusAI18]. Changing the finance department is hard, as finance people usually like yearly planned budgets and fixed forecasts. However, the need for flexibility is very strong across industries and shifts organizations toward rolling budgets. In the agile finance arena, the concept of Beyond Budgeting has been the most successful. "Beyond Budgeting means beyond command-and-control toward a management model that is more empowered and adaptive" [Beyond14b]. It's been adopted by many large and small organizations worldwide[3] with great results.

Many of the twelve Beyond Budgeting principles [Beyond14a] are not new to agile, but they are still useful to remember in the context of finance:

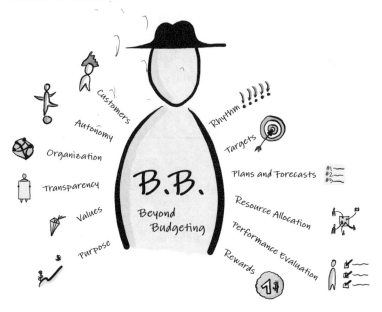

---

3. Key examples include Handelsbanken, Guardian Industries, tw telecom, Slim-Fast, Unilever, American Express, and M. D. Anderson Cancer Center — see https://planful.com/blog/are-you-ready-to-move-beyond-budgeting.

1. Be a purpose-driven organization.
2. Govern through shared values.
3. Focus on team culture.
4. Trust people.
5. Give them autonomy to act.
6. Be customer-centric.
7. Keep the rhythm.
8. Be dynamic.
9. Set directional ambitious goals.
10. Allocate resources as needed.
11. Encourage peer feedback.
12. Reward shared success over competitions.

This philosophy is familiar to true agilists, but it is very challenging for those who have spent their entire careers in the traditional environment based on fixed plans and budgets. The idea that an organization can be managed successfully without fixed annual budgets is sometimes hard to grasp. Interestingly, once you allow it to happen, you can be significantly more responsive to the business challenges and needs and can allow the organization to iterate toward the purpose, not just follow a plan that might not yet be relevant.

The tw telecom Story

Nevine White, VP Accounting at Hargray and former VP FP&A, tw telecom

In early 2004, my boss laid out a challenge for me—find a better way to financially plan for the company and replace the outdated and wasteful budget process. That was the beginning of a major organization-wide transformation that resulted in not only our moving to rolling forecasts but also in allowing a shift to a management system that was agile, effective, and exceptionally successful. For lack of any specific direction on how to move forward, I started researching ideas to find that "better way." This led me to a planning approach known as Beyond Budgeting. We quickly designed the new process and planning models. Taking care of these very tangible items was exciting and well within what my Finance team and I were good at. Then the realization hit that this was going to be a huge cultural change, and we had to embrace our newly enabled change management methodology, learning skills that were critical to the success of this finance-originated initiative.

We began to enroll people in this profound change and did something that is often foreign to finance teams—we listened to our front line. We very deliberately shifted from this being a "finance thing" to it being a corporate initiative. We became visible in the field, allowing us to be more responsive. We eliminated home-grown bureaucracy and pushed out approval authority to the front line to make decisions happen faster and make us more agile as an organization.

Our first new forecast process was rough, but we learned from our mistakes, adjusted, and tried again. We realized that this would require continuous adaptation to keep up with changes in the market and to stay aligned with strategic priorities. When we unraveled this "sacred cow" of budgeting, everything was suddenly fair game, and we adopted a mindset of continuous improvement and innovation. Even processes that were fixed and working would inevitably feel the strain of the market and customer needs shifting as we grew—we were constantly tinkering with removing obstacles.

The whole tone of the organization changed. People were listening, collaborating, and including new stakeholders. We embedded the Finance team with the field organizations to be able to make decisions faster—we were no longer seen as an obstacle. We were all suddenly part of a larger purpose, striving for a common goal. I will claim that eliminating the budget was the sole factor in the company's success—but by creating business agility, we allowed our front-line leaders to focus on the job they were hired to do. In the decade we operated without the constraints of outdated budgets, tw telecom delivered forty consecutive quarters of top-line revenue growth—and that includes the years of the great recession. By being willing to take some risk and truly engage in deploying some new ideas, we accomplished something remarkable. We created the necessary transformation in our business to be the most agile in our industry in terms of customer experience and innovation.

Books to Read

- *Agile People: A Radical Approach for HR & Managers (That Leads to Motivated Employees)*, Pia-Maria Thoren (Austin, TX: Lioncrest, 2017).
- *Implementing Beyond Budgeting: Unlocking the Performance Potential*, Bjarte Bogsnes (Hoboken, NJ: Wiley, 2016).

In a Nutshell

☐ Agile HR supports the growth of the agile culture.
☐ Agile HR = agile leadership + system coaching + large groups facilitation.
☐ Agile organizations decouple salaries and positions and make the roles emergent.
☐ Rolling budgets are flexible, dynamic, and keep the rhythm.

11
. . .
TOOLS AND PRACTICES

SYSTEM COACHING AND FACILITATION

Two of the most important skills for the agile organization are system coaching and facilitation.

We don't stop at individuals; we need to be able to coach teams and larger systems. As agile at the organization level is still very new, unfortunately, there are not many coaching programs that focus on systems. One is Organization and Relationship Systems Coaching (ORSC), which is very much aligned with agile and is widely used by agile coaches [Šochová17a]. In Chapter 6, I described three system coaching tools: the three levels of reality, High Dream/Low Dream, and

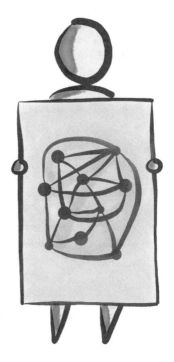

Bringing Down the Vision. System coaching is also the key skill the agile leadership model (Chapter 5) is based on, so you will use these skills every day.

The more organizations rely on collaboration and forming networks, the more facilitation of large group workshops, conversations, and brainstorming becomes indispensable. Facilitation brings neutrality and helps people find alignment and mutual understanding. They own the process, while the participants own the content. "Facilitation is like a complex dance of polarities. When teams come together to collaborate, rarely are topics or decisions black and white with a clear 'right' answer" [Acker19]. Like system coaching, there is no right and wrong in a complex system, there are just different perspectives, and the goal of the facilitator is to make sure the voices of the system are heard without being judged.

The Value of Facilitation Skills

Marsha Acker, author of The Art and Science of Facilitation: How to Lead Effective Collaboration with Agile Teams

Agility requires leaders to think differently—to break old habits of planning and controlling for the sake of finding new ways to learn quickly and be able to adapt. The kinds of problems organizations face today require many minds thinking together about how to solve challenges and move forward.

My wish for leaders at all levels of organizations today is that they come to value and appreciate the art of facilitation skills. That they do the work to learn and become practiced at what it means to be more neutral in how they listen and participate. That they create environments where all voices are equally heard, dedicate time to hearing different points of view, and find the right balance between not rushing to a final decision too quickly and not getting stuck in the soup of opinions.

OPEN SPACE

One of the very interesting formats of facilitation at the complex system level is Open Space. The Open Space format is a facilitation technique that enables system creativity and allows a large group of people to work on a common theme in a distributed way. It uses self-organization and gives people the opportunity to choose the specific topics they wish to discuss. Sounds complicated, but it's not that hard. It's just a different way of having a conversation about ideas.

The Open Space format has only one simple rule and four quite philosophical principles. I remember that I was discouraged by their abstractness at the beginning. They sound very complicated when you read them for the first time, but they simply describe self-organization. The moment I stopped analyzing the principles and applied them at a higher level, I realized that Open Space is an awesome tool.

The Law of Two Feet is the key rule of Open Space.

The Law of Two Feet sets the foundation for Open Space. It allows everyone to take responsibility for what their interests are, and if they find themselves in a conversation isn't holding their interest and to which they are not contributing, they must use their feet and go to another topic circle where the conversation is more interesting or relevant to them.

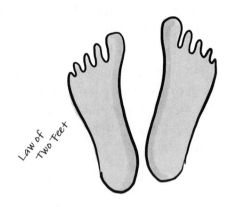

This is probably the key to Open Space's success. Just imagine using this law at work every day. How many meetings would you stay at? The conversations you attend would be much more interesting, and let's not forget how much more time you would have for them. The Law of Two Feet is a game changer, as it defines participation as voluntary. Everyone can participate, and they can leave when the Open Space no longer offers them relevant information or interaction.

While the law is the foundation, the four principles [Stadler19] define self-organization and help people to get the most out of participation.

Whoever come are the right people.

All those who are interested in a conversation are the right people to attend the Open Space. Participation is open to everyone. You cannot limit it by number of people, experience, or knowledge. Open Space must be open to everyone, and it sets no limitations for people to join.

Whatever happens is the only thing that could have.

Don't think about "what would happen if. . . ." The conversation runs in the direction it runs, those who came are the ones who are here, and what is happening right now is the only thing that has to happen. In our lives, we are all influenced to a certain extent by our experiences, ideas, and plans, which constantly force us to think about the past or the future. The "whatever happens" principle brings us back to the present moment, where we stop evaluating what could happen and fully focus on what is happening right now, in the present.

Whenever it starts is the right time.

Creativity cannot be planned, and our task is to not limit the flow of creativity. Whenever it starts, it's the right time. And if that means you need to continue the conversation longer than you planned, you continue the conversation for as long as necessary. If that means you start later, that's fine as well.

When it's over, it's over.

Creativity has its own rhythm, so pay attention to it. Time is not so important. If you feel it would be a good idea to end the topic, ask the group. When they agree, finish and go to the next thing that interests you; if not, you continue with it and investigate the topic in more detail.

As you can see, there is nothing difficult about it, but it requires an agile mindset as a prerequisite. Open Space would feel really weird in the context of a traditional mindset where people believe that every conversation must have a clear leader and decision maker, a fixed plan, and measurable goals. Open Space is anything but that—it's not planned in detail and it's not centralized. It takes the self-organization and distributed way of working to the next level and unleashes the power of creativity of the system.

Organizational Open Space

Jutta Eckstein and John Buck, authors of Company-wide Agility with Beyond Budgeting, Open Space & Sociocracy: Survive & Thrive on Disruption

Today's pressure on companies from VUCA and digitalization requires companies to be innovative at all times. Management typically assumes to be responsible for inducing innovation, for example, by inviting selected people to thinktanks. This approach misses the innovative power of the whole staff.

Open Space is a special events facilitation technique for achieving this increase in capacity. *Organizational Open Space* uses the same principles to leverage the innovative potential of everyone working for the organization every day—not just at special events.

For example, video game developer Valve Corporation invites staff to suggest ideas about a new game or improvements to existing games whenever the idea occurs to them during the work week. If there are any colleagues who believe in this new idea, they will join together to make it happen. Another example: at W.L. Gore (the outdoor equipper), everyone is invited constantly to suggest a new product, a new feature, or maybe even a new process. In both cases, if enough staff are interested in implementing this product, feature, or process, that interested group will pursue it. If there is not enough interest for the idea, the idea dies because the missing passion signals that it is probably not worth implementing. The opposite is also possible. If staff tires of an activity, they can stop doing it, so long as they take care of existing customers.

Innovation no longer relies solely on assignments via job descriptions, or on a few "innovative" people (like the R&D department), or on specific events like thinktanks. Innovation happens all the time by everyone.

Diversity of Roles

Every individual has different preferences, and flexible formats such as Open Space need to accommodate diversity and make it a guiding principle. That is why, besides the facilitator (the Open Space host) and the participants involved in discussion circles, Open Space defines two roles—Bumblebee and Butterfly. These roles simply describe the way you use the Law of Two Feet when you leave a discussion that lacks value or relevance for you and join a new one or when you just need a quiet moment to digest what you've learned.

Bumblebees fly freely from one group to another. They always listen to a piece of conversation and then jump to the next group and conversation. It often happens that the inspiration they have acquired in one group is transferred to  another and makes a bridge between conversations. Bumblebees are like a last-minute spice, added on a whim, that turns a mediocre meal into a culinary delight. That's what a Bumblebee does—on a whim, it lands in a topic circle and sometimes creates a buzz. It can't be planned. It's emergent, based on the situations and context. The randomness of it feels weird in the traditional environments but works great in complex systems.

The second role is the Butterfly. In contrast to Bumblebees, Butterflies are not participating in the planned conversations but create new opportunities to connect and learn. Some-times they overhear some-thing, and they need to keep their thoughts straight, so they sit somewhere along-side active conversations and take the time to reflect.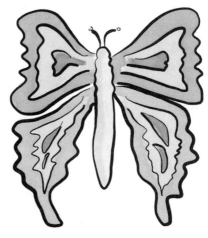

Sometimes it happens that other butterflies sit down and create a totally unplanned group on the current theme. They are the most decentralized and disorganized part of the Open Space, living the principles: Whenever it starts is the right time, whoever come are the right people, and most important, whatever happens is the only thing that could have.

Open Space's flexible format accommodates any idiosyncrasies in your preferred way of thinking, learning, and conversing. Consequently, it's a great tool for addressing complex problems with creative and innovative ideas. It's a completely free format, so don't be afraid to be yourself. Remember, during the Open Space, whatever is happening is the right thing. You'll see that once you get familiar with it, you will become a great fan of Open Space.

What You Need to Prepare

Let's now take a look at what you need to prepare. You need a big room where the so-called marketplace will be held, and you need ideas for conversations. It's not hard to arrange—just arrange chairs in a circle,  or in several rows for a larger group, with enough markers and paper in the middle. The Open Space facilitator explains the rules and principles, reminds the participants about the theme of the day's Open Space, and opens up the marketplace to ideas. Then, one by one, the participants present their area of interest to the others, write the topic and their name on a piece of paper, and place it on a specific space and time on the board to reserve a timeslot.

Sometimes, topic owners agree to combine their conversations if they have similar topics, and sometimes they change the timeframe at the last minute to be able to participate in a compet-ing conversation about another interesting topic. Anyone who has suggested a topic may present his or her own idea or just facilitate the discussion among the participants and leave the ideas to them. There is no limit to the form. Each site has a flipchart to allow par-ticipants to record substantial conversation points so that the out-comes are not lost. At the end, everyone meets again, and someone from each group presents a summary of their conversation. Note that Open Space usually provides a forum to *start* a conversation about a certain topic — it's not intended for participants to make big decisions; however, different experiments often emerge from Open Space conversations.

Example of Open Space marketplace from Agile Prague Conference 2017

Where Organizations Can Use Open Space

Once you understand what Open Space is, it's time to consider where organizations can use this format. Open Space is often used at conferences to bring the experience of lectures and workshops to a concrete level, giving everyone the opportunity to discuss their particular problem and to be inspired by what interests others. The largest Open Space group I've seen was about 1,200 peo-

ple; companies that organize Open Spaces regularly often have hundreds of participants. The number of people is not the limit here, as Open Space scales pretty well. All you need is to have a big enough room to run a joint marketplace and enough separate locations to have separate conversations.

So where is this format typically used? Basically, wherever we are dealing with a complex problem and are ready for real self-organization. Bringing together a large group of people is a great option to generate creativity and innovations and to brainstorm possible solutions to the problem, such as how to change the evaluation system; what types of goals, objectives, and measures we should have; what the new office space should look like; how to improve quality; how to get better access to the customers. It can also be used for Product Backlog refinement[1] or an organizational retrospective.

Open Space builds on emergent leadership. When you are interested, you stand up for it, take responsibility, and try to form a group of people around you who are also interested in the topic. It raises transparency, and it's voluntary and inclusive. It enhances the collaboration and creativity and thereby the overall agility of the organization.

---

1. Product Backlog refinement is where Product Backlog is created and ordered in Scrum.

The first time I participated in an Open Space was sometime in 2003, when our customers wanted to change their style of work. It was a few years before we had implemented Scrum and become agile. At that time, the customers just wanted to invest a hundred days in a better way of working. It was called "100 days of improvement," with teams working for one hundred days to improve processes, infrastructure, automation, and so on. The hundred days started with an Open Space, where we all brainstormed what could help us in product development and how we could invest the one hundred days to improve in the most efficient way. It was weird at the time; we were confused and wondering why they let us talk without any predefined structure. But the ideas that came from that day were great, and we improved several parts of the system, which brought great business value afterward.

A few years later, I used Open Space workshops for an overall HR change, to improve the people development system, to design a new bonus structure, and to redesign our office space. At the product space, one of my favorite workshops facilitated by Open Space is the overall retrospective, where teams that work together on one product think of how they could improve teamwork. You would be amazed by the brilliant ideas that can emerge from pure self-organization.

How to Start

Let's now see how to get started. Don't be afraid. What emerges from Open Space does not necessarily have to be implemented in that exact way. What one working group suggests is just a beginning. It might be a long way to go to convince the others about the idea, evaluate it, and implement it. Well, it doesn't have to be long, but what I want to emphasize is that what a group of people proposes is not automatically a decision. Sometimes, when there is agreement, a change can take just a few minutes. Other times, the final implementation takes months because lawyers need to get involved, finance needs to review it, and other departments have to finalize it. And sometimes an idea is never realized if it's not practical from the organizational perspective. It doesn't matter, because it's about finding creative solutions to a complex problem, and that takes time and a series of experiments.

Open Space is a voluntary format, so it has enthusiastic people from the start and does not have to deal with demotivation. It is a format that builds on diversity and allows people to focus on the part of the problem that seems most interesting to them and try to move a bit together. The rules are simple and familiar to people with an agile mindset, and in an agile organization, the workshop will run almost by itself. In a traditional organization, where people still have the feeling that you need to have reporting and central management to do anything, Open Space usually makes people nervous and someone in the management stops it. "What if employees come up with something we don't like, then what? It's better not to let them do it at all." Although facilitation is simple and the workshop itself cannot go wrong, some organizations and managers see it as a no go. After all, it's an advanced technique of the agile world.

Agile Prague Open Space conversation about a topic

Let's try this simple assessment. By evaluating responses to your idea to run an Open Space, you can tell if your organization is agile or not that much yet. Imagine a similar conversation in your organization:

"We would like to organize a half-day workshop on how to improve _____. _____ is our biggest problem. It costs us _____ in time and money monthly, and so far, we haven't been able to improve it. We would like to invite all team members to think about what we can do about it in an Open Space."

What will be the reaction in your organization?

0: "Don't even think about changing it. No change is possible in this area. All you have to do is to follow the processes."

1: "How much will it cost? We can't give it half a day—we have to work and deliver."

2: "You can't invite everyone. If you really want to do it, create a small working group."

3: "Is participation really voluntary? And what if . . . ?"

4: "Let me know how it went."

5: "Can I join as well?"

It's a simple test. Ask people around you and classify their answer according to the 0 to 5 scale. The number of points you get on average shows how agile your organization is:

0 means your organization is not ready for such agile practices and is deep in the traditional mindset. I would start with something smaller to show the organization that self-organization and decentralizing work can be successful.

3 gives you a chance to try, though you will have to explain it a lot and also increase the safety. When you sell the first such workshop within the organization as a success, you usually have a win and you will be allowed to use it again from time to time.

5 is a sign that you have gone quite far on your agile journey and agile is part of your organization's DNA. Agile is not only what you do but how you live. Open Space workshops will become a normal part of your organization, and other people within the organization will start organizing them whenever they need to address some complex problem.

Anything in between these thresholds shows you are already on the way to reaching the next level.

What can you do to increase the readiness of the organization to try the Open Space format?

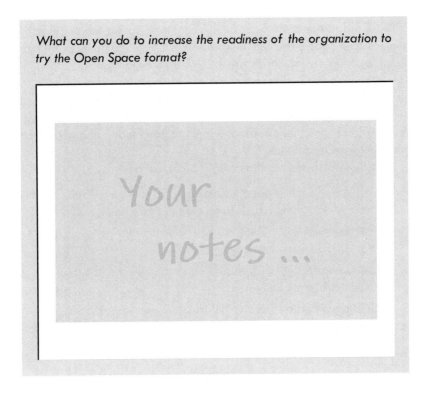

WORLD CAFÉ

World Café is another great tool for raising awareness about a topic. It's great for scaling a conversation and leveraging the wisdom of the system. The setup is very simple: people sit in small groups around tables, like in a café, so they can have a conversation in a comfortable way. Usually, each table has a flipchart or just a set of larger Post-it Notes and Sharpies so people can make notes from their conversation.

The World Café starts with the facilitator introducing the format and setting the expectations for it. World Café is a great tool to address the first step of the agile leadership model: get awareness. It's not a tool for making fast decisions, but it helps large and diverse groups to reflect on the current state, listen to the voices of the system, and become aware of the different perspectives.

Initially, we ask people to form cross-functional diverse teams, to cover as many perspectives as they can. We usually run three (or more) 20-minute conversations about the topic, where each conversation round is framed by a question. The questions don't cover three different topics but instead look at the same topic from three different angles, to help people investigate the area from different perspectives and listen to the voices of the system.

In every round, the group selects one person who stays in the group and at the beginning of the next round explains to the new participants the bottom line of the previous conversation. The flipchart is a useful visual tool for that. The rest of the people randomly choose a new discussion table to join, keeping in mind the diversity and cross-functionality of the groups.

After the last round is done, the groups present their outcomes to others and look for action steps.

Agile Lean Europe Network Vision

My first experience with World Café was at the Vision/Purpose session of ALE, the Agile Lean Europe network[2] at XP2011 in Madrid (you can watch the video from the session).[3] We used Lego StrategicPlay[4] to help creativity flow. It was an event where agilists from thirty-two countries came together and used the World Café format to discuss possibilities for the Vision of the newly created ALE network. Creating a community vision

2. Agile Lean Europe (ALE) is a network for collaboration of agile and lean thinkers and activists across Europe: http://alenetwork.eu.
3. Video from ALE Network Europe StrategicPlay Vision, XP2011, Madrid, Spain: https://www.youtube.com/watch?v=Zg2PMv8lFUA.
4. StrategicPlay: http://strategicplay.de.

is anything but a straightforward process. Everyone has an opinion, and everyone is right—but only partially. The World Café created the right diversity mix, while Lego helped us to go through the three levels of reality and leverage the power of sentient essence and dreaming before we brought it back to the consensus reality. Every group proposed a vision, along with an explanation of it. In the end, Jurgen Appelo, who initiated the idea of creating the ALE network, was able to compile the vision: "The Agile Lean Europe (ALE) network is an open and evolving network of people (not businesses), with links to local communities and institutes. It helps people in European countries by spreading ideas and growing a collective memory of Agile and Lean thinking. And by exchanging interesting people with diverse perspectives across borders it allows beautiful results to emerge" [ALE11]. It was almost magical how all the diverse voices unified after the session around one coherent vision statement.

Example of Lego StrategicPlay for ALE Network, XP2011 (Photo by Ralph Miarka)

Awareness about Processes

Another example is from a corporation where we invited about one hundred people and facilitated a discussion around how their current business process mapped against the formal process description and how it could be changed. We printed a big poster of the existing process and put it on a wall, and in three rounds let people investigate the differences between how it was used and how it was described, the obstacles they were facing, and the areas they wanted to keep unchanged. During the conversation, we mapped the current process to the picture representing the formal process to visualize the differences, and we concluded the workshop with a conversation about how we should change the way we work.

Example of the outcome of World Café mapping the existing processes to the expected way of working

Expectations from the Roles

The third example is from an agile organization where we needed to raise awareness of different mutual expectations from the roles of Scrum-Master, Product Owner, and Manager. We had three rounds of questions: "How can the ScrumMaster help the Product Owner and Manager?" "What can the Product Owner expect from the ScrumMaster and Manager?" and "The manager is primarily a leader. How does my leadership affect the ScrumMaster and Product Owner?" No decisions were made that day, but several ScrumMasters, Product Owners, and Managers left the room with the action item that they needed to have a deeper conversation and get aligned, as they realized their expectations didn't match. And that's exactly where the World Café is often used—to start the conversation and raise awareness.

As you can see from the given examples, the World Café is a very flexible format for sparking the creativity of the system. You can use it to address any complex problem, but it would be a waste of time on predictable problems where the solution is easy to figure out.

SYSTEMS THINKING

Tools such as systems thinking are interesting in the modern world, as they don't avoid complexity but show it in its entire ugliness so we can deal with it. The fundamental belief behind it is that everything is part of a larger whole and that the connections between all elements are critical [Acaroglu16], and therefore you need to be aware of the whole system and its complexity.

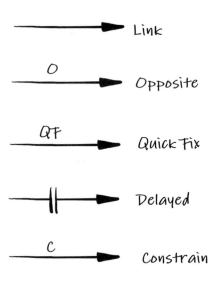

To visualize the complex system, we often use the causal loop diagram [LeSS19b], which creates a great opportunity for conversation and collaboration. There is no right or wrong in the complex system, just different perspectives, and the causal loop diagram is a good visualization technique to start seeing them and initiate a conversation around them. While it's a good technique for running a workshop, it's not intended to be self-explanatory once you see the result.

Causal loop diagrams are easy to start experimenting with. As you can see, the syntax is straightforward. We have a simple arrow to represent the causal link of how one item influences another, as well as the opposite effect—links representing constraints, quick-fix reactions, and delayed reactions.

As mentioned, this technique is easy to start with, but you need some practice to make sense of it. Remember, it's not a tool to show you one way to go but instead to help you visualize the interconnectedness and the overall complexity so that you can have a conversation about the complex system while drawing it.

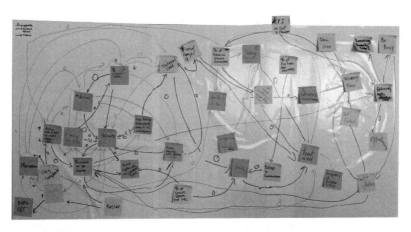

Example of the systems thinking causal loop diagram

Systems Thinking to Discover Conflicting Optimization Goals

Jurgen de Smet, Cofounder of Co-Learning

I have been supporting many large organizations with becoming more agile, and one of the major things one has to do in this context is redesign organizational structures and processes. There was a time when I was helping an organization to adopt LeSS Huge within the boundaries/mandate provided, and the managers providing support were struggling to connect to their existing project management office. Exploring the issues, I suspected that the project management office (PMO) had optimization goals conflicting with what we wanted to achieve with the research and development (R&D) and product marketing group. In order to validate my suspicion, and provide a higher level of transparency on the optimization goals of the systems in place, I organized a systems modeling workshop with representatives from the PMO, R&D, and product marketing departments.

Instead of creating smaller groups with a high diversity, which I do in most of the systems modeling workshops I design and facilitate, I went for groups that represented their departments. I had a group of project and program managers, a group of product marketeers and managers, and a group of engineers. The groups were guided to define their own system variables they cared about within the context of their organization. They then modeled the relationships between their own variables and chose their own, single optimization goal that was, for them, crucial to being effective in their context. With the optimization goal identified, they evaluated the impact on their system variables and thus acquired a good understanding about the why of everything they do and were changing. At the end, we had the three groups connect the three different models to each other, as everything is connected to everything. They discovered that the optimization goal set forward by PMO was conflicting (not consistent) with the optimization goals set forth by product marketing and R&D. Through having

> a higher level of transparency on their system design, their PMO decided to change gears and adapt to the optimization goals of the others. The result? Less frustration and fewer conflicts in the day-to-day operations and a faster change track.

RADICAL TRANSPARENCY

Transparency is the key building block of any agile environment. It looks simple, but it's very hard to practice in traditional organizations, where the competing environment makes people extremely protective as they believe that whoever has information can make a decision and therefore owns the power. Let's be truthful for a moment—how many organizations that you've worked for have real transparency, and how many are hiding information behind team or department walls, encouraged by processes and claiming the necessity of compliance? Lack of transparency is a strong weapon that eventually can kill any agile transformation, as it makes collaboration and self-organization almost impossible. Lack of transparency is a great friend of hierarchical structures supported by fear and politics. "If I'm the only one who has the information, no one can jeopardize my position, and I'm safe in my position as manager. All I need to do to be promoted is wait and make sure that no big mistake happens." Sound familiar?

Radical transparency is the key enabler of agility.

When you move from a hierarchical individual culture to a team-oriented culture, the information needs to flow at a much broader level. Once you are committed to your agile journey, radical transparency is the key enabler. Together with the empowerment resulting from self-organization, it energizes people, and they start to take over responsibility and ownership. They don't wait until someone promotes them to a specific function, and they don't wait for orders. They take over and collaborate on the solutions.

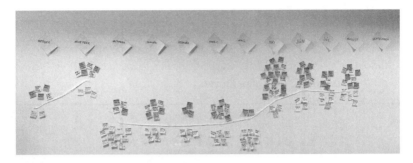

You can also make your monthly agile journey retrospectives visible on the wall.

Transparency doesn't have boundaries. It's not about tools. You can start by sharing Post-it Notes and visualizing the obstacles along your journey, making transparent the actions from the retrospectives or positivity charts—the only limit is the wall space.

Result of large group refinement workshop

You can implement real-time visualization and show the real-time data from your system performance and be more business-driven. Leverage the continuous delivery and fast feedback to see right away what feature created an intended impact and what feature did the opposite and needs to be changed.

Make all key business indicators transparent.

Radical Transparency

Eric Engelmann, Founder of Geonetric, Iowa Startup Accelerator, and NewBoCo, Board Chair at ScrumAlliance

My team explored radical transparency at Geonetric, opting to construct fully empowered, self-organizing teams with minimal hierarchy. I had noticed that small cross-disciplinary teams working on a clearly defined and focused goal could accomplish incredible things very quickly, and I decided to build a culture and even an entire company around it.

We created as much transparency as we could imagine— financial data, operational data, customer data—and asked the teams to respond to and prioritize their work using it. I had imagined that these changes would be mostly "operational"—in how the work got done. But it eventually became the core culture of the company, in every team: we had to change how we marketed and sold our products; we had to rewrite our approach to attracting and retaining talent; we had to revamp our accounting systems. All of these things combined changed our company strategy and our position in the marketplace, too.

From those early glimpses of agile success through fully embracing it as a company, we had no idea how deep the rabbit hole went—there was always more to learn and explore, no matter how radical the changes felt at the time. And there's still more to discover.

Nowadays, technologies help us to address transparency from new angles. Different online voting and survey tools[5] help raise system awareness about new perspectives and can make a difference even on a topic as complex and hard to describe as a culture. No matter where your participants are located, they can see the real-time results. It's fast, easy to use, and transparent. However, be aware that all such tools do only the task of data gathering and would not solve the issue itself.

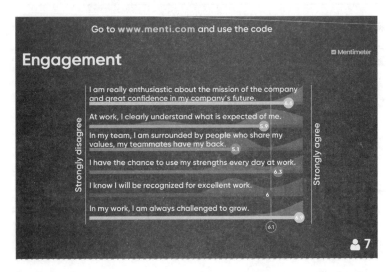

Example of Engagement survey results using Mentimeter online tool

---

5. I've been using mentimeter.com or pollev.com, but there are hundreds of similar tools.

Radical transparency is about showing *everything*, including sharing information about your business with the world. Some organizations blog about everything they do. One example is Dodo Pizza[6]—you can see the company's finances online, read about its Sprint reviews, and follow its journey. Dodo Pizza is not afraid someone might steal some secret information and compete with it. The company has embraced radical transparency and everything that comes with it. Another well-known example is Buffer.[7] It has moved transparency to the next level and shares all revenues, salaries, pricing, and product roadmaps as well as emails, how company personnel travel, and how they work as a remote team. Quite radical, you might say. Radical transparency gives Buffer the opportunity to learn faster. As its director of people, Courtney Seiter, says, "We learn so much faster than if we were to keep things to ourselves. We're able to gather all that information that's sort of wisdom of the crowd." Radical transparency is only one of Buffer's core values [Seiter15], and I would say that together with its people-oriented culture, transparency makes the biggest difference. "As long as we all share information, what's going on in our email, what's going on in our projects, or what's going on in Slack, that gives everyone full context to make connections we might otherwise have missed" [Cherry18]. Slack is, by design, a transparent tool for communication, but imagine if everyone could read everyone's emails and how that would minimize any attempt to engage in politics or be manipulative, since everyone can see everything. As Ray Dalio, another promoter of radical transparency, says, "The most important things I want are meaningful work and meaningful relationships. And I believe that the way to get those is through radical truth and radical transparency. In order to be successful, we have to have independent thinkers—so independent that they'll bet against the consensus. You have to put your honest thoughts on the table" [Hammett18].

---

6. Dodo Pizza Story: https://dodopizzastory.com.
7. Buffer Transparency Dashboard: https://buffer.com/transparency%20.

Relationships take time, and so does radical transparency. At the end of the day, time is the only downside. Like every culture change, it's hard to hardcode it in your behavior. As Courtney Seiter shared, "You really have to set aside time and keep making it a priority and keep making it something that you communicate" [Seiter15]. You also need to be ready to have a candid, open conversation and have the courage to voice constructive criticism and disagree with your colleagues.

Other organizations are running tours to let people experience what it is like to work there. The most famous example is Zappos.[8] Zappos runs tours of its building in Las Vegas, Nevada, to show the world its culture.

Menlo Innovations Collaborative Space

I recently visited the Menlo Innovations[9] offices in Ann Arbor, Michigan, and spent two days there. The level of transparency was

---

8. Zappos Insights: https://www.zapposinsights.com/tours.
9. Menlo Innovations: https://menloinnovations.com/tours-and-workshops/factory-tours.

outstanding. Indeed, you can see all the backlogs and story maps all over the walls and experience its huge organizational Daily Standup where everyone shares what they did and are going to do, but my favorite was the wall with all the people and their positions. Everyone can clearly see where they are and who among their colleagues can mentor them to grow. As everything is transparent and linked together, the Levels Board shown in the following photograph is visible to everyone and also determines their salary. Every column shows the maturity level and every box creates an experienced step on the learning journey.

Menlo Innovations offices and transparency about levels

Using a Transparent Pay Scale to Provoke Growth Opportunities at Menlo Innovations

Josh Sartwell and Matt Scholand, Menlo Innovations

It was Friday evening, and Tim took a quick stop at the Levels Board on his way to the coat room. He'd spent the past week working with Sam and wondered what level she was. He looked for her initials in the Consultant column. He couldn't find her. Then he looked at the Associate levels, and found her at level 3—below a consultant. Surprised, Tim reflected on the week's work. What stood out to Tim was Sam's exceptional skill in consulting the client on a difficult and expensive project decision. Tim was very grateful to have had Sam in those conversations.

While he was looking at the Levels Board, Kelly, a project manager, came up and asked him what he was contemplating. Tim suggested that, based on what he had seen from Sam in the past week, he thought it was time to move Sam up to the consultant levels. Kelly hesitated, then asked, "How do you think Sam would do with a technology that's new to her?" Tim thought for a moment and realized he didn't know. Kelly acknowledged that Sam demonstrated consultant-level skills in a number of ways, but the project managers were not comfortable putting her on a project with an unfamiliar technology, since she hadn't demonstrated an ability to make progress and pick up new things quickly. That led Kelly and the other project managers to believe that Sam wasn't operating at a consultant level.

The following week, Sam agreed to a short feedback session with Tim and Kelly. Tim shared his appreciation for the work Sam had done and the value she brought in their week of being paired together. He expressed his desire to move her up in order to recognize this value, but her skill set in working in unfamiliar technologies was holding her back. Sam understood and explained that her discomfort around unfamiliar technologies was rooted in a fear of letting the team down. The three of them discussed the issue and advocated for the project managers to pair Sam and Carl, another developer good at diving into unfamiliar technology, on a different project with a new technology in order for Sam to grow her skills with Carl as a mentor.

In an organization where growth opportunities are discussed once a year and employees are evaluated by people they don't work with, Sam might not have received the immediate feedback and support she needed to grow professionally. Without transparent levels and pay scale, Sam's team would not have had the opportunity to realize her growth potential. The transparency provided by the roles and Levels Board at Menlo is a catalyst for conversations that are needed in order to help employees and the business thrive.

EXPERIMENT, INSPECT, AND ADAPT

The next step on the radical transparency journey is to run experiments. At every level, you need to be transparent, openly share experiments at the early stage, and be ready to adapt on the basis of feedback. Though you can apply it to product development, the process is applicable to the entire organization. 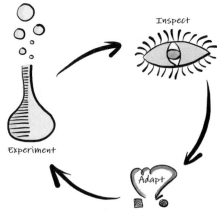 The downside is that before you learn how to collaborate and confirm that you have the same understanding of the vision, it's going to be very inefficient. And very frustrating. "If we can just do it our way," "They don't understand it," and "We know what to do, so why should we ask for feedback?" people often say. But if you are strong enough and stay away from shortcut prebaked solutions, very soon you will see the results in higher collaboration, better understanding, and harmony, which together contribute to a high-performing environment.

Run regular retrospectives and be transparent about action steps. Share the backlog internally and externally. There is very little information—if any—that needs to be hidden. If you believe you have found such information, double-check it by applying the Five Whys[10] technique, and make sure you have a plan for what needs to be done so you can make it transparent in the future.

---

10. Five Why is a root-cause analysis technique in which you ask why five times to help you understand the issue better.

When we decided to move toward a different way of running performance reviews, we didn't know if it was going to work, and I didn't have a backup plan either. I wanted to make it simple, with as light a process as I could, based on transparency, peer feedback, and coaching. I wanted to stop evaluating and help people to grow and to find their own role in the organization. Initially, we started on a quarterly basis and ran self-assessment followed by a coaching session. We got good feedback from all the employees as we listened to their dreams and desires, but very soon we realized that this might be too much. We started doing quarterly peer feedback and had coaching conversations about growth on a yearly basis or when there was a specific need.

As everybody got to experience it and we built trust in the system, people started coming when they felt a need to talk about their value or development. We also realized that quarterly peer feedback might not fit every situation, so eventually we made it more frequent in some teams and left it open for every team to design their own process according to their needs. We also made the coaching conversation irregular—we just made sure we got to talk to people at least once a year about where they wanted to go, what they wanted to learn, and how they saw their role in the organization. The whole process changed significantly on the basis of the feedback: certain ideas were not practical (like assessing all the technical domains), and some were too radical at the time (like making the peer feedback fully transparent). We were not looking for a fixed process. Step by step, we iterated on transparency, learned from the feedback, adapted, and found ways to experiment. The idea of adapting the whole system built trust in the teams and made it easier for them to embrace the change, as even when something was not working that well, it was clear that it was not set in stone. Everything was just an experiment that could be adapted through the feedback loop.

BE INCLUSIVE

The last necessary step on the radical transparency journey is to be inclusive. There should be no such thing as a closed meeting. They

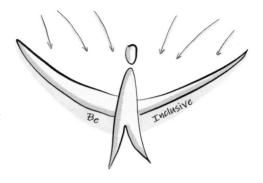

should be publicly visible, with an open invitation so people can join if they are interested and have something to say. If there are a lot of people, the facilitator can use some diverge-and-merge facilitation techniques, but no restriction should be applied for the sake of efficiency.

It's not about being fast without alignment; it's about building alignment that allows you to be even faster.

One of the key parts of our culture shift was to be more innovative and creative. It was not that simple, as most of our employees were used to working according to strict requirements. They thought that in our business there was no space to be creative and innovative because we work in a life-and mission-critical systems domain. Asking them to be part of the creative workshop and explore the potential of social networks, the internet of things, or autonomous systems sounded to them like language from a different planet.

Traditionally, building a new business pillar would work as a small pilot team isolated from the rest of the organization. We decided to do it differently: use the power of the system and make the whole initiative inclusive and voluntary. Participation varied; many people were skeptical at first, but at some point, we experienced an interesting shift whereby many different people you would never have expected to participate in such an initiative started coming up with new ideas, teams were trying new prototypes in their slack time, and the whole initiative was infused with new energy, which brought people who were initially skeptical back to the team. In about a year, one of the ideas was sold to a new customer. We used new technology, addressed a new business segment, and leveraged artificial intelligence experience in collaboration with the researchers. Through that experience, I learned that a volunteer-based inclusive approach is an enabler in many situations. Let the system self-organize and let the teams figure out what is the best solution to the problem. It's not the most efficient way if you already know what the solution is, but it works incredibly well to crack the VUCA challenges.

HAVE COURAGE

Radical transparency is hard. You first need to have the courage to say how things really are, not be afraid to hear difficult feedback, trust that people will help you, and be ready to help others because, after all, you have the same vision and the same evolutionary purpose to achieve. It's not easy, but it is a great investment, and it will pay back when you have formed a highly adaptive (agile), high-performing organization, one that is equipped to crack the challenges of our complex world.

From the following list, choose the item that most closely describes your organization:

In our organization . . .

People don't need to know everything; the information flow is purely hierarchical.

We are transparent at the team level.

We have full transparency within the organization.

We are open to sharing information publicly within the network of our customers and partners.

We are open with other organizations and the world; radical transparency is our biggest competitive advantage.

The list starts from a description of environments with very low transparency and continues with higher transparency applied to the broader areas in the organization or even outside of the organization.

What can you do at your organization to increase the transparency?

Your notes ...

Better to Ask for Forgiveness than to Beg for Permission

Jurgen de Smet, Cofounder of Co-Learning

Many people come to me for management support, asking how to acquire this in their context. The best thing I can come up with is to work from within the principles and not beg for permission. When done right, one will automatically have management support to get things to move forward. I was at the pub with some of my hometown buddies when this topic came up, and one of them challenged me to join his organization and he would show me, he said, that my statements were BS (not Basic Scrum). He arranged some budget, and I went to work with him and his team members; in this context, we had little to no mandate for true change, and many had the impression one could do only as much as the mandate allowed for. One of the first things I did was to synchronize their Sprint Planning and Sprint Review sessions across six teams, facilitating and organizing them in the same room with all the people involved. Yes, they all had their own Product Owner (well, team output owner) and their own Product Backlog (well, team backlog), of which they were not aware across the teams, but that didn't matter to me. I considered them working on the same product, and by having Sprint Planning and Sprint Review sessions together, the team members started to notice they were actually working on the same product (I increased transparency, and the teams inspected and adapted). In Sprint 3 or 4, the teams did their Sprint Retrospective around the topic "Why are we not one team?" They came up with argumentation for the R&D director (the one with the mandate) to change their structures and work with only one Product Owner and from only one Product Backlog as if they were one team. Parallel to this, I connected with the head of product management, explored the problems he had, and helped him see the benefits of a single, outcome-based Product Backlog across the teams. So the R&D director got a request from product management to redesign their structures in a way similar to what the teams were asking for. There is no director or manager who will refuse to take an action when the request is coming from their own teams and from the business at the same time. Today, my hometown buddy is telling his own stories instead of calling my stories BS.

The key is to have the courage to work from within the principles and to increase transparency and awareness within the organization. The rest will follow! Don't beg for permission: it's better to ask for forgiveness.

GROWING TRUST

Trust is the key prerequisite for a well-functioning team [Lencioni11]. Lack of trust happens if people are reluctant to be vulnerable with one another; they are often afraid to ask for help, they hide their mistakes from each other, and they are reluctant to give constructive feedback. Quite a disaster, as there is no way people who don't trust each other would collaborate on anything and be agile.

People usually think about trust in terms of predictability. If you can expect certain behavior from a person, you trust that he or she will do the same good job again. But that's only the first step toward full trust. As Patrick Lencioni says in his book *The Five Dysfunctions of a Team*, vulnerability-based trust brings with it much deeper confidence: "In the context of building a team, trust is the confidence among team members that their peers' intentions are good, and that there is no reason to be protective or careful around the group. In essence, teammates must get comfortable being vulnerable with one another" [Lencioni11].

Vulnerability-based trust is a prerequisite for high-performing teams. The environments with a high level of trust would embrace agile without a struggle. Let's take a look at several tips on how to build trust.

Team Building

Team building is the most impactful trust builder. When people spend some personal time together, talking not only about work but also about life, their hobbies, ideas, and passions, they form close interpersonal connections. You can go for a beer after work, go bowling, try to "Escape the Room"[11] together, take a trip together to explore, or just have a team lunch or spend time talking over coffee about non-work-related topics. Some teams play a game of "Tell me something that people don't usually know about you and it's not a secret." You would be amazed by the number of interesting stories you can learn even about people you've been working with for years.

---

11. Escape the Room game: https://escapetheroom.com.

Some time ago, I got a very dysfunctional team. The team members were demotivated, frustrated; the environment was full of blaming and contempt—so thick you could feel it in the air. However, they were in a stage of not seeing reality, pretending that they were just fine. I agreed to run a short workshop with them and see what I could do to help them out. From that short retrospective, using Patrick Lencioni's Five Dysfunctions of a Team concept, they reflected on the current state of the team and were able to see that it was actually very unhealthy. It was eye-opening. After the first moment of hesitation, when I told them no one could solve it for them and they needed to take responsibility for their environment and relationships, they started coming up with ideas. The conversation became very open but also surprisingly very constructive. We talked about building trust, the impact of positivity, and the need for strengthening relationships.

Long story short, the next day one of them, the most frustrated person from the team, came back and offered to organize some team building. He said he had already talked to several of his colleagues and they would go for it, and then he asked me to join. He thought we should start with an appreciation loop to raise the positivity. The following Friday, we went to the local pub, and before we had a few beers, we ran the appreciation loop. Everyone drew a name from a bowl, and the name you drew was the person you had to appreciate. If you got your own name, you had to change it. Simple and easy. Turned out, it went very well. It was amazing how a very simple event like going for a beer and spending some time talking to each other could make a difference. We ran several retrospectives after that, and they quickly became a well-functioning collaborative team.

Personal Maps

Another interesting method for getting to know one another better is to draw a personal map [Mgmt19]: you draw your own mind map with your name in the center and add interesting categories about yourself, such as education, work, hobbies, family, and friends. You can add pictures to make it more fun. The more you think about yourself, the more you raise your own awareness about the decisions you've made and the events that have shaped who you are, and you help others to see that. Leaders need to build high emotional and social intelligence before they are able to see the group as a single integrated whole and trust it [CRR13], so personal maps are a great starting point.

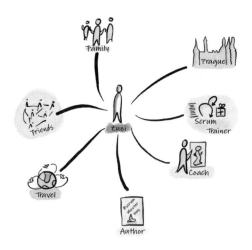

How Are You Leading Your Life?

Michael K Sahota, CEC Certified Enterprise Coach and CAL Educator

A key part of being an effective agile leader is having healthy relationships. Powerful leaders are ready to look at the quality of relationships they have with others and how they are showing up in those relationships.

A pivotal change in my leadership came to me when I was going through a challenging period in my life. I was reading Brené Brown's book *I Thought It Was Me*,[12] and there was a sentence that really grabbed me:

> You can only be kind to others to the extent that you are kind to yourself.

It was a wake-up call in my life. I became very aware of my "internal critic" and the talk track of self-judgment that

---

12. Brené Brown, *I Thought It Was Just Me (But It Isn't): Making the Journey from "What Will People Think?" to "I Am Enough."* New York: Brilliance Audio, 2014.

accompanied my perfectionist personality. I thought about the quote and I wondered: "How kind am I to my kids? To other people in my life?" At that moment, I set an intention for myself to be kind to myself and others. But how? I created a "simulation game" in my mind: An Epic Quest for Self-Kindness.[13] The next two years took me on a life journey as I "leveled-up" in my quest for self-kindness. I ran experiment after experiment to try anything that might support the journey. I found the "weird stuff that works." I started with meditation and experiential workshops. I then took a deep dive into personal growth by going to India, where intense psychological processes of clearing my mind initiated a permanent shift in my consciousness. This became my path to silence my mind and find peace and stillness among the stress of life. This opened my connections to self and others.

As I look back on my career, I can see how important this journey was in shaping my current ability to inspire and influence others.

It is important for you to find your own path of self-discovery.

The invitation is to consider, "How kind are you to yourself?" And perhaps set the intention to go on your own epic quest to create a powerful inner shift that not only will unlock you but will unlock all your relationships as well.

You can draw your own journey, visualizing important events and sketching them on your journey drawing. Some of them you will evaluate as more positive and put them closer to the smiling face. Other events you will see as less positive and therefore put them closer to the frowning face. In both cases, the visualization makes things easier to share with others, and the drawing makes it more fun. Overall, it increases the positivity, and people become more open in positive environments.

---

13. Inspired by Jane McGonigal's SuperBetter story. For more information, visit https://www.superbetter.com/about.

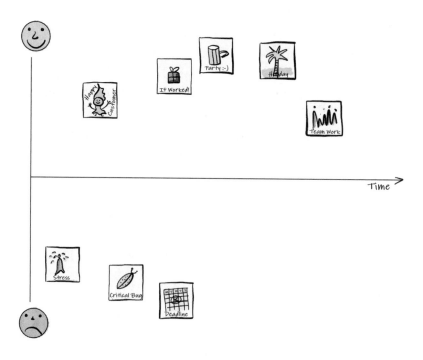

Assessment

If you wish to invest in a more structural approach to building trust, you can take the Table Group assessment,[14] which shows you in a very simple graphic, based on the Teamwork Dysfunctions[15] model [Lencioni11], how healthy you are as a team and

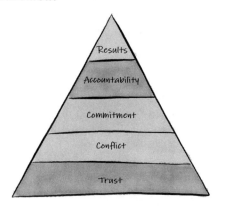

---

14. The Table Group provides team assessments based on *The Five Dysfunctions of a Team* [Lencioni11]: https://www.tablegroup.com.
15. The five team dysfunctions are absence of trust, fear of conflict, lack of commitment, avoidance of accountability, and inattention to results.

recommends steps for improvement. Regarding absence of trust, the Table Group recommends one additional step you may consider: using a personality assessment (e.g., MBTI,[16] DiSC[17]) to help team members understand one another's different preferences, patterns, and attitudes. Understanding people's personality helps team members to be nonjudgmental and leverages the diverse approaches and perspectives of the team. Also, the second team dysfunction, fear of conflict, which deals with artificial harmony, is very often grounded in the absence of trust. To deal with this level, you can use another personality assessment, TKI,[18] to help people understand how they deal with conflict together—which, combined with creating team agreements and acknowledging that conflict is neither good nor bad but just a voice of the system (as described in Chapter 5), grows the trust.

TEAMWORK

The most complicated shift for traditional managers working to become agile leaders is learning to deal with teams instead of individuals. An important part of your leadership competencies is collaboration. At the end of the day, in agile organizations, since the structure is flat, everyone is a member of some team and most likely of some community as well. That makes things easier, as everyone has experience with self-organized teams and with emergent leadership.

If you are not there yet, starting the communities or virtual teams on initiatives that will let them experience emergent

---

16. MBTI is the Myers-Briggs Type Indicator, a personality-type assessment: https://www.myersbriggs.org.
17. DiSC (Dominance, influence, Steadiness, Conscientiousness) is a personality test: https://www.onlinediscprofile.com.
18. TKI is the Thomas-Kilman Instrument, which assesses the conflict mode: https://kilmanndiagnostics.com/overview-thomas-kilmann-conflict-mode-instrument-tki.

leadership is a good first step. Also, even with a very traditional structure of departments and managers, you can look at the managers as a team. This is where agility at the organizational level often starts mak-

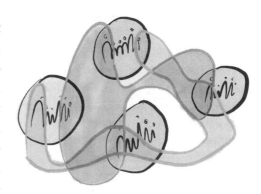

ing all managers part of two teams—the one they are leading and one of their peer managers. While, for most of them, the team they are responsible for feels closer and more important, the opposite needs to happen: they need to feel a closer relationship with their peers than with their subordinates. They need to stop competing for power and influence and instead collaborate to achieve their common goal. Only then can they take a step back and become coaches and facilitators rather than decision makers and be closer to becoming agile leaders. The prerequisite for all teams is that they have one goal, which derives from the organizational purpose. Without team spirit, there is no agile. Every agile journey should start with defining strategic goals and forming teams around them.

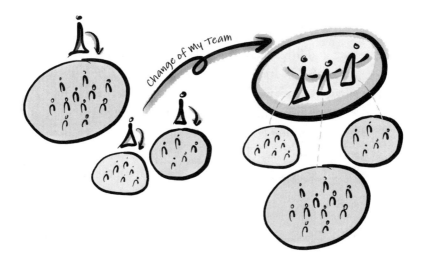

One of the most interesting shifts I've seen from a traditional structure to a team-oriented structure happened not at the development team level but with the executive team. Originally, it was a bigger group of individuals who fought for power, number of people, and better space, blaming each other at every occasion, focusing on local optimization over the common goal. For example, the IT director was refusing to order computers before a new employee started working, the testing director always had his people busy on ongoing projects so they couldn't help in cross-functional teams, and the operations director was trying to optimize the process for his assistant even if that meant hundreds of extra hours spent by other employees. When anyone in the organization had a creative idea that challenged the status quo, it was almost impossible to make it happen.

Once we reorganized into a flat agile structure, we also narrowed down the executive team to four directors and created a good team spirit, investing ourselves into trust and open communication. It was amazing how fast we were able to react to creative and innovative ideas, run experiments, try different ideas, and support each other. It was fun, it was energizing, and most important, it was working and bringing business results.

BUILDING COMMUNITIES

Agile organizations have their basis in self-organization. While the team structure makes the org chart less important, the communities take over and drive many initiatives that in the traditional world used to be centrally driven. The community is a free, inclusive, volunteer-based entity with a common goal to achieve. Once the goal is achieved, the community can be disbanded or can continue working toward another goal.

Organizations usually have different communities of practice[19]—an agile community, a community focused on better

---

19. A community of practice is a group of professionals who share the same interests in resolving an issue, improving skills, and learning from each other's experiences.

development practices, a community focused on increasing quality, a community focused on good design, a community focused on improving the architecture, a community for the customer segment, and so on. Anyone can start a community. Because everything is transparent, the idea is that the community is vetted by the rest of the organization, and if no one joins, it's a signal that the issue is not interesting enough for others to spend their time working on it. If people are interested and find regular time to meet and work on the task, it's a signal of its importance to the organization.

Nowadays, communities can also be active online, over Slack or social media, especially if you create a community that extends beyond the organizational boundaries. Agile organizations are built on the enthusiasm and energy of communities. They share the way they work with others, they collaborate with external parties in wider networks, and they sometimes even do most of their business through volunteer work. You don't have to rely on traditional employees. Modern organizations build networks of supporting teams that are aligned around the same purpose. Traditional organizations with employees is only one way of working. Engaging communities is in some cases a more powerful way of achieving the common vision.

Leaders Ask for Help

Evan Leybourn, Founder of Business Agility Institute

I never set out to create a community or research organization. It was never part of my career path or what I trained for. And yet, when the opportunity arose, there was no other decision I could make. Hence, the first question I had to ask myself was, *What does it take to be a leader in this role?*

No one could answer this question for me. And no one can answer this question for you either. While there is plenty of advice and there are plenty of role models to follow, the delta between who you are and what you need to be is uniquely your own. I had to be honest about my own weaknesses—those skill limitations and cognitive biases that could easily destroy the Business Agility Institute before it had a chance to grow. In my case, I put aside my ego and arrogance and asked for help. A lot of it.

I realized that I needed more than just staff. I needed thought leaders, experts, and practitioners to join us. People who, like me, could put aside their ego and share their insights and experiences. Not for money or self-promotion, but in service of a common-vision.

The first part of this, and possibly the hardest, was to communicate the vision. This is fundamentally important no matter what organization you are in. Why do you exist? How do you make the future better? And why should anyone else care? It's that last question that many organizations struggle with. They spend so much time looking inward that they assume that everyone sees the world through the same eyes. We needed to clearly articulate why our vision was important—not just to us but to you.

But a vision without action is worthless. We needed people. And this was the biggest lesson for me personally. People want to help as long as it's not a transaction. People are naturally curious, sharing, and giving. But we had to make it easy for them to join us. Every step between you and them is a barrier. So we made everything as clear as possible. We made it easy to start a local community. We opened the Library to everyone. And we designed clear approaches to our research so volunteers understood the time and effort involved.

And it has been more successful than I could have possibly imagined. Today, we have more than 150 volunteers. They run our local Business Agility Meetups, organize global conferences, write case studies and references, take stewardship of the Business Agility Library, and undertake leading research on the future of business.

Books to Read

- *The Five Dysfunctions of a Team: A Leadership Fable*, Patrick Lencionis (Luzern, Switzerland: GetAbstract, 2017).
- *The OpenSpace Agility Handbook: The User's Guide*, Daniel Mezick, Mark Sheffield, Deborah Pontes, Harold Shinsato, Louise Kold-Taylor (New Technology Solutions, 2015).

In a Nutshell

- ☐ Trust is the prerequisite for a well-functioning team.
- ☐ Radical transparency is the key enabler of agility.
- ☐ Agile organizations are built on the enthusiasm and energy of communities.
- ☐ Modern organizations build networks of supporting teams that are aligned around the same purpose.

12
. . .
SUMMARY

When I started to write this book, I had the idea that I could layer all the concepts on one summarizing map. Visualization is key to gaining understanding. It stimulates our brain in a different way than just reading or listening.

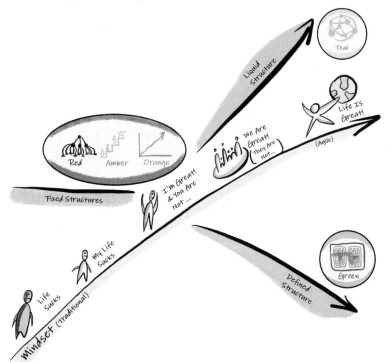

So, I created this map, visualizing the core concepts in one picture. You might need to spend some time looking at it and analyzing it so you can make a connection and think about implications in your environment.

The practices, concepts, and models all have their place and time where they're a great fit and will help your organization to be successful in the VUCA world. In other cases, they might not be beneficial to the organization in any way. For example, transitioning from being a red to a teal organization in one step might be too much and only create chaos. Going to teal or green—which rely on emergent leadership and intrinsic motivation—when most people are in the My Life Sucks tribe can be too hard and end in failure. Implementing agile at the organizational level when most leaders are experts or achievers might not go well either. Structure, leadership, and mindset need to be aligned and go hand in hand on your agile journey.

ORGANIZATIONAL PERSPECTIVE

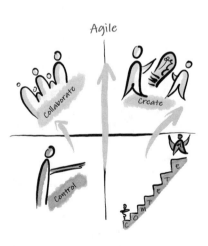

Agile moves the focus from individuals to teams and shifts the culture from control and compete quadrants to the collaboration and create quadrants of the competing values framework. You may not see it on the first day you decide to go for agile, but collaboration, people, and creativity are what drive the leadership shift. The competing values framework doesn't tell you which culture is right or wrong for your organization. At the end of the day, who knows what is right and what is not?

To take the connection a bit further, here is how the color model defined in *Reinventing Organizations* fits in. The red and amber organizations have their center of gravity deep in the control and competition hemisphere, while green and teal organizations live in the higher levels of the collaborate and create hemisphere. Orange organizations fall somewhere in the middle.

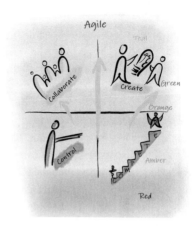

Culture can't be disconnected from the structure or practices, which stimulate the behaviors and values. Therefore, your agile journey always starts with recognizing where the organization is right now, followed by an articulation of the desired state, supported by a clear and strong vision of where you would like to be and why that is important to you. When the organization has a good evolutionary purpose and this dream is appealing enough at the organization level, people will go for it and initiate the culture shift from the inside out.

It's not a surprise that most of the practices often used in the agile organization—peer feedback, customer collaboration, rolling budgets, flexible scope, team interviews, flat structure, self-organized cross-functional teams, no positions, emergent leadership, and so on—are on the collaboration and create part of the competing values framework map. On the other hand, most of the traditional practices take place in the control and compete space: individual key performance indicators (KPIs), performance reviews, positional power, fixed time and scope contracts, yearly budgets, defined career paths, detailed position descriptions, and siloed component teams, among others. Remember, there is no right mix of practices—they are all driven by the desired change of the culture.

I will give you a short example of how we changed our practices when we decided to move the culture to be more collaborative and creative (see Example 1 in the Competing Values section of Chapter 8). It all started by building true cross-functional teams. We already had them in one part of the organization, but never as a key principle. Some teams were more like a group of individuals, and some were narrowed by functional silo or component focus, so for a big part of the organization, the idea of the cross-functional team was pretty radical. What was in the way were functional departments, so, as you know from the introduction, we decided to merge software testers, software developers, and hardware designers into one department called Engineering: a multirole department where people could collaborate across their domains. To minimize the impact of the roles, we made positions more general—such as engineer instead of software developer or tester. Having one department allowed us to have a pretty flat structure where, instead of hierarchy, we relied on teams and their self-organization not only at the single team level but also through cross-team collaboration.

The shift was challenging for parts of the former organization that used to have team leads, as team members were initially lacking the motivation and were reluctant to take over the responsibility because they didn't trust the new way of working. Most of the former team leads felt threatened by the change and showed various symptoms of resistance, so it took a lot of energy to explain the overall vision needs of the organization and coach them to help them find their new role. Ultimately, most of them ended up as experts, running one of our communities (automated testing, tools, architecture, Java, etc.).

Coaching was a critical aspect in our success because we also removed all the traditional KPIs and performance reviews, as those never worked in our dynamic environment anyway. We redesigned the salary structure to have a higher base and no variable parts in most cases, and we built the entire performance review based on radical transparency, peer feedback, and coaching for growth. We encouraged people to work as a team, and in the first few quarters, had a small bonus tied to that; however, the overall vision was that we needed to collaborate across the teams to help the organization to be successful: we don't fight with each other, we don't compete, and we collaborate across teams and products because one plus one is always more than two. Recruiting followed the culture shift. Instead of the multi-round formal interview process focused on technical skills, we did a behavior interview and tried to give candidates the opportunity to experience our culture, join the team for lunch, and see if there was a mutual fit.

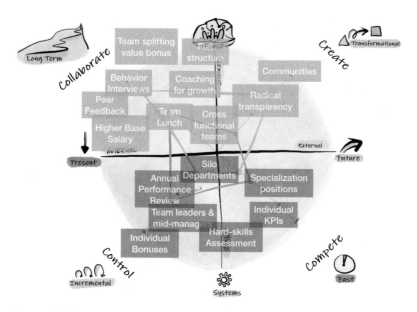

Example of practices we avoided (red) and implemented (green) to enhance the desired culture shift

Long story short, it was a journey. Such things take time. It was frustrating and exhausting. Not everything went well. Nonetheless, if I were in the same situation again, I would do the same—not because the organization became more successful in doing business but because of the energy the overall culture shift created in people. The enthusiasm, the pride in who we are, the motivation. We truly lived the We Are Great mindset and were on our way to Life Is Great. We formed something between a green and a teal organization. We didn't follow any frameworks or models. We were fully value- and culture-driven, and the change was worth all the trouble.

AGILE LEADER PERSPECTIVE

Agile leaders are guides for the organization on its agile journey. From the meta-skills perspective, you need patience, as such change takes time. Even if your current state is far away from your dreams and desires for the organization, you need to be only one step ahead with the practices and not push too hard for the change.

Don't push the change — let it grow.

The let-it-grow approach is easier said than done: you need to be a good servant leader, have a Catalyst mindset, and apply the leader-leader approach to grow the "we" culture. Every day, you will get better at the agile leader competencies: practice coaching and facilitation, collaborate, and train your brain to become better at using different meta-skills, such as patience, curiosity, openness, courage, and trust in the system.

It took me a while, and I'm still on the journey of becoming a better agile leader. Am I more patient than I used to be? Yes. Can I more easily let my ideas go and help others to come up with their ideas? For sure. The ability to see organizations from the system perspectives was an eye-opener for me. Be able to trust the system and let it go. You need to live according to the agile leadership model (see Chapter 5). It's not as simple as it seems. I myself need to overcome my old habits and gain new skills. But it's a journey, and every step makes me a better leader, closer to being a Catalyst, closer to being a better coach, creating cultures and environments where people can collaborate rather than compete and be creative and do their best.

Organizations need to invest in system coaching, large group facilitation skills, and agile leadership development. Business agility is not just about applying some framework; it's a total shift of organizational values and  culture, and such change always needs to happen from the inside out. You can never be successful by delegating it or telling others to change. Leaders need to change first, and the organization will follow.

Agile leaders are the key success factor to organizational agility success in the VUCA world.

Finally, having a critical mass of agile leaders is the key factor to organizational success in the VUCA world. Supporting agile leadership and growing agile leaders is one of the most important tasks on your agile journey. The effort will pay back faster than you would ever have expected. Agile is a journey: it can never be completed and it will never be perfect, but it's always going to be exciting.

How would you assess the level of the following aspects in your environment on a scale of 1 to 10, where 1 is low and 10 is full?

	1	10
Agile leadership	◆—————◆	
Autonomy	◆—————◆	
Creativity	◆—————◆	
Engagement	◆—————◆	
Emergent leadership	◆—————◆	
Experimentation	◆—————◆	
Fun	◆—————◆	
Purpose-driven	◆—————◆	
Team spirit	◆—————◆	
Transparency	◆—————◆	
Trust	◆—————◆	

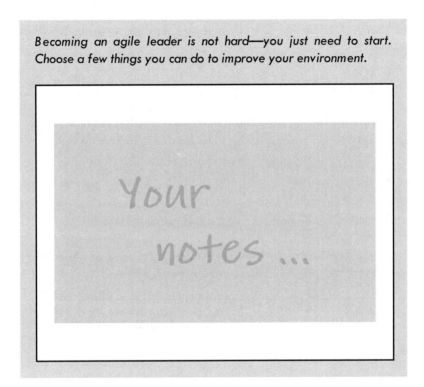

Becoming an agile leader is not hard—you just need to start. Choose a few things you can do to improve your environment.

WHAT'S NEXT

Being an agile leader is a never-ending journey of continuous education, development, and learning. It will never be done, and it will never be perfect. The variety of the concepts, models, and practices is unlimited, so you will not lack for inspiration. I hope you have enjoyed this tasting menu of agile leadership. Now you can start building your own set of tools and skills that work for you. There is no one-size-fits-all approach. Your leadership style must suit your unique personality, circumstances, and constraints. I hope this book has helped you find the ideas that will support you in your own personal journey.

For those who might ask, "I know you shared all those tips along the way, and recommended books at the end of each chapter, but is there anything else you can recommend?" I guess there is always more. Here are a few tips on possible next steps in your leadership development:

- Certified Agile Leadership CAL:[1] A unique leadership development program in an agile space. I'm one of the Scrum Alliance[2] CAL educators, and while this book crystalizes experiences from my Certified Agile Leadership program, the program also deepens the concepts described in this book through practical experience. The program starts with a class, followed by the seven-month virtual CAL II program.
- Organizational Relationship System Coaching ORSC:[3] For system coaching at the team and organizational levels.
- Leadership Circle Profile:[4] For a better understanding of your reactive and creative site.
- The Leadership Gift:[5] For growing faster as a leader.
- Table Group:[6] For investing in your team's health.
- Business Agility Institute:[7] For stories and case-studies from organizations that have embraced agility at the entire organizational level.

You can get help from world-class experts on agile transformation. Any certified agile coaches and trainers—Certified Scrum Trainer (CST), Certified Enterprise Coach (CEC), Certified Team Coach (CTC)—from the Scrum Alliance is going to be a great guide on your agile journey.

---

1. https://sochova.cz/cal-certified-agile-leadership-course.htm
2. https://www.scrumalliance.org
3. https://www.crrglobal.com
4. https://leadershipcircle.com
5. http://www.the.leadershipgift.com
6. https://www.tablegroup.com
7. https://businessagility.institute

In a Nutshell

☐ Being an agile leader is not about positional power but about your ability to leverage the power of influence.

☐ Agile leaders are guides for the organization on its agile journey.

☐ Invest in system coaching, large group facilitation skills, and agile leadership development.

☐ Agile is a mindset of continuous improvement in order to unleash the creativity of the system.

☐ Each practice, concept, and model has a place and time where it is a great fit and will help your organization to be successful.

☐ More collaborative and creative cultures are more adaptive and flexible and therefore more suitable to deal with the VUCA world challenges.

☐ Leaders need to change first, and the organization will follow.

BIBLIOGRAPHY

[1] [Acaroglu16] L. Acaroglu, "Problem Solving Desperately Needs Systems Thinking," *Medium*, August 2, 2016. https://medium.com/disruptive-design/problem-solving-desperately-needs-systems-thinking-607d34e4fc80

[2] [Acker19] M. Acker, "Five Guiding Principles of an Agile Team Facilitation Stance," teamcatapult, 2019. https://teamcatapult.com/5-guiding-principles-of-effective-facilitation

[3] [Agile19] Agile Alliance, "Business Agility," 2019. https://www.agilealliance.org/glossary/business-agility

[4] [ALE11] Agile Lean Europe (ALE), "Agile Lean Europe (ALE): Vision and Purpose," May 10, 2011. http://alenetwork.eu/about/vision-and-purpose

[5] [Ancona19] D. Ancona, E. Backman, and K. Isaacs, "Nimble Leadership," *Harvard Business Review*, July–August 2019. https://hbr.org/2019/07/nimble-leadership

[6] [Anderson15a] B. Anderson and B. Adams, "Reactive Leadership," The Leadership Circle, November 11, 2015. https://leadershipcircle.com/en/reactive-leadership

[7] [Anderson15b] B. Anderson and B. Adams, "Five Levels of Leadership," The Leadership Circle, November 19, 2015. https://leadershipcircle.com/en/five-levels-of-leadership

[8] [Arbinger12] The Arbinger Institute, *Leadership and Self-Deception: Getting Out of the Box*. Richmond, British Columbia, Canada: ReadHowYouWant, 2012.

[9] [Avery16] C. Avery, *The Responsibility Process: Unlocking Your Natural Ability to Live and Lead with Power*. Pflugerville, TX: Partnerwerks, 2016.

[10] [Beck01a] Kent Beck, Jeff Sutherland, Martin Fowler, et al. "Principles behind the Agile Manifesto," 2001. https://agilemanifesto.org/principles.html

[11] [Beck01b] Kent Beck, Jeff Sutherland, and Martin Fowler, "Manifesto for Agile Software Development," 2001. https://agilemanifesto.org

[12] [Bennett14] N. Bennett and J. G. Lemoine, "What VUCA Really Means for You," *Harvard Business Review*, January–February 2014. https://hbr.org/2014/01/what-vuca-really-means-for-you

[13] [Beyond14a] Beyond Budgeting Institute, "The Beyond Budgeting Principles," 2014. https://bbrt.org/the-beyond-budgeting-principles

[14] [Beyond14b] Beyond Budgeting Institute, "What Is Beyond Budgeting?" 2014. https://bbrt.org/what-is-beyond-budgeting

[15] [Bockelbrink17] B. Bockelbrink, J. Priest, and L. David, "The Seven Principles," Sociocracy 3.0, 2017. https://sociocracy30.org/the-details/principles

[16] [BusAI18] Business Agility Institute, "The Business Agility Report: Raising the B.A.R.," 2018. https://businessagility.institute/wp-content/uploads/2018/08/BAI-Business-Agility-Report-2018.pdf

[17] [Chamorro13] T. Chamorro-Premuzic, "Does Money Really Affect Motivation? A Review of the Research," *Harvard Business Review*, March–April 2013. https://hbr.org/2013/04/does-money-really-affect-motiv

[18] [Cherry18] M. Cherry, "Buffer: What It's Really Like Being Radically Transparent," *Medium*, January 19, 2018. https://medium.com/make-better-software/buffer-what-its-really-like-being-radically-transparent-2416ad4dbbdb

[19] [CRR_nd] CRR Global, "ORSC™ Organization and Relationship Systems Coaching," CRR Global, accessed 2019. https://www.crrglobal.com/orsc.html

[20] [CRR13] CRR Global, "An Introduction to Relationship Systems Intelligence™ Advanced Coaching for Individuals, Groups & Organizations," 2013. https://www.crrglobal.com/uploads/5/6/9/0/56909237/rsi-white-paper.pdf

[21] [CRR19] CRR Global, "ORSC™ PATH: Vision & Potential," 2019. https://www.crrglobal.com/path.html

[22] [Derby19] E. Derby, *7 Rules for Positive, Productive Change: Micro Shifts, Macro Results*, Oakland, CA: Berrett-Koehler Publishers, 2019.

[23] [Duncan19] R. D. Duncan, "Are You a Creative or Reactive Leader? It Matters," *Forbes*, 2019. https://www.forbes.com/sites/rodgerdeanduncan/2019/02/13/are-you-a-creative-or-reactive-leader-it-matters/#7c0113524d8b

[24] [Esser_nd] Hendrik Esser, Jens Coldewey, and Pieter van der Meché, "Decision Making Systems Matter," Agile Alliance, accessed 2019. https://www.agilealliance.org/decision-making-systems-matter

[25] [Fridjhon14] M. Fridjhon, A. Rød, and F. Fuller, "Relationship Systems IntelligenceTM Transforming the Face of Leadership," CRR Global, 2014. https://www.crrglobal.com/uploads/5/6/9/0/56909237/rsi_-_transforming_the_face_of_leadership.pdf

[26] [Friedman14] T. L. Friedman, "How to Get a Job at Google," *New York Times*, February 2, 2014. https://www.nytimes.com/2014/02/23/opinion/sunday/friedman-how-to-get-a-job-at-google.html

[27] [Greeenleaf07] R. Greenleaf, "The Servant as Leader." In W.C. Zimmerli, M. Holzinger, and K. Richter (eds.), *Corporate Ethics and Corporate Governance*. Berlin, Germany: Springer, 2007.

[28] [Grgić15] V. Grgić, "Descaling Organizations with LeSS," The Less Company B.V., May 8, 2015. https://less.works/blog/2015/05/08/less-scaling-descaling-organizations-with-less.html

[29] [Hammett18] G. Hammett, "3 Steps Ray Dalio Uses Radical Transparency to Build a Billion-Dollar Company," *Inc.*, May 23, 2018. https://www.inc.com/gene-hammett/3-steps-ray-dalio-uses-radical-transparency-to-build-a-billion-dollar-company.html

[30] [Hayes19] Mary Hayes, Fran Chumney, Corinne Wright, and Marcus Buckingham, "Global Study of Engagement Technical Report," ADP Research Institute, 2019. https://www.adp.com/-/media/adp/ResourceHub/pdf/ADPRI/ADPRI0102_2018_Engagement_Study_Technical_Report_RELEASE%20READY.ashx

[31] [Heffernan15] M. Heffernan, "Forget the Pecking Order at Work" [video], TED Women, 2015. https://www.ted.com/talks/margaret_heffernan_why_it_s_time_to_forget_the_pecking_order_at_work/transcript#t-82427

[32] [ICF20] International Coaching Federation (ICF), "About ICF," 2020. https://coachfederation.org/about

[33] [Isaacs99] W. N. Isaacs, "Dialogic Leadership," *The Systems Thinker*, 10(1): 1–5, 1999.

[34] [Jeffries16] R. Jeffries, "Dark Scrum," September 8, 2016. https://ronjeffries.com/articles/016-09ff/defense

[35] [Joiner06] W. B. Joiner and S. A. Josephs, *Leadership Agility: Five Levels of Mastery for Anticipating and Initiating Change.* San Francisco, CA: Jossey-Bass, 2006.

[36] [Joiner11] B. Joiner, "Leadership Agility: From Expert to Catalyst," ChangeWise, 2006/2011. https://reggiemarra.files. wordpress.com/2012/01/leadership20agility20white20paper20-20320levels.pdf

[37] [Kantor12] D. Kantor, *Reading the Room: Group Dynamics for Coaches and Leaders.* San Francisco, CA: Jossey-Bass, 2012.

[38] [Kerievsky19] J. Kerievsky, "Modern Agile," accessed 2019. https://modernagile.org

[39] [Kessel-Fell19] J. Kessel-Fell, "The 12 Dimensions of Agile Leadership," LinkedIn, April 6, 2019. https://www.linkedin. com/pulse/12-dimensions-agile-leadership-jonathan-kessel-fell

[40] [Kotter_nd] J. P. Kotter, "The 8-Step Process for Leading Change," accessed August 2020. https://www.kotterinc.com/ 8-steps-process-for-leading-change

[41] [Kotter12] J. P. Kotter, *Leading Change.* Boston, MA: Harvard Business Review Press, 2012.

[42] [Laloux14] F. Laloux, *Reinventing Organizations.* Brussels, Belgium: Nelson Parker, 2014.

[43] [Lead19] The Leadership Circle, "Leadership Circle Profile," 2019. https://leadershipcircle.com/en/products/leadership-circle-profile

[44] [Lencioni11] P. M. Lencioni, *The Five Dysfunctions of a Team: A Leadership Fable.* San Francisco, CA: Jossey-Bass, 2011.

[45] [Lencioni12] P. M. Lencioni, *The Advantage: Why Organizational Health Trumps Everything Else in Business.* San Francisco: Jossey-Bass, 2012.

[46] [Lencioni19] P. Lencioni, "Patrick Lencioni: What's Your Motive?" Global Leadership Network, August 13, 2019. https://globalleadership.org/articles/leading-yourself/patrick-lencioni-whats-your-motive

[47] [LeSS19a] The LeSS Company, "Overall Retrospective," 2014–2019. https://less.works/less/framework/overall-retrospective.html

[48] [LeSS19b] The LeSS Company, "Systems Thinking," 2014–2019. https://less.works/less/principles/systems-thinking.html

[49] [Lisitsa13] E. Lisitsa, "The Four Horsemen: Criticism, Contempt, Defensiveness, and Stonewalling," The Gottman Institute, April 23, 2013. https://www.gottman.com/blog/the-four-horsemen-recognizing-criticism-contempt-defensiveness-and-stonewalling

[50] [Logan11] D. Logan, John King, and Halee Fischer-Wright. *Tribal Leadership: Leveraging Natural Groups to Build a Thriving Organization.* New York, NY: HarperBusiness, 2011.

[51] [Marquet13] D. Marquet, *Turn the Ship Around!: A True Story of Turning Followers into Leaders.* Austin, TX: Greenleaf Book Group Press, 2013.

[52] [McGregor60] D. McGregor, *The Human Side of Enterprise.* New York, NY: McGraw-Hill, 1960.

[53] [Mgmt19] Management 3.0, "Personal Maps," 2019. https://management30.com/practice/personal-maps

[54] [Mindell_nd] A. Mindell and A. Mindell, "Consensus Reality, Dreamland, Essence: The Deep Democracy Of Experience," accessed 2019. http://www.aamindell.net/consensus-reality-dreamland-essence

[55] [Partner10] Partnerwerks, "An Introduction to the Power Cycle," ChristopherAvery.com, 2011–2019. https://christopheravery.com/blog/intro-power-cycle

[56] [Partner17] Partnerwerks, "The Power or Control Process," 2000-2017. https://www.leadershipgift.com/wp-content/uploads/2010/03/The-Power-or-Control-Process-Poster-Partnerwerks.pdf

[57] [Pflaeging14] N. Pflaeging, *Organize for Complexity: How to Get Life Back into Work to Build the High-Performance Organization*. New York, NY: BetaCodex Publishing, 2014.

[58] [Pflaeging17] N. Pflaeging, "Org Physics: The 3 Faces of Every Company," *Medium*, March 6, 2017. https://medium.com/@NielsPflaeging/org-physics-the-3-faces-of-every-company-df16025f65f8

[59] [Pflaeging18] N. Pflaeging, "The McGregor Paradox: The Most Tragic Misunderstanding in the History of Work & Organizations," LinkedIn, February 18, 2018. https://www.linkedin.com/pulse/mcgregor-paradox-most-tragic-misunderstanding-history-niels-pflaeging

[60] [Pink09] D. H. Pink, *Drive: The Surprising Truth about What Motivates Us*. New York, NY: Riverhead Books, 2009.

[61] [Pink18a] D. H. Pink, *When: The Scientific Secrets of Perfect Timing*. New York, NY: Riverhead Books, 2018.

[62] [Pink18b] D. H. Pink, "Daniel Pink on the Effect of Midpoints" [video], FranklinCovey On Leadership, August 2, 2018. https://www.youtube.com/watch?v=eKA5uHKRZjU

[63] [Reinvent_nd] Reinventing Organizations wiki, "Evolutionary Purpose," accessed September 2020, http://www.reinventingorganizationswiki.com/Evolutionary_Purpose

[64] [Rød15] M. F. Anne Rød, *Creating Intelligent Teams: Leading with Relationship Systems Intelligence*. Randburg, South Africa: KR Publishing, 2015.

[65] [Schein17] E. H. Schein, *Organizational Culture and Leadership*. San Francisco, CA: Jossey-Bass, 2017.

[66] [Seiter15] Courtney Seiter, "The 10 Buffer Values and How We Act on Them Every Day," Buffer, January 7, 2015. https://open.buffer.com/buffer-values

[67] [Šochová17a] Z. Šochová, *The Great ScrumMaster: #ScrumMasterWay*. Boston, MA: Addison-Wesley, 2017.

[68] [Šochová17b] Z. Šochová, "The Synergies between ORSC™ Coaching and Agile Coaching," CRR Global, 2017. https://www.crrglobal.com/orsc-agile.html

[69] [Stadler19] A. Stadler, "Doing an Open Space: A Two Page Primer," 2019. https://www.openspaceworld.org/files/tmnfiles/2pageos.htm

[70] [Szabolcs18] E. Szabolcs and K. Molnár, "Reinventing Organizations Map," 2018. https://reinvorgmap.com

[71] [Whitmore09] J. Whitmore, *Coaching for Performance: GROWing Human Potential and Purpose—The Principles and Practice of Coaching and Leadership*. London, England: Nicholas Brealey Publishing, 2009.

[72] [WPAH16] Western PA Healthcare News Team, "Creative vs Reactive Leaders," *Western PA Healthcare News*, December 30, 2016. https://www.wphealthcarenews.com/creative-vs-reactive-leaders

INDEX

Agile Development
Books, eBooks & Video

Whether are you a programmer, developer, or project manager InformIT has the most comprehensive collection of agile books, eBooks, and video training from the top thought leaders.

- Introductions & General Scrum Guides
- Culture, Leadership & Teams
- Development Practices
- Enterprise
- Product & Project Management
- Testing
- Requirements
- Video Short Courses

Visit **informit.com/agilecenter** to read sample chapters, shop, and watch video lessons from featured products.

Photo by izusek/gettyimages

Register Your Product at informit.com/register

Access additional benefits and **save 35%** on your next purchase

- Automatically receive a coupon for 35% off your next purchase, valid for 30 days. Look for your code in your InformIT cart or the Manage Codes section of your account page.

- Download available product updates.

- Access bonus material if available.*

- Check the box to hear from us and receive exclusive offers on new editions and related products.

Registration benefits vary by product. Benefits will be listed on your account page under Registered Products.

InformIT.com—The Trusted Technology Learning Source

InformIT is the online home of information technology brands at Pearson, the world's foremost education company. At InformIT.com, you can:

- Shop our books, eBooks, software, and video training
- Take advantage of our special offers and promotions
- Sign up to receive special offers and monthly newsletter
- Access thousands of free chapters and video lessons

Connect with InformIT—Visit informit.com/community

the trusted technology learning source

Addison-Wesley • Adobe Press • Cisco Press • Microsoft Press • Pearson IT Certification • Que • Sams • Peachpit Press

 Pearson